SharePoint Developme the SharePoint Framework

Design and implement state-of-the-art customizations for SharePoint

Jussi Roine
Olli Jääskeläinen

BIRMINGHAM - MUMBAI

SharePoint Development with the SharePoint Framework

Copyright © 2017 Packt Publishing

First published: September 2017

Production reference: 1260917

Published by Packt Publishing Ltd.
Livery Place
35 Livery Street
Birmingham
B3 2PB, UK.

ISBN 978-1-78712-143-0

www.packtpub.com

Credits

Authors
Jussi Roine
Olli Jääskeläinen

Reviewer
Bill Ayers

Commissioning Editor
Amarabhab Banerjee

Acquisition Editor
Siddharth Mandal

Content Development Editor
Mohammed Yusuf Imaratwale

Technical Editor
Prashant Mishra

Copy Editor
Safis Editing

Project Coordinator
Ritika Manoj

Proofreader
Safis Editing

Indexer
Rekha Nair

Graphics
Jason Monteiro

Production Coordinator
Shantanu Zagade

About the Authors

Jussi Roine started working with SharePoint with the very first version, SharePoint Portal Server 2001, in late 2000. With a strong infrastructure and development background by then, and also having worked quite a bit on Linux-based solutions, SharePoint fascinated him with its seemingly endless potential and easiness for end users. He continued working with SharePoint through all the versions since, including SharePoint Portal Server 2003, MOSS 2007, and SharePoint 2010, 2013, and 2016. He also enjoyed working with customers when they started moving beyond on-premises to the early cloud-based offerings on BPOS and Office 365, later in 2011.

He has been a Microsoft Most Valuable Professional since 2014, and a Microsoft Certified Trainer since 2006. In 2012 and 2014, he had the honor of attending the Microsoft Certified Master (later Microsoft Certified Solutions Master) program, which he passed among the very selected few in the world at the time. In 2017, Jussi became a Microsoft Regional

Director, a member of 150 of the world's top technology visionaries chosen for their community leadership and cross-platform expertise.

Having providing his clients with solutions, architectures, and trusted advisor services for 25 years now, he has also had a chance to dive deeply into Microsoft Azure, which connects and integrates with Office 365 robustly. Over the years, he has written several books on SharePoint, the Office clients, productivity, flexwork, and Microsoft platforms. This book is his first international book aimed at a more diverse audience, and he hopes that this book will help current and future developers working on the Office 365 platform to more easily provide superior solutions for their clients using SharePoint Framework.

Olli Jääskeläinen is a Microsoft MVP, **Microsoft Certified Master (MCM)**, and **Microsoft Certified Trainer (MCT)**. Olli has been working in the field for over 15 years. He knows SharePoint inside out and is currently focusing on building productivity solutions using Office 365. Olli works as an architect for Sulava and as an organizer for the Office 365 and SharePoint User Group Finland. He has been giving technical presentations since 2013 at events such as TechDays Finland, European SharePoint Conference, TechTalks Finland, SharePoint Saturdays, and Office 365 Engage.

About the Reviewer

Bill Ayers is a consultant developer and solution architect who has been working with SharePoint since the 2003 version of the product. He is a Microsoft Certified Master and Charter MCSM, and a Microsoft Certified Trainer and Office Development MVP. He specializes in Microsoft Office, SharePoint, Office 365, and mobile solutions, with a particular focus on agile software development practices. He has over 25 years of experience in the software industry and speaks regularly at international conferences and user groups. He is also a moderator on `SharePoint.StackExchange.com`, and blogs occasionally at `http://SPDoctor.com/`. He is based in Sheffield, UK.

www.PacktPub.com

For support files and downloads related to your book, please visit www.PacktPub.com.

Did you know that Packt offers eBook versions of every book published, with PDF and ePub files available? You can upgrade to the eBook version at www.PacktPub.com and as a print book customer, you are entitled to a discount on the eBook copy. Get in touch with us at service@packtpub.com for more details.

At www.PacktPub.com, you can also read a collection of free technical articles, sign up for a range of free newsletters and receive exclusive discounts and offers on Packt books and eBooks.

https://www.packtpub.com/mapt

Get the most in-demand software skills with Mapt. Mapt gives you full access to all Packt books and video courses, as well as industry-leading tools to help you plan your personal development and advance your career.

Why subscribe?

- Fully searchable across every book published by Packt
- Copy and paste, print, and bookmark content
- On demand and accessible via a web browser

Customer Feedback

Thanks for purchasing this Packt book. At Packt, quality is at the heart of our editorial process. To help us improve, please leave us an honest review on this book's Amazon page at `https://www.amazon.com/dp/1787121437`.

If you'd like to join our team of regular reviewers, you can e-mail us at `customerreviews@packtpub.com`. We award our regular reviewers with free eBooks and videos in exchange for their valuable feedback. Help us be relentless in improving our products!

Table of Contents

Preface

SharePoint Framework is the new, modern, and fresh approach for implementing customizations in SharePoint and SharePoint Online. It's a client-side approach to a server-side problem, allowing developers already familiar with JavaScript, HTML, and CSS to implement lightweight custom functionality for SharePoint.

In the past, SharePoint-based development has been challenging, complex, poorly documented and full of changing directions from Microsoft.

Originally, in early 2000, the guidance, was not to modify or customize SharePoint. Microsoft was saying at the time not to touch anything and simply to use SharePoint as a portal service that hosts your content and documents. With newer versions of SharePoint for on-premises deployments, Microsoft initially introduced a somewhat home-brewed approach to implementing custom web parts (widgets on a page) and UI elements. This included legacy `.bat` files, weird file formats, numerous modifications to XML files with minimal documentation and a cryptic approach to provisioning your solutions between different environments.

Between then and now we've also had different models for developing solutions for SharePoint in the cloud; this included a better approach to implementing features without deploying server-side code, but by the time this was made available developers were already familiar with Microsoft .NET-based customizations on the server-side. Giving a replacement client-side model that had strict rules and security restrictions did not go down easily for seasoned SharePoint developers.

Finally, now with the SharePoint Framework, we have a documented framework for implementing UI elements, custom web parts, and features for SharePoint 2016 in on-premises and SharePoint Online in Office 365. It is still early days, but we're already seeing good uptake from developers who can now finally and confidently migrate their existing code to the cloud while simultaneously switching from .NET-based development languages to TypeScript, which is a superset of JavaScript.

This book will take you from a Hello World-implementation in SharePoint Framework to implementing enterprise-ready functionality with ease. We'll walk you through the essential knowledge you need in order to survive in a modern project that aims to use SharePoint Framework as the core development model. In addition, the necessary tools are explained, as well as debugging and troubleshooting. Obviously, you might still be using other JavaScript frameworks, such as jQuery, AngularJS, and React so we have guidance on that too – because SharePoint Framework does allow and support you to use other frameworks while implementing SharePoint functionality.

This book will provide an invaluable resource for all those seeking to use and learn the SharePoint Framework as their development model for SharePoint.

What this book covers

Chapter 1, *Introducing SharePoint Online for Developers*, will give you a short history lesson to understand the limitations of the previous development models for SharePoint. You will begin to see how and where SharePoint Framework differs the most and why it matters.

Chapter 2, *Developing Solutions for SharePoint*, will introduce you to SharePoint Framework in more detail. It covers the types of project you can implement and reveals how to code and start using the necessary tools quickly.

Chapter 3, *Getting Started with SharePoint Framework*, walks you through installing the toolchain and verifying everything is installed correctly. You'll learn how project files are laid out and where to find what.

Chapter 4, *Building Your First Web Part*, you will code your own SharePoint Framework-based web part and deploy it locally for testing and in SharePoint for real use.

Chapter 5, *Using Visual Studio Code and Other Editors*, shows you how to get started with Visual Studio Code, the free editor from Microsoft that fully supports SharePoint Framework projects. You will also learn how to use Visual Studio 2015/2017 if you are more familiar with them.

Chapter 6, *Packaging and Deploying Solutions*, once development is done, developers need to package and deploy their code in an orderly and managed fashion. You'll learn about the tools to aid you in this task and how to manually deploy your code to SharePoint.

Chapter 7, *Working with SharePoint Content*, is the next logical step when implementing solutions with SharePoint Framework. You'll frequently need to access SharePoint-hosted data such as lists and documents. You will also learn using mock data to quickly get your code working before further testing against live data.

Chapter 8, *Working with the Web Part Property Pane*, shows you how to create solutions that allow parameters and values from user input, such as settings data for a web part. This way your code can run dynamically regardless of where it is deployed.

Chapter 9, *Using React and Office UI Fabric React Components*, explains that Microsoft realized early on that developers prefer other frameworks, such as React, and might need to provide a unified UI that implements Microsoft's design language for SharePoint and Office. With React and Office UI Fabric React you'll learn how to combine these two frameworks with SharePoint Framework projects.

Chapter 10, *Working with Other JavaScript Frameworks*, will teach you how to use other popular frameworks, such as jQuery and Angular, to implement your solutions while still using SharePoint Framework

Chapter 11, *Troubleshooting and Debugging SharePoint Framework Solutions*, discusses efficient troubleshooting techniques to help you find common problems you might encounter. Debugging a SharePoint Framework solution is slightly different from traditional server-side debugging, and this chapter will teach you how to debug your code.

Chapter 12, *SharePoint APIs and Microsoft Graph*, will give you a run-down of the SharePoint APIs and how they differ from each other. You'll learn how to access the APIs, and also how to employ Microsoft Graph, the fabric that provides knowledge for most things in Office 365 and Azure Active Directory.

Chapter 13, *The Future of SharePoint Customizations*, provides a glimpse into the future and what SharePoint Framework means for developers from now on. As development models come and go, we give you several ideas how developers should approach this major change.

What you need for this book

- SharePoint 2016 Farm or SharePoint Online tenant (as part of an Office 365 subscription)
- Visual Studio Code or Visual Studio 2015/2017
- Web browser (Chrome or Internet Explorer or Firefox)
- Internet access

Who this book is for

This book is for developers who want to start developing solutions for SharePoint 2016 and/or SharePoint Online using SharePoint Framework. It is also for developers who are already familiar with SharePoint's development models of the past and who are ready to start using SharePoint Framework for their future projects. Though SharePoint experience is not required, you should have a general understanding of the capabilities that SharePoint provides. We'll provide a brief overview of SharePoint as well. It is also helpful to have an understanding of JavaScript-based web development.

Conventions

In this book, you will find a number of text styles that distinguish between different kinds of information. Here are some examples of these styles and an explanation of their meaning.

Code words in the text, database table names, folder names, filenames, file extensions, pathnames, dummy URLs, user input, and Twitter handles are shown as follows: "Create another file, called `MockSharePointClient.ts`, in the same folder that the web part is located."

A block of code is set as follows:

```
import { Environment, EnvironmentType } from '@microsoft/sp-core-library';
import { ISPListItem } from "./ISPListItem";
import MockSharePointClient from "./MockSharePointClient";
```

Any command-line input or output is written as follows:

```
gulp serve
```

New terms and **important words** are shown in bold. Words that you see on the screen, for example, in menus or dialog boxes, appear in the text like this: "Write in **Team site name**, for example, SPFX-testing."

Warnings or important notes appear in a box like this.

 Tips and tricks appear like this.

Reader feedback

Feedback from our readers is always welcome. Let us know what you think about this book-what you liked or disliked. Reader feedback is important to us as it helps us develop titles that you will really get the most out of.

To send us general feedback, simply e-mail `feedback@packtpub.com`, and mention the book's title in the subject of your message.

If there is a topic that you have expertise in and you are interested in either writing or contributing to a book, see our author guide at `www.packtpub.com/authors`.

Customer support

Now that you are the proud owner of a Packt book, we have a number of things to help you to get the most from your purchase.

Downloading the example code

You can download the example code files for this book from your account at `http://www.packtpub.com`. If you purchased this book elsewhere, you can visit `http://www.packtpub.com/support` and register to have the files e-mailed directly to you.

You can download the code files by following these steps:

1. Log in or register to our website using your e-mail address and password.
2. Hover the mouse pointer on the **SUPPORT** tab at the top.
3. Click on **Code Downloads & Errata**.
4. Enter the name of the book in the **Search** box.

5. Select the book for which you're looking to download the code files.
6. Choose from the drop-down menu where you purchased this book from.
7. Click on **Code Download**.

You can also download the code files by clicking on the **Code Files** button on the book's web page at the Packt Publishing website. This page can be accessed by entering the book's name in the **Search** box. Please note that you need to be logged in to your Packt account.

Once the file is downloaded, please make sure that you unzip or extract the folder using the latest version of:

- WinRAR / 7-Zip for Windows
- Zipeg / iZip / UnRarX for Mac
- 7-Zip / PeaZip for Linux

The code bundle for the book is also hosted on GitHub at `https://github.com/PacktPublishing/SharePoint-Development-with-the-SharePoint-Framework`. We also have other code bundles from our rich catalog of books and videos available at `https://github.com/PacktPublishing/`. Check them out!

Errata

Although we have taken every care to ensure the accuracy of our content, mistakes do happen. If you find a mistake in one of our books-maybe a mistake in the text or the code-we would be grateful if you could report this to us. By doing so, you can save other readers from frustration and help us improve subsequent versions of this book. If you find any errata, please report them by visiting `http://www.packtpub.com/submit-errata`, selecting your book, clicking on the **Errata Submission Form** link, and entering the details of your errata. Once your errata are verified, your submission will be accepted and the errata will be uploaded to our website or added to any list of existing errata under the Errata section of that title.

To view the previously submitted errata, go to `https://www.packtpub.com/books/content/support` and enter the name of the book in the search field. The required information will appear under the **Errata** section.

Piracy

Piracy of copyrighted material on the Internet is an ongoing problem across all media. At Packt, we take the protection of our copyright and licenses very seriously. If you come across any illegal copies of our works in any form on the Internet, please provide us with the location address or website name immediately so that we can pursue a remedy.

Please contact us at `copyright@packtpub.com` with a link to the suspected pirated material.

We appreciate your help in protecting our authors and our ability to bring you valuable content.

Questions

If you have a problem with any aspect of this book, you can contact us at `questions@packtpub.com`, and we will do our best to address the problem.

1

Introducing SharePoint Online for Developers

SharePoint Online is a core part of Office 365, which is a **Software as a Service** (**SaaS**) cloud service from Microsoft. **SharePoint Online** (**SPO**) is one of the services in Office 365 that companies and organizations typically purchase when they move parts or all of their infrastructure and services to a public cloud service.

In this chapter, we'll take a lap around Office 365 and SharePoint Online, with a strong focus on development models and features that are relevant to you as a developer. In addition we'll provision a new SharePoint site collection that will aid us in testing code we'll write in upcoming chapters. At the end of this chapter, you'll have a good overview of SharePoint Online and the development models that have been, and some of which still are, available to you in on-premises SharePoint and SharePoint Online.

What is SharePoint Online?

SharePoint Online is, depending, who you ask, a development platform, collaboration service, file management system, and intranet service. It's the logical successor and partially a replacement for SharePoint, the on-premises collaboration and productivity platform. It also (partially or fully depending on the business case) replaces file shares, email attachments (through Outlook's support for OneDrive for Business, which is technically part of SharePoint/SharePoint Online), messaging boards, and similar needs for intra-organization or cross-organizational collaboration.

SharePoint Online is a collection of services bundled together, and these are

- SharePoint team sites
- SharePoint publishing sites
- Search
- User profiles
- InfoPath Forms Service for rich and fillable online forms
- **Business Connectivity Services** (**BCS**) for integrated backend data to SharePoint
- SharePoint add-ins (formerly apps)

In marketing terms, OneDrive for Business is a separate service, but it shares a lot of the same thinking, vision, and in some parts, APIs with SharePoint Online.

Depending on who is accessing SharePoint Online, it can act as a simple team site offering a common storage for documents (typically Office files, such as Word and Excel documents), a messaging board, a blog, and a place to store organizational data such as software licensing information or employee contact information.

SharePoint Online supports accessing content through a web interface, through Office clients and APIs. In some scenarios, content can be accessed through a mapped network drive using WebDAV but this is more or less a legacy way of accessing documents and files stored in SharePoint.

In the following sections, we'll walk you through the essential concepts of SharePoint Online, on a level that we feel is relevant for any developer aiming to work with SharePoint Online.

SharePoint sites and site collections

Each SharePoint site is a separate place for storing content. Each site belongs to not more than one site collection. Think of SharePoint sites as folders, and site collections as a drive letter or hard drive partitions. The analogy is slightly lacking, but for now, it's sufficient for relaying the essential concepts of SharePoint Online.

Organizations create one or more site collections and use site collections typically as security boundaries. One site collection could be the intranet, another could be an extranet for specific partner companies or customers. A third one could act as the Board of Directors' secure site collection for storing highly sensitive documents. Each site collection can hold one or more sites, but they always have one site, which will be the root site of a given site collection.

Sites are the common building block for SharePoint Online services, such as intranet and extranet. You could build a very nice intranet using just one site collection, and then using just one site within the site collection. In the real world, however, you would typically need to structure your content and data among multiple sites, and possibly multiple site collections.

In the following illustration, you can see a high-level overview of what SharePoint Online is. On the left-most side, you see site collections, which are made up of sites and possible subsites. Each site can then hold relevant configuration data and SharePoint artefacts such as document libraries and lists.

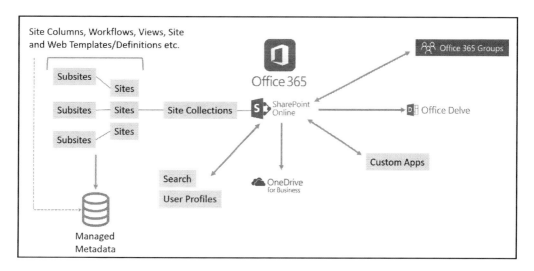

SharePoint document libraries

SharePoint sites store information, which requires different types of containers. One type of container is a document library. A document library can be used to store files, including Office documents, text files, media files, and similar content. Most SharePoint sites have, by default, one or more document libraries provisioned and you are free to create more as needed.

Document libraries can either have a modern user experience or a classic user experience. This is due to the changes Microsoft is rolling out over several months (or sometimes even years), which in turn allows for customers to decide when to deploy new and drastic changes, such as a new user experience for something as central as a document library.

The modern user experience is fully responsive and has a fresh look. All essential tooling is available in a simple toolbar and the ribbon interface from the Office 2007/2010 era is gone:

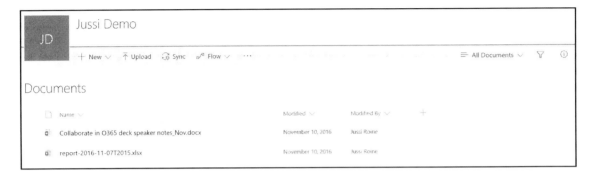

The classic experience is still very much in use; it is supported and, in certain scenarios, works better. This holds especially true for situations where users have used SharePoint Online for several years and are very accustomed to the classic experience:

Both views relay almost identical information, but the classic experience also exposes the ribbon UI, which in turns hides (or shows, depending on context) a lot of additional tooling:

One of the challenges for developers with the ribbon UI has always been the cumbersome approach to modifying, hiding, or adding custom buttons in the ribbon. While it's possible, it's certainly not a task customers would request initially. Users are familiar with the default buttons, and changing or disabling essential buttons for something else will most certainly confuse users.

Each document in a document library holds metadata. Metadata is a larger topic, and not in the scope of this book, suffice to say that metadata in SharePoint Online document libraries is used to reveal and store information about files, and data in general. Metadata can be used to search files and different views on data can be shown, based on metadata filtering, sorting, and selections.

The classic view for modifying metadata is very bare bones but also easy to use:

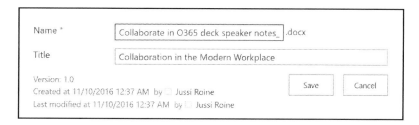

The modern view for modifying metadata is more modern, but might involve a little learning curve for users accustomed to the classic view:

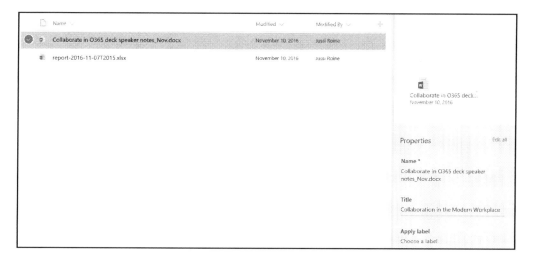

Notice how metadata in the modern view is shown upon selection of a file, while in the classic view the view is completely different and the context of other files is hidden.

SharePoint lists

Besides document libraries, SharePoint sites can hold lists. Technically, lists are identical to document libraries but rather than storing binary files, they store other data such as text, numbers, selections, or even attachment files. Lists are typically used to create ad-hoc data structures to hold data that can be sorted, filtered, and queried. Document libraries often act as a file store and lists act as a data or information store without really storing physical files.

While document libraries are just that: document libraries, lists come in all sizes and varieties. The common base list is a custom list, which is essentially an empty list with just a few data columns as a template. Other list templates include contact lists (predefined person data columns), links (URLs and descriptive text columns), and announcements (news-style items with headlines and summary text), to mention a few:

By creating a custom list you can easily build a data store for any kind of data your application might require at a later time. The list can be queried similarly to how you would query a relational database table. It's a graphical representation of an SQL table, with the addition of built-in functionality such as graphical views, sorting, filtering, and integration to other Office 365 services.

By adding new columns (metadata) to a list, you effectively provide additional ways to store data. The **Title** column is the base column, which you can later rename if you choose to.

To add a new column, simply define the datatype and other properties and it will automatically be added to the default view:

When you add a new column of the datatype **Multiple lines of text**, you effectively create a new text box that can be filled out when adding a new line to your custom list:

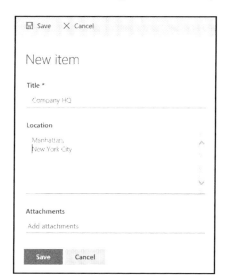

This data can now be saved and is immediately visible and accessible on the list:

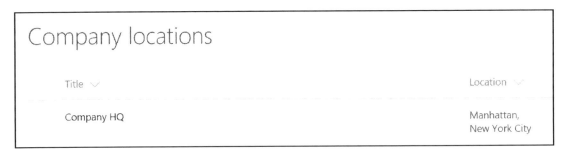

It's crucial to understand that you have a built-in, scalable, secure, and ready-to-use platform for storing data within SharePoint lists and document libraries. Instead of always designing, provisioning, and maintaining a separate SQL database with custom-created tables, you can always provision your application's data to a SharePoint list or library, depending on which works best for you.

SharePoint web parts

Web parts are the building blocks for SharePoint pages. Pages sit in a document library and provide a graphical view that can be customized or hand-built depending on need.

Each document library and list, upon provisioning, create a web part representation of itself that can be embedded on a SharePoint page. As such, web parts are an easy way to create a clickable portal page to quickly access document libraries and lists or for simply resurfacing information from within SharePoint structures.

There are also a few dozen pre-created web parts that provide additional functionality, such as embedding comments on a page or retrieving an RSS feed and rendering a nice formatted list out of the feed items. Developers often create custom web parts that do the kind of actions that default web parts lack. This could include custom buttons, views, fields, and using data stored within SharePoint and providing a nicer interface for modifying said data.

By editing a SharePoint page, users can rearrange existing web parts on a page or add new ones and remove existing ones:

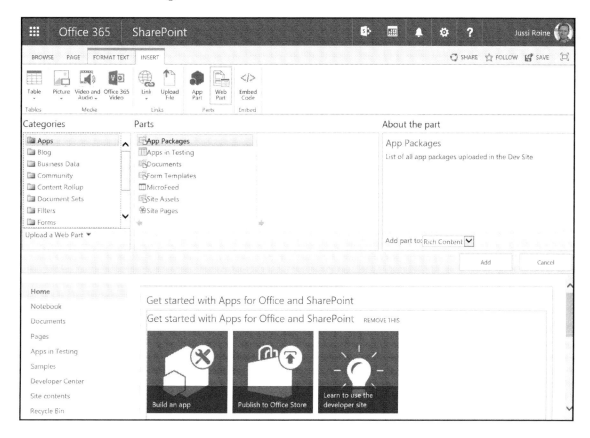

Adding a web part by editing the page and then selecting **Insert | Web Part** provides a list of all supported and installed web parts on the service.

The interface is a bit retro in the sense that it involves a lot of dragging, dropping, and popup menus to finalize the web part settings:

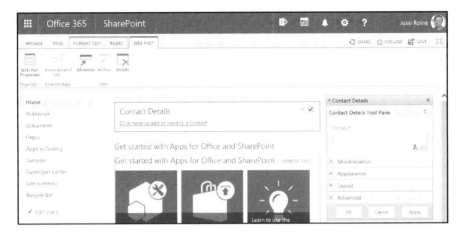

When editing a web part, the **WEB PART** tool pane (on the right) becomes visible, allowing manipulation of the **Web Part Properties**. This includes the title text and possible parameters to instruct the web part to act differently.

Why SharePoint Online?

So far, we've taken a whirlwind tour of SharePoint Online, barely scratching the surface of the default functionality within a SharePoint site. Considering the first version of SharePoint was introduced in 2001, a lot of has evolved since then. But at the same a lot has surprisingly stayed the same: document libraries, lists, and sites more or less share the same concepts as they did over 15 years ago.

Today, companies choose SharePoint Online for several reasons. In our opinion, the three main reasons companies choose SharePoint Online are:

- Compatibility and cooperation with Office suite applications, including cross-platform support on macOS and Office Online browser users
- A readily available intranet and extranet platform that works with single sign-on (using Azure Active Directory as the identity provider)
- It works natively with Exchange, Skype for Business, and OneDrive for Business, which are the default choices of productivity tools for many organizations

Most probably the development aspects of SharePoint Online are not the primary reason for companies to choose SharePoint Online. Interoperability, common standards, and well-documented APIs are critical, but often not the main driver for choosing SharePoint Online to start with.

Microsoft claims* that over 90 percent of Fortune 500 users are using Microsoft's cloud services; this, of course, includes both Microsoft Azure and Office 365. While the claim is very impressive, it does not mean that *all* 90 percent of Fortune 500 companies are solely using Office 365 and/or Microsoft Azure; they might be using Amazon's AWS or any number of other hosting or public cloud offerings available, together with Office 365. The reality, though, is that over 100 million users are accessing Office 365 workloads every month. This is an amazing number of users who have enrolled to a paid license and are actively using any number of the multiple services Office 365 has to offer. As such, development for SharePoint Online is something that is in demand from both small and large organizations and enterprises, as well ISVs who need to implement their own products to fit with Office 365.

* Microsoft 2017 earnings call; see `https://www.microsoft.com/en-us/Investor/earnings/FY-2017-Q3/press-release-webcast`.

Another reason that organizations choose SharePoint Online is that they might already be paying for it. When they initially purchased a license for Office 365 to maybe use Exchange Online for their emails, they typically also purchased a SharePoint Online license for users. Nowadays this includes 1 terabyte of storage to hold all SharePoint Online content, as well as the majority of SharePoint Online functionality. Comparing this *free* offering to an on-premises SharePoint 2013 or SharePoint 2016 deployment often means that SPO becomes a compelling option. While the on-premises deployment of SharePoint typically requires at least 3-6 months for full installation, roll-out for users, customization, configuration, and managing--the equivalent in Office 365-SharePoint Online is already there and ready to use. This is not to say that SharePoint Online and SharePoint on-premises are identical; however, they do share more or less the same set of features that most users tend to need.

Office 365 licensing

While licensing is out of the scope for this book, we feel it is important for developers to understand the rough edges and limitations of a given service in order to be able to build performant and robust cloud solutions.

Office 365 licensing is a fixed per-user license that is billed monthly (or yearly if you choose to pre-pay for a full year). You can have one or more different types of licenses, but only one license type at any given time for a specific user. You can, of course, purchase a higher tier license, assign it to a user, and later change that to a lower tier license when the needs of the user change.

When writing about public cloud services such as Office 365, it is an assumption nowadays that prices fluctuate. You can always verify the current prices at http://www.office365.com. Make sure to change your country at the bottom of the page to get pricing in your preferred currency.

Office 365 licenses are sold for home use, business use, and enterprise use. When researching suitable licenses for yourself or your users, make sure you choose the correct category of licenses in order to find the best one for your needs.

Choosing an Office 365 license for development use

When you choose developer solutions for SharePoint Online, you have to choose one of the organization licenses for Office 365. The available licenses are in two license families; the **B** (**Business**) and **E** (**Enterprise**) license families. Most developers working on SharePoint Online commonly use E-licenses. This is mostly for minimizing any impending issues when deploying your code in the future, as E-licenses have most of the features one might need within SharePoint Online.

Over the years, many have complained about the complex licensing models Microsoft imposes on some of their products. SharePoint on-premises tended to have all kinds of small limitations, connector licenses, and similar things, to look out for that plagued many development projects in the early 2000 and 2010's. Office 365 is a different breed as licensing is very opaque and easier to understand. As stated before, you will need at least one license for your development use and additional licenses for any users who might be accessing your solutions that you aim to deploy to SharePoint Online.

We recommend you use a license from the E-family of plans, such as E1, E3 or even E5, which, at the time of writing, is the license offering the most features for Office 365 services. It is also the most expensive license.

You can see a detailed listing of all E-family plans and their respective features at https://products.office.com/en-us/business/compare-more-office-365-for-business-plans.

SharePoint Online is available for E1, E3, and E5, so from that perspective, there is little difference when starting development on SharePoint Online. Keep in mind that certain minuscule features might differ or might not be available in E1 if they are available in E3 and E5. These special situations might arise at a later time, so this is something to keep in mind if you choose to go with the E1 license. Remember that you can upgrade from E1 to E3/E5 at any time in the future (unless you pre-pay for the yearly license).

This book assumes you will be using an E3 or E5 capable license, as they provide the most functionality and are generally the license model organizations choose to use for their information workers.

To enroll to Office 365, you can purchase a license at https://products.office.com/en-us/business/office-365-enterprise-e3-business-software.

Getting started with SharePoint Online

SharePoint Online has a separate administration and management interface called the SharePoint Admin Center. To access the page, click **Admin** on the Office 365, landing page (https://portal.office.com). This takes you to **Office 365 Admin Center** and requires you to be a SharePoint Admin or a Global Admin for your organization:

Under **Office 365 Admin center**, on the left-hand side, you'll get a navigation pane with all Office 365 management pages. Scroll down and click **Admin centers** and then click **SharePoint:**

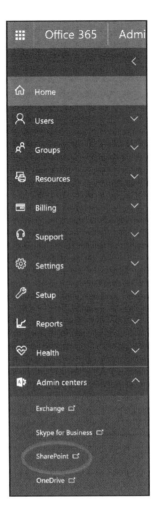

This takes you to **SharePoint admin center**, with a direct address of the format `https://{tenant}-admin.sharepoint.com/`, where `{tenant}` is your Office 365 tenant name that you specified during Office 365 provisioning and sign-up phase:

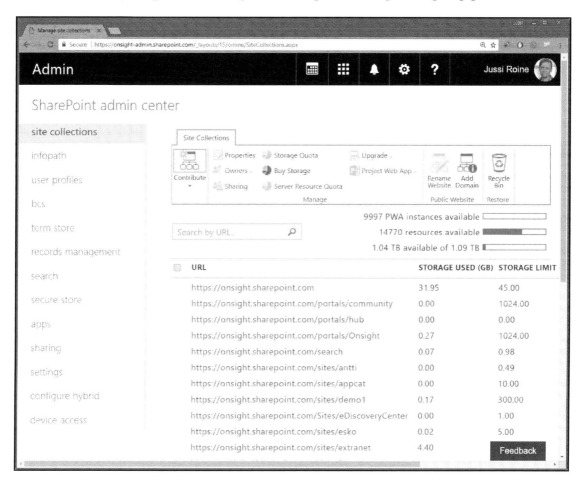

In **SharePoint admin center**, you can create new collections of SharePoint sites, called **site collections**, configure any of the built-in services, and access any existing site collections within your tenant.

The interface is somewhat different from the more modern Office 365 admin center, but certainly still very usable. Many times, developers need to access this interface mostly to check on something, rather than spending time doing daily management tasks such as provisioning new site collections or fiddling with quotas. We anticipate the SharePoint admin center to get a refresh sometime in the future.

Your tenant should have at least the root (home) site collections provisioned at `https://{tenant}.sharepoint.com`. We recommend that, in the following chapters, when you build your solutions and try out the sample code, you provision new site collections and do not deploy any code in the root site collections. This way, other users in your tenant do not get confused if you leave around sample code or code that is still being worked on and might not work as intended.

Creating new site collections

A site collection is a core concept in SharePoint Online and works more or less the same as it has worked in SharePoint on-premises versions for years. You can create one or multiple site collections and each site collections can hold one or more sites. You cannot, however, create a site collection that holds another site collection underneath. You can only have site collections that consist of sites and subsites.

To create a new site collection, you can use **SharePoint admin center**, which is typically the easiest way for one-off site collections you might need for development use. If you need multiple site collections, it might be easier to use a scripting language, such as PowerShell, to create multiple site collections.

A word or two on SharePoint site templates

Each SharePoint site is based on a template. This makes sense as SharePoint (on-premises) and SharePoint Online typically provision tens or hundreds of sites for any given tenant, and most sites share a common set of functionality and features.

Site definitions

Templates used to be XML-based definitions, called Site Definitions. These would reside on the SharePoint servers in an on-premises deployment, but one couldn't directly modify these. The reason was that all SharePoint default files, that reside in the so-called SharePoint Hive (or SharePoint Root) on the file system, might be updated in any upcoming service pack, cumulative update, hotfix, or public update. Thus, if you edited even one XML file just slightly, you would run into unforeseen provisioning troubles, or even render yourself in a state that your SharePoint deployment would be unsupported.

Site templates

Site templates could then be used to provision new sites, with modified templates. Site templates were database-only copies of Site Definitions, and they could include content such as SharePoint document libraries, lists, and even files within document libraries. The challenge with Site templates was (and still is) that they are only supported in non-publishing sites, meaning sites that do not use SharePoint Publishing Features capabilities. This would include site templates (not Site Templates, note the capitalization difference here) such as Developer Site, Team Site, and Blank Site. A Site Template would, upon creation, save itself, and a reference to the original site definition it was based on, and create a `.STP` file within the SharePoint content database. As you might guess, this proved to be problematic as well, since content in the database was strictly only accessible through a set of (then) very-limited APIs or through the user interface of SharePoint. For developers, this was not adequate.

Web templates

Microsoft made a third type of template, called the Web Template. This was an evolution on Site Definitions but also took the better parts from Site Templates. A Web Template was a single XML file that only contained the deltas (changes) from a Site Definition without the need to first create a custom Site Definition. A developer could then have a peek at all the available Site Definitions as they were on the disk of the SharePoint server, figure out which was the best *base* template for the intended need, and provides a simple XML file that would provide the instruction set for a custom Web Template. This template would then show on the template selection list upon creating a new SharePoint site (or site collection, for that matter), and would not differ for the end user but, at the same time, could provide additional or customized functionality from the original Site Definition. The XML file for the Web Template could also be packaged in a manageable package and distributed as fit.

SharePoint Online and site templates

So far, we've covered Site Definitions, Site Templates, and Web Templates. One would think that with these three template types, developers could create any style of SharePoint site with full freedom and flexibility to customize sites. There is a slight roadblock here that subsequently forces us to move *away* from all these template types in SharePoint Online.

In SharePoint Online, developers do not have direct disk access. As such, developers are unable to take a peek at the SharePoint Hive and select from the list of available Site Definitions what kind of Web Template they are about to create. Of course, Microsoft has published the full list of supported Site Definitions, but the limitations of Web Templates is often a major challenge. For this purpose, and other smaller but persistent issues, developers needed something more manageable and something that could better be molded into whatever needs a project might have for a custom SharePoint site.

The solution is *remote provisioning*. We will cover remote provisioning in much more detail later in this book, but suffice to say that this approach allows for most freedom for developers while also maintaining full fidelity and supportability to any of the existing Site Definitions that SharePoint Online currently supports. With remote provisioning, developers either scan through newly-created sites or get an event (a sort of trigger) that a new site is being provisioned. Upon finding one, they can programmatically verify the origins of the site and the base template it was provisioned from--typically this would be a Team Site, Developer Site, or a Blank Site. Armed with this information, developers can then use the APIs to instruct the new site to re-configure itself based on another template-- which would be a templating system the developer has coined.

It's not important to understand all the intricacies of the cumbersome SharePoint site template system as it has a 15 year history and most of that history is irrelevant for SharePoint Online developers. But it is essential to understand the basics of the templating system, especially the limitations developers might face when initially creating new SharePoint deployments.

When developing SharePoint Online-based solutions, you always need to base your solutions on the assumption that sites are based on a pre-defined site definition. You could also force the selection of the base template and discourage the user from selecting a template that might not be suitable for your needs. If you scan through the templates in the site collection creation dialog, you'll see there are a lot of templates that might not make sense today, such as the Visio Process Repository template that has a very specific usage.

Creating a new site collection

To start creating a new site collection, click **New** in the toolbar and select **Private Site Collection**. This is the preferred choice for intranet-style deployments or sites you aim to share later for external users. **Private Site Collection with Project Web App** is a special type of site collection that also enables the use of **Project Online**, a project management and sharing platform that can be purchased with a separate license for Office 365. A public website might still be visible in your tenant, depending on when and how your Office 365 was initially provisioned. This is a functionality that will soon fade away and should not be used as it was originally intended for public-facing and anonymous SharePoint Online sites:

Next, fill out the provisioning form for a new **Site Collection**. For **Title**, you can choose whatever name you feel is suitable for your needs. For the **Web Site Address**, your tenant address is pre-filled and cannot be changed. The second part of the upcoming site collection URL will be a pre-defined managed path, either **/sites/** or **/teams/**. We prefer using **/sites/** as it is commonly used for all kinds of SharePoint sites regardless of their usage. For the last part of the URL, type in a name (no whitespace or special characters) for the site, such as `MyDevSite` and there is less risk to accidentally confuse these as Microsoft Teams-based sites.

Thus, your new site collection can then be accessed through
`https://{tenant}.sharepoint.com/sites/mydevsite`:

For **Template Selection**, you should always choose **English** as the primary language. The reason for this is that if at any later time you run into errors or issues with your code and need to do troubleshooting, this language dictates the language used for error pages and exceptions. We've sometimes seen customers who originally provisioned their site collections in a language other than English, and since, this is a setting that cannot be changed (without destroying the whole site collection), troubleshooting code-specific or SharePoint Online specific gets very problematic. Template language does not dictate the language for SharePoint page content or any other setting for users later on.

For the actual template, the same rule applies--it's a one-time setting. It's best to spend a bit of time here, as the template selection is a crucial selection and developers should understand why this is as it is.

As explained earlier, there are a lot of different templates available in SharePoint Online. When starting your development adventures in SharePoint Online, it's always good to go with the **Developer Site** template, as it provides some advantages over the other templates.

For **Time Zone**, choose whichever timezone is most fitting for you. For **Administrator**, use your own credentials to ensure you have full access to your new site collection.

For **Storage Quota**, while being important, it's not really relevant for development sites so 1 GB should be more than enough for any development needs you might require for now.

The **Server Resource Quota** is reminiscent of the time when development mostly occurred in sandbox development models and it is not in active use anymore. You can leave the default value of 300 and then commit the provisioning of a new site collection by clicking **OK**.

Creating a new site collection takes a little bit of time, anywhere from a minute to more than 15 minutes depending on the load on the service. In normal circumstances, a new site collection should be provisioned in no more than five minutes.

When the site has been provisioned, you can access the site at `https://{tenant}.sharepoint.com/sites/{sitename}`.

When you access the new site collection, you initially land on the root site of the given site collection. Sometimes this is confusing since you're accessing both the site collection and the root site at the same time. Just keep in mind that you are most often working with individual sites not specifically with individual site collections:

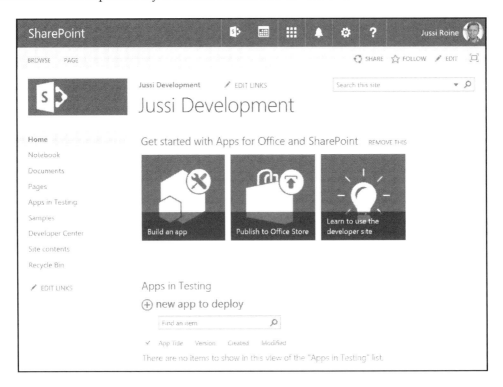

Note that the developer site, which we chose as the site template, is not updated for modern experience yet. As such, we're mostly receiving the classic experience when working on a developer site.

Developer sites versus team sites

A developer site has a few differences from regular team sites that you would typically provision for users. First and foremost, developer sites allow add-in sideloading. This is a method for developers to quickly deploy a custom-developed add-in for their site for testing, thus bypassing the safety procedures and possible governance models SharePoint Online admins tend to prefer in production environments.

As such, if you choose to develop your own add-in, you could deploy it directly to your own developer site. Later, when you are certain your add-in behaves as it should and is ready for production, you can submit the add-in to a separate site, called the Application Catalog, that admins use to provision the custom add-in for wider consumption.

Second, besides the add-in sideloading functionality, developer sites have a few quick links in the left-most navigation bar to aid in quickly navigating between core features within a developer site. The **Apps in Testing** link takes you to a list of add-ins you currently have sideloaded on your site so that you can quickly hop back and forth between multiple add-ins. **Developer Center** is a static link in Microsoft's own public Office Developer Portal at `https://dev.office.com/docs`. **Samples** are also a static link to Microsoft's public repository of sample code.

Don't worry about the navigation bar items or the overall look and feel of your developer site. The purpose of the site is to allow you to kickstart your add-ins for further testing, not to act as a landing site for your users to access your custom add-ins in the future. Typically developers re-create new developer sites when the need arises and might not use the same developer site eternally.

SharePoint Online APIs

Developers need APIs in order to successfully integrate their solutions with other workloads and services. SharePoint Online exposes a good set of APIs, which we'll introduce in this chapter. In later chapters we'll walk through how to best employ the APIs, including authentication and authorization, as well as proper use cases for different kinds of APIs.

Currently, SharePoint Online exposes three types of APIs.

REST APIs, that can be found under the `/_api/` URI, for example, `https://{tenant}.sharepoint.com/_api/{commands}/{parameters}`. This is the most common use case for accessing SharePoint Online structures, data, and information. A sample API call would be a call to the Lists API, which exposes all site lists. The URL for this would be `https://{tenant}.sharepoint.com/_api/web/lists`.

Note, that we need to first call `/web/` underneath `/_api/`, in order to instruct the API to look at the current SharePoint site, and then call the `Lists API`:

```xml
<?xml version="1.0" encoding="utf-8" ?>
- <feed xml:base="https://onsight.sharepoint.com/sites/jussidev2017/_api/" xmlns="http://www.w3.org/2005/Atom"
    xmlns:d="http://schemas.microsoft.com/ado/2007/08/dataservices"
    xmlns:m="http://schemas.microsoft.com/ado/2007/08/dataservices/metadata" xmlns:georss="http://www.georss.org/georss"
    xmlns:gml="http://www.opengis.net/gml">
  <id>006f14c1-ef1c-4060-aa56-c236f80b502a</id>
  <title />
  <updated>2017-05-02T19:03:34Z</updated>
- <entry m:etag=""1"">
    <id>https://onsight.sharepoint.com/sites/jussidev2017/_api/Web/Lists(guid'5bf37e14-670e-4eef-9449-b9366ffd82ac')
    </id>
    <category term="SP.List" scheme="http://schemas.microsoft.com/ado/2007/08/dataservices/scheme" />
    <link rel="edit" href="Web/Lists(guid'5bf37e14-670e-4eef-9449-b9366ffd82ac')" />
    <link rel="http://schemas.microsoft.com/ado/2007/08/dataservices/related/FirstUniqueAncestorSecurableObject"
      type="application/atom+xml;type=entry" title="FirstUniqueAncestorSecurableObject" href="Web/Lists(guid'5bf37e14-
      670e-4eef-9449-b9366ffd82ac')/FirstUniqueAncestorSecurableObject" />
    <link rel="http://schemas.microsoft.com/ado/2007/08/dataservices/related/RoleAssignments"
      type="application/atom+xml;type=feed" title="RoleAssignments" href="Web/Lists(guid'5bf37e14-670e-4eef-9449-
      b9366ffd82ac')/RoleAssignments" />
    <link rel="http://schemas.microsoft.com/ado/2007/08/dataservices/related/Activities"
      type="application/atom+xml;type=feed" title="Activities" href="Web/Lists(guid'5bf37e14-670e-4eef-9449-
      b9366ffd82ac')/Activities" />
    <link rel="http://schemas.microsoft.com/ado/2007/08/dataservices/related/ContentTypes"
      type="application/atom+xml;type=feed" title="ContentTypes" href="Web/Lists(guid'5bf37e14-670e-4eef-9449-
      b9366ffd82ac')/ContentTypes" />
    <link rel="http://schemas.microsoft.com/ado/2007/08/dataservices/related/CreatablesInfo"
      type="application/atom+xml;type=entry" title="CreatablesInfo" href="Web/Lists(guid'5bf37e14-670e-4eef-9449-
      b9366ffd82ac')/CreatablesInfo" />
    <link rel="http://schemas.microsoft.com/ado/2007/08/dataservices/related/DefaultView"
      type="application/atom+xml;type=entry" title="DefaultView" href="Web/Lists(guid'5bf37e14-670e-4eef-9449-
      b9366ffd82ac')/DefaultView" />
    <link rel="http://schemas.microsoft.com/ado/2007/08/dataservices/related/DescriptionResource"
      type="application/atom+xml;type=entry" title="DescriptionResource" href="Web/Lists(guid'5bf37e14-670e-4eef-9449-
      b9366ffd82ac')/DescriptionResource" />
    <link rel="http://schemas.microsoft.com/ado/2007/08/dataservices/related/EventReceivers"
      type="application/atom+xml;type=feed" title="EventReceivers" href="Web/Lists(guid'5bf37e14-670e-4eef-9449-
      b9366ffd82ac')/EventReceivers" />
    <link rel="http://schemas.microsoft.com/ado/2007/08/dataservices/related/Fields"
      type="application/atom+xml;type=feed" title="Fields" href="Web/Lists(guid'5bf37e14-670e-4eef-9449-
      b9366ffd82ac')/Fields" />
    <link rel="http://schemas.microsoft.com/ado/2007/08/dataservices/related/Forms"
      type="application/atom+xml;type=feed" title="Forms" href="Web/Lists(guid'5bf37e14-670e-4eef-9449-
      b9366ffd82ac')/Forms" />
    <link rel="http://schemas.microsoft.com/ado/2007/08/dataservices/related/InformationRightsManagementSettings"
      type="application/atom+xml;type=entry" title="InformationRightsManagementSettings" href="Web/Lists(guid'5bf37e14-
      670e-4eef-9449-b9366ffd82ac')/InformationRightsManagementSettings" />
```

The output, by default, is XML. This sample call exposes all SharePoint lists in the given SharePoint site.

The REST APIs available for SharePoint Online are listed here: `https://msdn.microsoft.com/en-us/library/office/jj860569.aspx?f=255 MSPPError=-2147217396#Reference`.

In addition to REST APIs, SharePoint Online still exposes a smaller subset of **SOAP Web Services**. These Web Services are from the SharePoint 2007 era, but still, work and can sometimes turn out to be useful in specific situations where the REST APIs can't be used or where they might not provide the needed information. In truth, the SOAP Web Services are randomly used and not something SharePoint Online developers should resort to unless absolutely needed.

The SOAP Web Services available for SharePoint Online are listed here: `https://msdn.microsoft.com/en-us/library/office/gg454740%28v=office.14%29.aspx?f=255MSPPError=-2147217396`

Last, but definitely not least, are the **Microsoft Graph APIs** or, more specifically, endpoints. As the name implies, these are not specific to SharePoint Online but more of an overall collection of APIs that Microsoft Graph provides.

A quick primer on Microsoft Graph

Microsoft Graph is an ever-growing collection of APIs that can be uniformly accessed through a common contract. The idea with Microsoft Graph is that developers would only need to learn one set of authentication, authorization, and access models to access any kind of cloud-based service within Office 365. For now, Microsoft Graph does not provide parity for all SharePoint Online REST APIs, but it has a fairly good collection of modernized APIs developers may wish to use for their applications.

Using Microsoft Graph is essentially more helpful with Graph Explorer, which is a web-based tool for figuring out what data there is and where it lies. It can be accessed through the Microsoft Graph marketing page at `https://graph.microsoft.io/`, by clicking **Graph Explorer** on the top navigation:

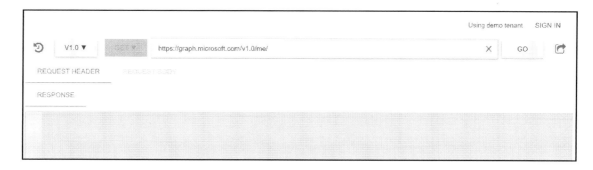

You can try out the APIs in a demo tenant, or by clicking **Sign in**, you can access your real data. Keep in mind that the Graph Explorer is built and operated by Microsoft, but it's still a good idea to avoid logging in with your global admin account unless you absolutely and unconditionally trust the service.

After logging in and running the default query against Microsoft Graph, the /me/ object resolves to your current account's metadata:

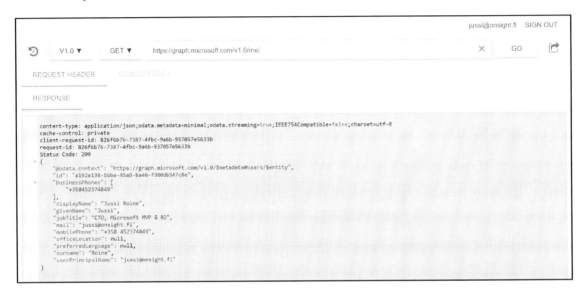

To target the queries against my SharePoint Online site, I need to change queries from /v1.0/me/ to /beta/, as SharePoint Online APIs are still in beta for Microsoft Graph.

Under /beta, I can point my queries to /beta/sharePoint/ (note the lowercase 's', and capital 'P') and then to /beta/sharePoint/site/lists:

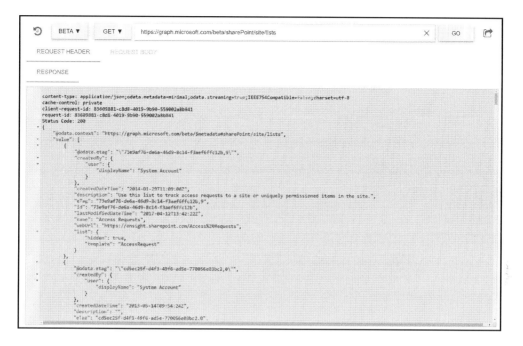

This returns a clean list formatted in JSON for us to use within our code. The purpose of the Graph Explorer is to allow the developer to rapidly test against live data and figure out the correct API queries.

Graph Explorer has an intellisense-style helper built-in, so when you're constructing your queries, you should see a small window popup and provide suggestions for the current query:

All Microsoft Graph SharePoint Online APIs are referenced and documented here: `https://developer.microsoft.com/en-us/graph/docs/api-reference/beta/resources/sharepoint`.

You are free to combine your calls to different APIs between SharePoint Online REST APIs, Microsoft Graph calls, and perhaps also the SOAP Web Services. In addition, you could also build your own custom APIs using Microsoft Azure API Apps, Azure Functions, and similar services. A good practice is to first check Microsoft Graph for your needs. If you find it lacking for your specific requirements, check the SharePoint Online REST APIs, and only if these do not provide you with the necessary functionality, consider building your own custom APIs.

Developing solutions for SharePoint Online

By now, you should have a basic understanding of what SharePoint Online is, how information is structured within SPO, and how you can provision your own developer site that can be used as a playground for your upcoming custom deployments.

Next, we'll look at what kind of solutions developers can build for SPO. We'll start with the classic and oldest models and move up the ladder to the add-in approach. This excludes the latest addition to the family, the SharePoint Framework (SPFx), which the book will cover in deep detail in the following chapters.

We feel it's crucial to understand how things were built for previous (and sometimes current) versions of SharePoint, even if at a pretty high level, in order to respect and understand the decision and options we have at our disposal today.

Solutions for SharePoint and SharePoint Online

Solutions for SharePoint (primarily versions from 2007 to 2016) and SharePoint Online can be built in numerous ways. Next, we'll go through a bit of history because we feel it is important to have a glimpse of how (bad) things were in the beginning. It is often helpful to understand why things work in a certain way with SharePoint, as many technical functionalities in SharePoint are based on the pre-SharePoint Online era.

SharePoint 2001-2003: direct modification of files

As the title of this section states, this relates to the early days of SharePoint, between SharePoint Portal Server 2001 and SharePoint Portal Server 2003. These two versions did not have a way to formally package, deploy, or retract custom code. Developers resorted to all kinds of hacks and kludges that kind of work, but did not really respect any solid development approaches, such as application lifecycle management or version control.

Developers would simply open a remote connection (typically via Remote Desktop) to a SharePoint 2001/2003 server, find the file they needed to modify, and use either Notepad on the server or copy the file for additional editing on their own workstation. Files would reside in the SharePoint Hive, under such directories as `C:\Program Files\Common Files\Microsoft Shared\Web Server Extensions\<version>\`. Each SharePoint server, if you had several in a farm configuration, would have identical files. Thus, changing one file on a single server would require you to change the same file identically on other servers as well.

In a way, this was a quick, fast, and reasonably well-understood approach. If you needed a change within SharePoint, you could simply figure out which file was responsible for the change and inject your changes to that file only. The result would often be so-so and kind of acceptable--until the next Service Pack was released and installed on the very same SharePoint server. At best, it would simply wipe customizations and force you to re-do all your changes once more. At worst, it would break something horribly as some files would now be patched with the Service Pack's version, while others would be customized and there would be no knowing what had gone wrong and where. Pages wouldn't load and random errors would occur for users.

One inventive, although certainly unsupported approach, was to tinker with Windows' **Internet Information Services (IIS)** web server settings to fool SharePoint just a tiny bit. SharePoint typically, at the time, mapped the infamous `/_layouts/` virtual directory to the SharePoint Hive under `C:\Program Files\Common Files\Microsoft Shared\Web Server Extensions\<version>\` subdirectories. Clever system administrators and developers would copy the hive directory structure to a sibling directory structure, and map the virtual directory from `/_layouts/` in IIS to this new copy of the original files. In practical terms, this allowed one to tinker with the files without fear that original files would be destroyed. Upon new Service Pack deployments, you could point the virtual directory back to the original hive, allow patching to complete, and then do a file diff comparison between the original (patched) hive and your customized hive. Talk about spending a lot of time to get to your results!

Luckily, SharePoint versions 2001 and 2003 are not supported and we haven't seen these versions in production in years. But this is where it all started back in the day.

SharePoint 2007--Full-trust code

Microsoft Office SharePoint Server 2007, or MOSS as it was known then, introduced the first true and quite proper development approach to SharePoint. This vehicle became known as SharePoint solution packages, that packaged our native .NET code to files with a `.WSP` extension.

This was also known as the full-trust code, as all code you wrote, packaged, deployed and used would run as fully trusted within SharePoint's memory space. A poor developer could easily write horribly sloppy code that iterated through hundreds of SharePoint sites recursively, then iterated through each list and document library and changed something in one or two of the document libraries. This would then be embedded in a web part, that is a building block that acts as a widget on a SharePoint page. Initially, the developer might have tested this on his or her laptop, and everything could have executed flawlessly. Change this to a production environment, with possibly hundreds or thousands of people loading the very same page, and you quickly run into all sorts of unforeseen performance issues.

Full-trust code initially did not have proper support within Visual Studio at the time, so developers would build custom tooling to compile, define, and package the deployment packages. Deployment would also be part of custom scripts and tooling executed locally on one or more SharePoint servers. Debugging would then occur on a separate server and would often be time-consuming and error-prone.

Solutions would be crafted around Features, which acted as a kind of lights on/lights off containment model for SharePoint artifacts. One or more Features would be packaged within a SharePoint solution package (the `.WSP` file) and uploaded to SharePoint's database for deployment. Each Feature would consist of at least one XML file introducing the deployment logic, and each solution package would consist of exactly one manifest file that held everything together. Combine this with possibly multiple solution packages per the overall solution and you often had a time-sensitive and highly detailed deployment script that needed to be executed just so, in the hope that everything would work.

What's important to realize is that MOSS 2007 gave us the Feature framework and the Solution framework. Much of the development between SharePoint versions 2007 and 2010 was tinkering and fiddling with XML file structures, essentially describing in pre-defined XML structures how a certain feature might act within SharePoint. Here and there developers could inject a little bit of HTML, combined with JavaScript, CSS and, if lucky, possibly also some C# code. We still remember countless meetings and review discussions with talented developers who swore never to work with SharePoint again, as it was not real coding, but would rather modify cumbersome XML structures that at times were poorly documented and lacked a strongly typed approach.

You wouldn't have compile-time error handling, and deployment to SharePoint might have taken 10 or 15 minutes for each try.

SharePoint solution packages (and Features) are still supported for all SharePoint versions from 2007, 2010 and 2013 to 2016. It's not advisable to continue building solution packages but, at times, a transformation from a legacy solution might be required. It should also be clear without saying, but just to be clear solution packages *are not* supported in SharePoint Online. As such, developers aiming to build cloud-supported solutions for SharePoint Online, should not build solution packages or solutions using the Feature framework.

SharePoint 2010 and SharePoint Online: sandbox solutions

With SharePoint 2010, Microsoft introduced a subset of the full-trust code development model. This was called sandbox solutions and, on paper, the idea was great. Not fabulous, but great.

The thinking at the time was that since organizations were starting to move more and more of their on-premises workloads to hosting environments or even public clouds (pre-Office 365 era), something needed to be done so that SharePoint deployments littered with full-trust code could safely be lifted and shifted or migrated to a multitenant platform. Since full-trust code was, well, fully trusted, it wouldn't take more than a few hours for someone to deploy bad-behaving code that would crash the whole application pool of a given IIS, and possibly even consume all available virtual memory within the SharePoint server.

Sandbox solutions were introduced for both SharePoint 2010 and SharePoint Online. These were initially meant for SharePoint 2010 and were offered as a multitenant platform for organizations so that they could share a common platform, and were later ported to SharePoint Online as a means to govern what kind of custom code would be deployed to a shared platform.

The idea with sandbox solutions was that running code within a package could only access a very limited set of APIs and namespaces within the SharePoint Object Model. One limitation that was set, meant that all calls to methods within the SharePoint development models could only access elements under a single site collection by using the `SPSite()` object. This way developers couldn't access any structures or data above the site collection that was running the code. Access to direct file I/O was also prohibited, as well as access to directly call HTTP interfaces through SharePoint.

This approach worked well, on paper. But in reality, porting existing code from full-trust packages proved to be troublesome, time-consuming, and sometimes just impossible. Existing code often resorted to using certain methods and features of the SharePoint Object Model, so that a replacement within the `SPSite()` object was not simply available. Therefore, either big pieces of custom code had to be cut in order to move the platform to the cloud, or fully rewritten without having proper APIs.

As part of this ideology, Microsoft introduced the idea of resources. Each call from the code would consume a small piece of resources from a pool of resources, and administrators could designate pre-allocations for each site collection. When the customization exceeded its allotted resources, it would simply be shut down. Imagine having a graphical component running on your SharePoint site that exposes a tool for your users. Suddenly, the tool simply disappears from the page because it exceeded a hidden resource allocation that end users weren't aware of. Administrators would have to reallocate more resources or start digging through code to understand where and how the resources were spent and how to best optimize this piece of code for a small subset of users complaining loudly.

As such, sandbox solutions never really took off. A couple of years after introducing sandbox solutions in SharePoint Online, Microsoft quietly deprecated the ability to run custom .NET code within a sandbox solution package. This effectively rendered the whole model to a vehicle for provisioning XML-based artifacts for a given SharePoint site or site collection. Not much changed, as developers were now complaining (again) that developing solutions for SharePoint were merely pointless exercises in understanding archaic XML structures in Notepad.

From time to time we still see customer deployment in SharePoint Online happily running sandbox solutions. This is fine but in no way advisable for the future. A good approach is to export the sandbox solution files, rename the packages from `.WSP` to `.ZIP` files, and explore what's in the package. This way you can learn and understand what the solution truly implement, and how to best replace the solution.

SharePoint 2013, SharePoint 2016, and SharePoint Online: add-ins

With SharePoint 2013, Microsoft felt it was time to introduce a new approach to partially (or fully) replace the now aging Feature and Solution framework development model. This model was initially launched to market with a catchy name, the **Cloud App Model** (**CAM**). As its name implies, CAM was crafted on purpose to provide a cloud-enabled development approach that fully supported SharePoint Online without the missteps of sandbox solutions. Later, CAM was renamed the App Model (AM) for a brief moment, and a while later it was renamed the Add-in model. For now, the Add-in model seems to have stuck, so in the context of development, we'll be referencing all types of apps as add-ins when they relate to SharePoint add-ins.

The winning ticket within the Add-in model was the de-coupling of server-side code from SharePoint. Developers were now able to code in their preferred programming language, the server-side implementation of their customization, and simply run that outside SharePoint. As such, it was never similar to full-trust code from the SharePoint 2007-2010 era, but more a model that allowed developers to execute code elsewhere.

This was also fairly close to the time when Microsoft Azure started gaining more and more ground and popularity within organizations. Ideally, companies could implement custom add-ins that would run in Microsoft Azure's **Platform as a Service** (**PaaS**) environment, and the surface on SharePoint with the help of the Add-in model's **Client-Side Object Model** (**CSOM**).

Add-ins initially came in three flavors:

- **SharePoint-hosted Add-ins**, which are add-ins without any server-side code or additional logic that would need to run outside SharePoint. They would use SharePoint's data structure, including a separate subsite within the current SharePoint site where the add-in was being provisioned. The subsite (called the AppWeb) would be used as a fixed storage for everything the add-in might need to record. The AppWeb could, obviously, store only data that fit the artifacts available for a SharePoint site: lists, document libraries, and similar quite limited elements. All user interface elements had to be built with CSS, HTML, and JavaScript, and all assets had to be hosted within the AppWeb to provide better security and in order to avoid cross-site scripting attacks.

- **Provider-hosted add-ins**, which are true add-ins in the sense that server-side code can be included as part of the add-in. The development consists of a separate website, that can be implemented with several supported frameworks and languages--even in non-Microsoft programming languages such as Python or Ruby on Rails. The idea is to implement a separate website and then call upon that site and embed the output of the site to a SharePoint site using a specifically crafted IFRame. For the most part, this solution turned out to be a fairly reasonable approach to running custom code outside SharePoint. For many scenarios though, performance was subpar, and security was problematic to configure and understand. The whole framework relied on carefully created public-key cryptography certificates that had to be deployed just in the right order in the hope of getting the platform to securely call the external website within the user's security realm. Provider-hosted add-ins are still built today, but they are not as common as one might expect. For several larger deployments with tens of thousands of users, we are seeing one or maybe two provider-hosted add-ins, and they tend to be rather complex implementations of internal applications that must play nicely with SharePoint's interface and look and feel.

- **Auto-hosted add-ins** were a novel idea to run add-ins in the cloud and if code required additional resources, they would be automatically provisioned from Microsoft Azure. There were too many questions on this approach--especially from customers who would ask which credit card or billing contract was used for the Azure-provisioned assets. Since then, Auto-hosted Add-ins have been retired and they have not supported or in use anymore.

Today, the Add-in model is still supported and alive. Not much progress has occurred with the model and it's mostly been stale since 2015.

SharePoint Online--add-ins and client-side scripts

In addition to add-ins, developers often need to drop small functionality and bits of features to individual pages within SharePoint sites. A common approach is to add a Script Editor Web Part on a page and drop a piece of JavaScript and/or HTML within the page. This is a very simple approach but can be both powerful and troublesome in the long run.

The benefits of using a **Script Editor Web Part (SEWP)** is that it's very easy to add as an ad-hoc solution when in a meeting with the site owner and simply code on-the-fly whatever is needed. This is assuming the developer is quite capable and fluent with JavaScript and the SharePoint APIs.

Adding a SEWP on a page allows developers to write JavaScript through the browser and save it into SharePoint Online's own database:

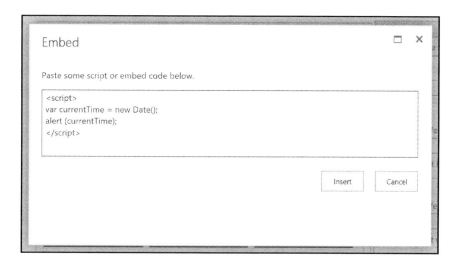

Upon page load, the script is executed and the user gets the result of the preceding code in a popup since the sample is using the classic JavaScript `alert()` message box:

The downside is that pages tend to become littered with all sorts of small JavaScript tidbits that no-one can keep track of. One piece of code could reference an external library that has a locally stored copy of a SharePoint document library, while another piece of code (even on the same page!) might reference the very same external library but a different version through a public CDN URI. Thus, the payload for a user loading the page would be at least double, as the client browser would need to resolve both external frameworks, load the payload, and figure out which version to use and when. Imagine having hundreds of sites, thousands of pages, with customizations using the SEWP-approach on five percent of all pages. You very quickly run into performance and supportability issues, as well as troubleshooting errors that are not obvious as frameworks are not referenced in a proper manner.

Development tooling for SharePoint Online

So far we've established that solutions built for SharePoint Online historically have been mostly about sandboxed solutions, custom scripts embedded on pages with the Script Editor Web Part, and custom add-ins that are either hosted within SharePoint or separately in Microsoft Azure (or a similar environment).

Developers use a reasonably new version of Visual Studio development tooling to build, package, and deploy their code to SharePoint Online. This can be Visual Studio 2015 or 2017, or newer when one becomes available. By installing Office Development Tools during Visual Studio installation, developers get to enjoy the pre-built templates for new projects that target SharePoint Online.

The only template that can be reasonably used today is the SharePoint Add-in template:

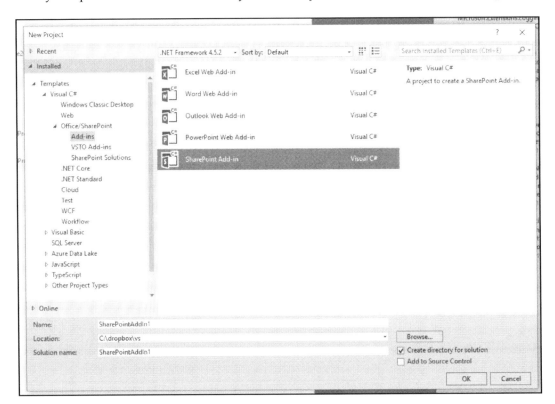

1. This template allows for the creation of a SharePoint add-in that can be either a SharePoint-hosted add-in or a Provider-hosted add-in. During the initial creation of the project, you can specify the target site for development, and this can be the developer site you created earlier within your SharePoint Online tenant:

2. Note that if you choose to create a provider-hosted add-in, you'll need to do additional configuration with certificates in order to secure the deployment. For a SharePoint-hosted add-in, no additional configuration is needed and you can start building your solution right away.

3. The solution consists of a single Feature, the Add-in package, and necessary support files and assets:

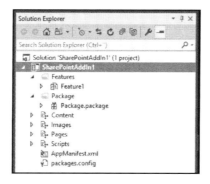

4. When deploying the solution, you can right-click on the **project**, and select **Publish**.

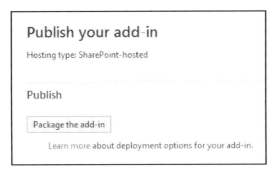

5. This allows you to publish the add-in as a package for manual deployment, or deploy the package to Office Store. Office Store is a marketplace run by Microsoft, allowing for reselling and marketing of your add-in to other organizations.

6. The packaged add-in can now be manually deployed to your developer site. First, simply upload the add-in package file to your developer site's **Apps in Testing** document library. Upon completion of the upload, you can simply deploy the app to the same site:

7. As the add-in is merely a sample add-in, we haven't introduced any additional user permissions we might be needing while impersonating the logged-in user (executing the add-in). As such, we can simply trust the add-in:

8. The add-in will now install and self-provision within the site:

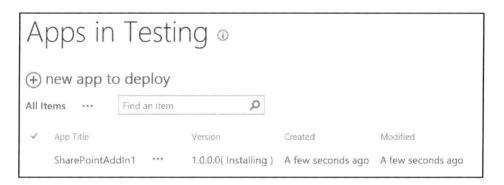

9. Installation might take a minute or two. After it completes, the ribbon has a **Launch AppButton** that becomes enabled when the app is selected in the document library. Clicking the button will call the add-in:

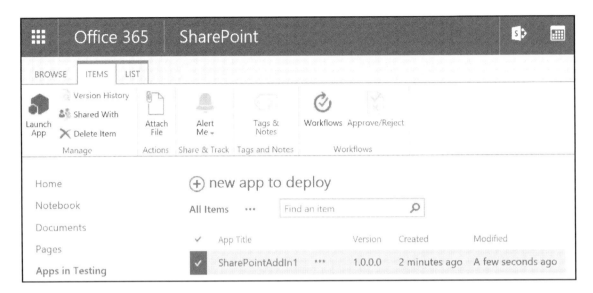

10. Since we didn't configure the add-in at all and just compiled the default template, the add-in is a full page app. It inherits the SharePoint Online look and feel, but is running in a different base URL to the SharePoint Online site it was launched from:

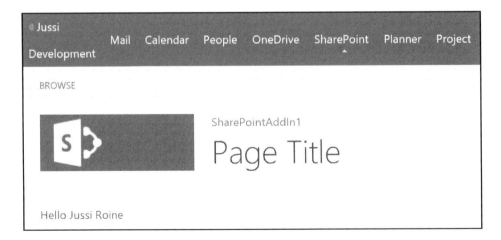

11. The add-in calls a small piece of JavaScript to resolve the logged-in user's full name. Everything else is static on the page, including the top-most navigation. The same add-in could also be embedded in a SharePoint page if we add an App Part instruction to tell SharePoint Online it can embed the add-in safely.

Summary

In this initial chapter, we had a tour of the core SharePoint Online building blocks, including document libraries, lists, and web parts. Additionally, these are always stored within SharePoint sites, which are then constructed within a given SharePoint site collection.

A somewhat simplified logical view of the structure of SharePoint Online is shown in the following graphic:

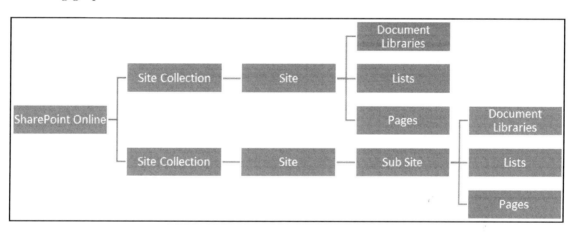

Typically, you would create one or more site collection and one or more site within these site collections. One site collection could be an intranet and another could be a dedicated site collection for project sites. Each site could then host your customizations and custom add-ins.

Development for on-premises versions of SharePoint differs quite a bit from SharePoint Online, as SharePoint Online only supports either client-side code with the use of JavaScript, CSS, and HTML, or code executed outside SharePoint--typically within a Microsoft Azure service such as Azure App Service.

For development, developers tend to use Visual Studio when building add-ins, as the templates are immensely helpful in managing the necessary file structures and packaging. Deployment can be done manually against a SharePoint Online developer site for real-life testing before production deployment through a special Application Catalog site.

In Chapter 2, *Developing Solutions for SharePoint Online*, we will start our journey of developing solutions for SharePoint Online. We will first have a look at SharePoint Framework, which partially replaces but also augments some of the existing development models in SharePoint Online. In addition, we'll dip our toes the usual development aspects of any type of project, including application lifecycle management and the best ways to manage your development efforts in SharePoint Online.

2
Developing Solutions for SharePoint

In this chapter, we'll take an in-depth look into the SharePoint Framework, and how it relates to the other, and often older, development approaches. In addition, we'll also need to understand what the limitations of the SharePoint Framework are and what can be done to implement solutions that are beyond the scope of this development approach. From there, we'll introduce the **Application Lifecycle Management (ALM)** capabilities for SharePoint developers.

Any type of framework typically requires a fair amount of time from developers to understand its essence and usage. As such, we'll introduce the basics of the SharePoint Framework in this chapter, and in the following chapters, we will open the features and possibilities even further. This includes:

- A general introduction and overview to get more familiar with the SharePoint Framework as a development framework
- The toolchain, which includes the necessary tools that developers must be familiar with when developing solutions for the SharePoint Framework
- Office developer patterns and practices, a community-supported project that is highly active and produces a lot of great tools, guidance, and sample code for SharePoint developers, including the SharePoint Framework
- ALM considerations for the SharePoint Framework-related deployment

Introducing the SharePoint Framework

The SharePoint Framework is a rather new approach to implementing and customizing SharePoint. We use the term *customization* quite loosely in this chapter, meaning mostly all types of custom implementations that organizations typically request as part of their SharePoint projects.

In order to understand the essence of the SharePoint Framework, we'll start with extensibility.

SharePoint extensibility

Ever since SharePoint was introduced, and the add-in model was introduced, the thinking from Microsoft for SharePoint extensibility has been that a supported model must exist, and it should be in the long term. Now, you might be thinking that after the previous chapter, where we had a brief encounter with many different approaches--where is the long-term thinking? Granted, some of those models, such as **sandboxed solutions**, should maybe have been more refined and possibly even not released in their past forms. But at the same time cloud computing, together with a **Platform as a Service (PaaS)** thinking, has surged and is constantly evolving.

The qSharePoint Framework aims to mitigate the past mistakes and challenges of SharePoint customization models in two major areas.

First, the SharePoint Framework aligns very closely with current industry standard frameworks and models. As such, Microsoft is not introducing yet another framework from zero and planning to spend the next 3 years refining this model to make a stable version. Instead, the SharePoint Framework has evolved quite rapidly from the initial preview builds to a general availability-stability that enterprise customers require.

Second, the SharePoint Framework is leaning heavily on tried and tested approaches, in that it is built on leading client-side solutions. As such, it will work for both on-premises deployments and in the cloud. The SharePoint Framework is supported in **SharePoint Online** and **SharePoint 2016** with **Feature Pack 2**.

All solutions built with the SharePoint Framework extend SharePoint, one way or another. Instead of trying to rip out a core piece of SharePoint, and replace that with your custom implementation, the SharePoint Framework will simply inject a new functionality and the existing one could be hidden from users. It's a lightweight approach to a heavyweight problem, and it works.

Philosophy of the SharePoint Framework

The philosophy of the SharePoint Framework takes many cues from past missteps of the add-in model and full-trust solution model. As developers have been moving to a more lightweight approach using script injection, embedded HTML within a script editor web part, and similar models, the SharePoint Framework aims to provide a unified and consistent way to create customizations in SharePoint.

All development for the SharePoint Framework is modern client-side development. This does not imply that nothing can be implemented on the server side. It merely means that most SharePoint customizations tend to be functionality that can be encapsulated on the client-side quite easily. For those features that require server-side logic, it can be implemented outside SharePoint; typically using a serverless platform such as Microsoft Azure Functions, Azure API apps, or similar concepts.

The modern approach also means that the SharePoint Framework will evolve over time. This, of course, is not a promise on our part, as we've already seen several development frameworks and approaches for SharePoint in the past decade. But this seems to be a commitment by Microsoft, that this time the framework is here to stay and will evolve based on industry needs, requirements, and shifts.

The SharePoint Framework's philosophy also includes a lightweight approach to implementing solutions. Existing logic, APIs, and functionality from other frameworks and platforms can be used as needed. The SharePoint Framework brings in the toolset and capabilities to better customize the overall user experience of SharePoint, rather than dissecting the internal workings of SharePoint in order to achieve something that the user can experience.

We need the SharePoint Framework and its controlled approach to custom code to avoid the problems of the past. These problems include complex migrations or upgrades, as the code was stored within the content or in multiple document libraries as JavaScript files. The SharePoint Framework will remedy these challenges by providing packaging, deployment, distribution, and version control for your code.

Types of projects the SharePoint Framework supports

As the SharePoint Framework is not a fixed set of functionalities that Microsoft chooses to release once, and then update at leisure years later, the types of projects it supports varies.

At the time of writing this book, the SharePoint Framework supports the following capabilities and project types:

- **Client-side web parts**: These are equivalent to your typical SharePoint web parts, or client-side web parts you could build with the add-in model. This is the most common requirement for any SharePoint project: to build a widget or element on a page that can be configured and parameterized to provide new functionality on a given page.

Client-side web parts are, as the name implies, implemented using assets the client browser understands; namely **Cascading Style Sheets** (**CSS**) for element branding and positioning, HTML for structure, and JavaScript for logic and functionality. You are free to include your preferred JavaScript frameworks inside a client-side web part, or use one of the recommended client-side frameworks, such as React or AngularJS, if you're already familiar with those.

- **The SharePoint Framework extensions**: These allow developers to extend and modify existing elements on SharePoint pages and views. These include the toolbars of SharePoint, the views of list data, notification areas, and similar facets. With the addition of the SharePoint Framework extensions, developers can customize and create new functionality outside client-side web parts, which was initially the only approach to using the SharePoint Framework in SharePoint Online.
- **Web part connections**: Similarly to classic (server-side) web part connections, these allow developers to create richer client-side web parts that can communicate with other web parts on a given page. This feature allows for functionality, such as selector view, that provides detailed information on another adjacent web part based on the selection.

As you can see, the SharePoint Framework already provides most of the needs that typical SharePoint projects, such as intranets, require. As the framework evolves, we can expect to get more abilities and possibilities that allow us to extend or even replace existing SharePoint features, in a clean and supported approach.

Key features of the SharePoint Framework

Besides the types of projects the SharePoint Framework supports, there are other key aspects of the approach that developers need to be aware of.

First, and foremost, the SharePoint Framework-based customizations and custom code runs in the context of a logged-in current user and connection with the browser.

Elevation of privileges, which would often be a way for developers to circumvent the permission model of SharePoint in full-trust code, are not used with the SharePoint Framework. As no IFrames are used, all code that you deploy that is based on the SharePoint Framework always executes with the permissions, privileges, and access of the current user. Keep this in mind when implementing your solutions, as you might need to store additional data elsewhere and the user either must have access to that location, or you need to resort to external code to shield your data or make it harder to access directly.

Each solution that you choose to make available for users can be deployed either on classic SharePoint pages or modern SharePoint pages. The difference between the two is that classic pages are what most users are accustomed to using and modifying. Modern pages are, as the name implies, a newer model based on a canvas rather than individual zones (called the web part zones). When implementing your solutions, you typically do not have to worry whether or not the hosting page will be classic or modern; they both work, and presumably more and more pages in the future will simply be modern pages.

Toolchain

The toolchain for the SharePoint Framework is based on open source tools and ideology. This section will walk you through all the necessary tools you will have in your toolchain when implementing solutions using the SharePoint Framework.

These tools aid you in managing your projects, building and deploying your code for test and production environments, and running your code locally when doing initial debugging and testing. If you've been already building solutions for SharePoint before the SharePoint Framework was available, you'll see that a lot has changed from the earlier SharePoint development models.

In Chapter 3, *Getting Started with the SharePoint Framework*, we will be using the toolchain to build our first SharePoint Framework package.

npm

npm is a package manager for JavaScript. It includes a command-line tool, coincidentally called npm, and it uses an online repository known as the npm registry to find, retrieve and deploy new packages your code might need. The SharePoint Framework uses npm packages in the base template you'll typically be using. In addition, new SharePoint Framework templates and functionality will be published as npm packages.

Think of npm as the tool that allows you to interact with a vast library of pre-made packages, that in turn will aid you in building SharePoint Framework packages. The rough equivalent of npm in the .NET world would be NuGet.

For example, the package named `@microsoft/sp-client-base` is a base package that the SharePoint Framework uses in the base project template, and the latest stable version will be automatically fetched from the npm repository at `https://www.npmjs.com/package/@microsoft/sp-core-library`.

You can find more information on npm at `https://www.npmjs.com/`.

Yeoman and Yeoman SharePoint generator

Yeoman is a generator tool, helping developers create new project and solution directories. You'd use npm to get individual packages, and you'd use Yeoman to generate a new SharePoint Framework project, which in turn would fetch the correct npm packages and other dependencies.

Microsoft has published a Yeoman generator for SharePoint, which includes all the necessary workflow actions to create the SharePoint Framework base project. This way, developers do not have to start each project from line 0, trying to figure out what goes where. As things evolve and change, the Yeoman generator for SharePoint will be updated and new projects will simply get updated project structures and updated npm packages.

Think of Yeoman as a tool that provides you with access to a pre-defined checklist and build file for constructing your project base. You will typically install Yeoman with npm, as Yeoman is published as an npm package.

Yeoman is used with the shorthand command `yo`, and it will call for SharePoint Framework generators for you, such as the `@microsoft/sharepoint` template.

You can find more information on Yeoman at `http://yeoman.io/`.

Gulp

Gulp is yet another tool that you will find highly useful, and a required tool in your overall toolchain for SharePoint Framework development projects. Whereas you will use npm to fetch the necessary packages and Yeoman to generate your projects, you will use Gulp to build your projects with all the necessary parameters and dependencies.

Gulp automates and allows you to enhance your build workflow. This is done with a configuration file called `gulpfile.js`, which allows you to add custom actions and tasks when building your project.

With .NET development, where you typically use Microsoft's Visual Studio development environment, you would typically just select the **Build** menu from the top toolbar, and then click on **Build solution**. This would compile and build your full-trust solution for SharePoint.

However, when using Gulp, you type `gulp <action>`, such as the `package`, to start packaging your code into a re-distributable and deployable package.

 You can find more information on Gulp at `http://gulpjs.com/`.

Visual Studio Code

With previous SharePoint frameworks, such as in the add-in model and the full-trust models, a developer would use Visual Studio to build and package everything in the project. As the code editor, this would often be a version released around the same time as the SharePoint version, such as Visual Studio 2013 together with SharePoint 2013.

For the SharePoint Framework, Microsoft envisioned that as things evolve rapidly and open source frameworks shift constantly, then the main development environment does not follow the pace set by Visual Studio. Visual Studio Code is a free, open source alternative to Visual Studio commercial editions from Microsoft, and it is the preferred integrated development environment for SharePoint Framework based projects.

Compared to a full and commercial version of Visual Studio, Visual Studio Code (or VS Code for short) is lightweight and quick to install. You can download the latest version of VS Code at `https://code.visualstudio.com/`, and it runs on Windows, macOS, and 64-bit Linux platforms. As it is much more lightweight, it lacks certain features of a full **Integrated Development Environment (IDE)** such as Visual Studio, but for the SharePoint Framework related work, it is more than sufficient. Think of VS Code as a glorified text editor that supports IntelliSense (providing automatic sensing of what you are writing and suggestions for methods, property names, and similar), several types of scripting and programming languages, debugging, source control, file management, and many third-party extensions.

> If you're ever in Command Prompt and need to start up VS Code, just type
> `code .`

VS Code also automatically updates itself, and you will frequently get a prompt for deploying a fresh update or forfeiting the update.

Compared to an IDE such as Visual Studio, VS Code's interface is fairly bareboned, to enhance productivity and to optimize code writing. In the following screenshot, you can see the toolbar on the far left, the open folder second, and a file being edited in the main area. As you can see in the following screenshot, VS Code does not have a toolbar but rather a command palette which opens up many options and features that are not immediately visible.

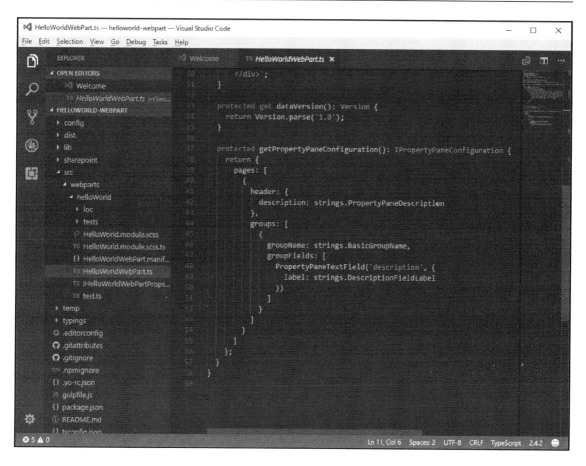

It's important to understand that VS Code works with files and folder structures, and it does not impose its own project or solution format that is typical for working with projects in Visual Studio.

VS Code is not only meant to be used with the SharePoint Framework it can be used for almost any type of development projects that include script-based languages, such as JavaScript, Python, PowerShell, HTML, and CSS.

You are free to choose any other text editor or IDE of your preference, as VS Code is not enforced in any way for developing SharePoint Framework solutions. The benefit of using VS Code, however, is that it's free, lightweight, and evolves very rapidly. Most sample code, tutorials, and guidance also assume that you are using VS Code so, as such, we strongly recommend you look at VS Code and consider using it as your primary editor for the SharePoint Framework solutions.

Browser developer tools

As an invaluable tool in your toolchain, a proper browser developer toolset is required. You are free to choose whichever browser you feel most comfortable with; it can be Google Chrome, Mozilla Firefox, Internet Explorer, Microsoft Edge, or similar.

Developer tools within a browser are typically accessed with *F12* while a page is open in the browser. This provides a toolset that is highly useful for debugging the SharePoint Framework issues and problems.

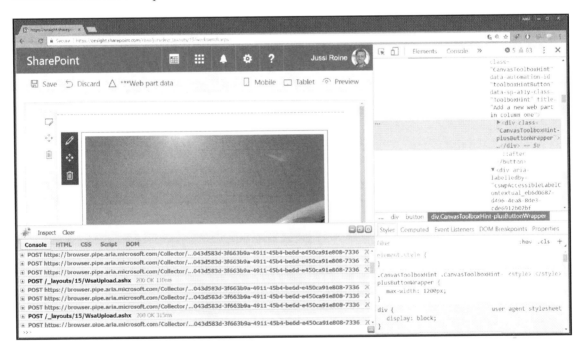

SharePoint Workbench

The last, and probably one of the most often used tools in your SharePoint Framework toolchain, is the SharePoint Workbench. This HTML page is served from a local filesystem by Node.js and loaded in a browser instance when you run `gulp serve`.

By default, SharePoint Workbench is dynamically loaded as `workbench.html` locally and is only accessible from your localhost. In addition, SharePoint Workbench also exists in SharePoint and can be used against a real Office 365 tenant or SharePoint 2016 to see how your code truly works.

In a typical development workflow with the SharePoint Framework, you'll mostly use the locally hosted `workbench.html` to test and see how your code works. When you're ready to package and test your code against SharePoint, you'll be using the hosted version from SharePoint 2016 or Office 365.

It's worth pointing out that the local version of SharePoint Workbench (`workbench.html`) does not require SharePoint installed locally. In fact, it only requires the packages from npm, that Yeoman generator kindly fetches for you, and nothing else! A network connection is not needed once npm install has been done.

In the following screenshot, you can see the status logs when SharePoint Workbench is being loaded locally:

```
Starting api server on port 5432.
Registring api: /getwebparts
Registring api: /*.*
Registring api: /workbench
[19:48:43] Finished subtask 'serve' after 538 ms
[19:48:43] Finished 'serve' after 4.84 s
[19:48:43] Server started https://localhost:4321
[19:48:43] LiveReload started on port 35729
[19:48:43] Opening https://localhost:5432/workbench using the default OS app
  Request: [::1] '/workbench'
  Request: '/temp/workbench.html'
```

When SharePoint Workbench has loaded, your default browser (in this case, Google Chrome for our sample) will try to load it from the localhost.

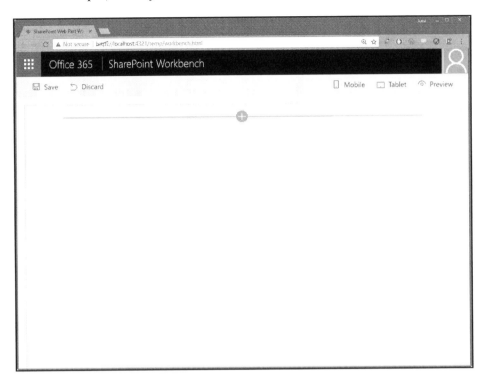

Upon loading **SharePoint Workbench**, you'll get a simple UI that mimics SharePoint. Microsoft even went to the trouble to add Office 365 in the top-left corner to make you feel as if you're truly debugging your code in the cloud. The reason SharePoint Workbench is highly efficient when used locally is that everything is running locally, thus there is no network latency. You can test, debug, and trial your code in mere seconds, and you don't have to wait for your code to first package, upload, and deploy to SharePoint. This latter approach would often take you anywhere from a minute to 5 minutes, and just to test small changes would mean that precious development time would be spent waiting for pages to load and for Office 365 to process your data first.

SharePoint Workbench provides a sample canvas (the large white area with the + -sign) where you can now add your sample code. In this example, an **HelloWorld** (client-side) web part was created and it's currently being debugged.

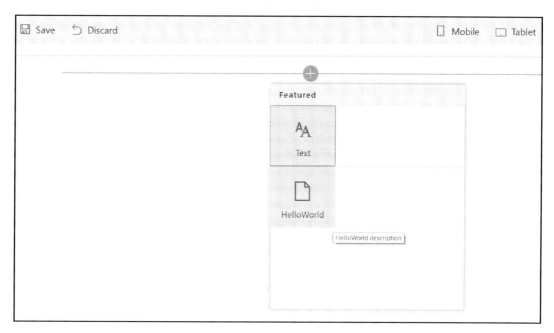

We can see that SharePoint Workbench is clever enough to automatically load our code from local disk, and by selecting the web part, we can drop it on the canvas.

We can also edit web part settings by clicking the pen icon.

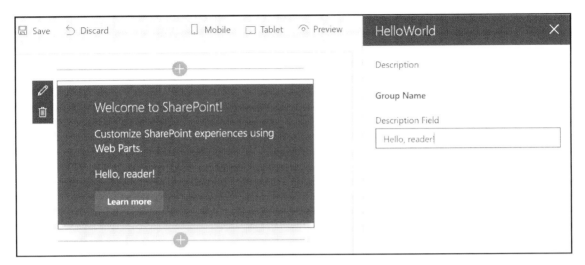

The sample project only has one editable text field. The contents of this text field will be automatically rendered on the web part itself. When editing the text field, it is simultaneously updated on the actual web part on the left.

Obviously, we cannot save our changes if we choose to change the configuration settings for the web part, as there is nowhere to persist the changes. We can even try adding the very same web part multiple times on the page and this is a good practice to test when writing your code. Quite often, developers need to add external frameworks on the page, and by adding the web part multiple times, we can test that the frameworks are not loaded over and over again and that they do not cause havoc by being loaded more than once.

As responsiveness is built-in, and almost always preferred in the SharePoint Framework components, there is a simple but useful tool for testing your customizations against common devices. By clicking either **mobile** or **tablet** in the toolbar, we can easily check how content flows with different dimensions and capabilities.

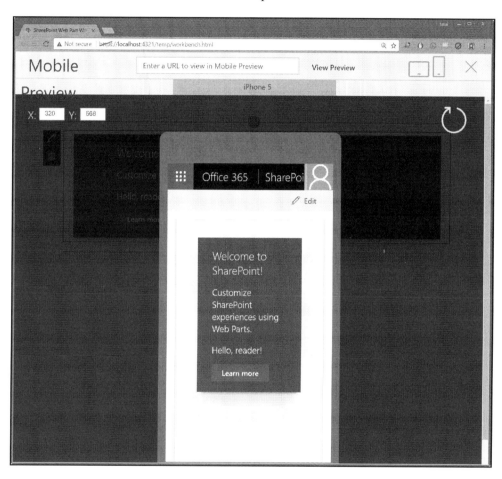

Testing against an iPhone 5, we get a mock-up of the canvas and our web part. We can also change orientation from horizontal to vertical, and change between multiple devices.

In your development workflow, you typically run SharePoint Workbench when you need to test that your elements load correctly, or to debug client-side issues with browser developer tools.

The hosted version of SharePoint Workbench is always accessible under the `/_layouts/workbench.aspx` page. So a working address could be `https://<tenant-name>.sharepoint.com/_layouts/workbench.aspx`. If you access this page directly (without Node.js servicing your code), SharePoint Workbench will initially complain that it's not able to find any SharePoint Framework-based web parts running on your local machine.

There's some clever trickery involved here, as SharePoint Workbench is trying to figure out if you have a local SharePoint Framework web part running, and it's helping you as a developer by hosting that within the page in SharePoint.

When you have such a component being served locally (similarly to how you serve it with Gulp for a locally hosted SharePoint Workbench), the cloud-hosted version acts almost identically except within the context of the SharePoint site.

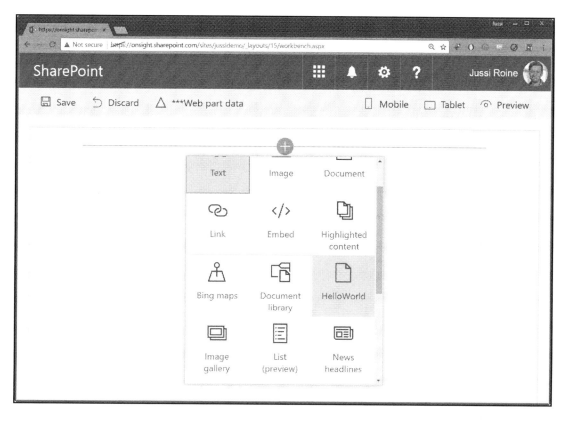

Note that when you're testing your code against the hosted version of SharePoint Workbench, you can also test how your web parts act together with other SharePoint web parts such as site news, image galleries, and other rich web parts.

Introducing Office Developer Patterns and Practices

Ever since SharePoint Portal Server 2001 was released at the start of the millennium, developers and businesses have tried all types of approaches to customize and bend SharePoint, one way or another.

SharePoint, after a default installation (which in itself is a discussion for a whole other book!), is referred to as an Out-of-Box (OOB) SharePoint. In its history of 15 years of releases for on-premises versions, and more than 5 years of updates with SharePoint Online, developers have always found ways to modify, change, or even remove built-in SharePoint functionality. This could be because of business requirements, usability reasons, or simply that a developer feels that he or she can implement a better implementation of a SharePoint feature.

This has resulted in numerous issues and headaches for both Microsoft, ISVs, Microsoft partner companies trying to make a living providing SharePoint-based solutions, businesses and their IT departments trying to support SharePoint, and end users trying to figure out how to do their work within SharePoint. There were, and still are, dozens of ways to do a simple change, such as changing the overall look and feel of a given SharePoint site, and while some of those are strictly not recommended, others are more or less either supported or at least not forbidden.

Developers accustomed to implementing SharePoint-based solutions might not often be aware or any sorts of best practices or common guidelines on how specific changes should be done. With SharePoint Online, the problem is two-fold: on one hand, developers might not have an API or an approach to change a facet of a given SharePoint feature. On the other hand, developers are not always sure *how* to do something, even if there's an API or an approach. Chances are that for any type of change a quick Google search will reveal at least five similar approaches. Some of those approaches might not work anymore, some might not be recommended, and some are poorly documented.

Office Developer Patterns and Practices in practice

For this particular reason, with a few driving forces within Microsoft and the community, the **Office Developer Patterns and Practices** emerged some years ago. **Office Dev PnP**, for short, is a massive project aiming to provide a centralized hub for most of the issues listed earlier.

The project currently has the following subcategories for SharePoint:

- YouTube videos help developers understand how things can be built for SharePoint and SharePoint Online. You can find the videos at `https://aka.ms/sppnp-videos`.
- MSDN help guidance providing a guidance on all things relating to SharePoint development. You can find the guidance at `https://aka.ms/sppnp-msdn`.
- The Microsoft Tech Community forums, for community discussions, peer-to-peer help, and announcements. You can find the forums at `https://aka.ms/sppnp-community`.
- A Twitter account at `OfficeDevPnP`.
- `Dev.office.com` documentation for an overview and additional information on the SharePoint Framework at `https://dev.office.com/sharepoint/docs/spfx/sharepoint-framework-overview`.
- Monthly Skype for Business calls showcasing new features and updates for SharePoint and Office developers. You can find the calendar invitation at `https://aka.ms/sppnp-call`.
- The Office 365 PnP Partner Pack, providing a package for Microsoft partner companies with tried and tested sample code, tools, and features. You can download the latest Partner Pack at `https://aka.ms/sppnp-partner-pack`.
- Over a dozen GitHub repositories with code, samples, and tools. You can access all the repositories through this link: `https://github.com/SharePoint/`.

In addition, the Office Dev PnP team is highly active on `https://dev.office.com`, providing more refined guidance and patterns for developers.

In practice, the Office Dev PnP aids developers wishing to become better on their journey with the SharePoint Framework by providing a wealth of guidance and code that can be freely reused.

The obvious one is the SharePoint Framework web parts, which is a GitHub repository that can be accessed at `https://github.com/SharePoint/sp-dev-fx-webparts`. This repo has several ready-made client-side web parts that can be freely used, enhanced, and modified.

The other very important and useful Office Dev PnP repository is the collection of PowerShell tools, found at `https://github.com/SharePoint/PnP-PowerShell`. This is a huge archive of PowerShell cmdlets, that allows developers and IT pros to remotely access, modify, and change most aspects of SharePoint and SharePoint Online sites. This becomes essentially more useful when you consider the use cases for a scripted installation of a SharePoint project.

As you cannot deploy all your artifacts and changes within the SharePoint Framework project, you will typically need a supporting project that provisions and pre-creates elements for your SharePoint Framework components. Imagine an out-of-the-box intranet solution that requires several client-side web parts, but also artifacts that are typically found in SharePoint sites, such as metadata structures (content type, site columns), SharePoint lists, and document libraries and subsites. You can easily use the PowerShell cmdlets to pre-create these during the initial deployment of your solution. When you then drop the relevant SharePoint Framework client-side web parts on the canvas, you can rest assured that the supported data and structures are in place.

You can download a ready-made installation package that includes all relevant PowerShell cmdlets you might ever need to modify your SharePoint sites from the same repository.

Contributing to Office Dev PnP

As so many people rely and depend on the Office Dev PnP efforts and results, it's worth considering contributing back to the community. As all content within the PnP effort are essentially free of charge and open source, it only works if others who benefit from this work contribute back for the greater good. As someone wise once said, *sharing is caring!*

You are not obligated to ask for permission if you wish to contribute. You can simply follow the guidance on what makes a good contribution, and what the technical approach to performing a commit back to a given repository is. The updated guidance can be found here: `https://github.com/SharePoint/PnP-Guidance/blob/master/CONTRIBUTING.md`, `which includes information on how to make a copy of a repository and submit pull requests using GitHub.`

Application life cycle management with SharePoint customizations

One of the key elements that all developers need to think about the long-term is life cycle management for your solutions. Application lifecycle management, or ALM, is a huge topic in itself, but we feel it's important to underline the aspects of ALM as it touches the SharePoint Framework.

One of the larger missing pieces with the add-in model since 2013 was that it mostly lacked a proper model for managing the life cycle of your deployments and solutions. The act of life cycle management involves multiple tasks within any given development project, including:

- Managing source code and assets
- Versioning source code
- Building solutions
- Testing code
- Deploying solutions
- Retracting solutions
- Managing solutions
- Updating solutions

ALM for the SharePoint Framework is still at a fairly nascent, but evolving stage. This does not mean that managing the life cycle of the SharePoint Framework project is impossible or a complex undertaking. It is still something that will take time, effort, and resources to get right for your project. But at the same time, it's more than critical to implement or otherwise future updates, or simply changing anything in your code becomes next to impossible to manage.

The SharePoint Framework does not include ALM tooling, such as for continuous integration, as it's client-side code is packaged and deployed to SharePoint. Microsoft does, however, provide support for multiple toolsets and services that can be hooked into your development workflow. We'll list the typical ones next, but if you have a preferred choice of your own, feel free to replace any of these with your own.

Managing and versioning source code and assets

Source code should be versioned so that changes to your code can be undone, should you run into unforeseen issues. We should also have clear visibility on who did what, when, how, and why. With classic SharePoint solutions, such as full-trust code projects, the versioning system was typically Microsoft's **Team Foundation Server** (**TFS**), an on-premises service that could be deployed locally. It would provide a portal for accessing different team projects, managing tasks, bugs, project schedule, and resources. TFS is still widely used, but it's fairly complex to deploy and configure, and numerous version upgrades in past years have proven that such services can also be provisioned as cloud-based services.

For the SharePoint Framework-style projects, you should typically choose either GitHub.com (a third-party cloud service), which allows you to store your project data and code in a private or public repository, or **Visual Studio Team Services** (**VSTS**), which is a service from Microsoft and hosted through the Microsoft Azure public cloud offering. GitHub is hugely popular, as basic use is free, and it's widely accepted as a trusted party for hosting your code. As you saw before, all Office Dev PnP repositories are hosted on GitHub. Enterprise developers might be inclined to choose VSTS, TFS, or a similar platform for source control, as that might be the platform their IT department supports and maintains.

GitHub

`GitHub.com` allows for cloning of existing repositories (such as the Office Dev PnP repos), or creating your own empty repositories.

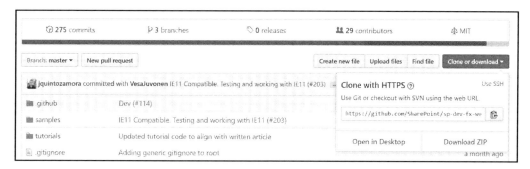

You can then either edit projects and code copied from someone else's repository or commit your own code back to your own empty repository.

For efficiently working with GitHub, we recommend you to install the GitHub Desktop from `https://desktop.github.com/`. This small tool allows you to browse and modify the repositories easily with a rich desktop client.

As such, GitHub is typically the primary tool for open-source projects with needs for project management tools. There is also a commercial option for closed-source projects within GitHub.

 Source code for the sample code of this book can be found on GitHub also: `https://github.com/jussiroine/MasteringSharePointFramework` or `https://github.com/PacktPublishing/SharePoint-Development-with-the-SharePoint-Framework`.

Visual Studio Team Services

VSTS is a service company typically prefer using, as it's more private, and lacks the community-style approach to sharing and publishing your code. VSTS builds upon the older TFS style, but at the same time, it's a modern and fresh take on performing the whole ALM process and Agile project management tooling within a single service.

You can provision a new VSTS account at `https://www.visualstudio.com/`. The basic service is free for up to five users, which typically is sufficient for smaller SharePoint Framework projects.

If you own a Visual Studio subscription, you can also access the basic services of VSTS.

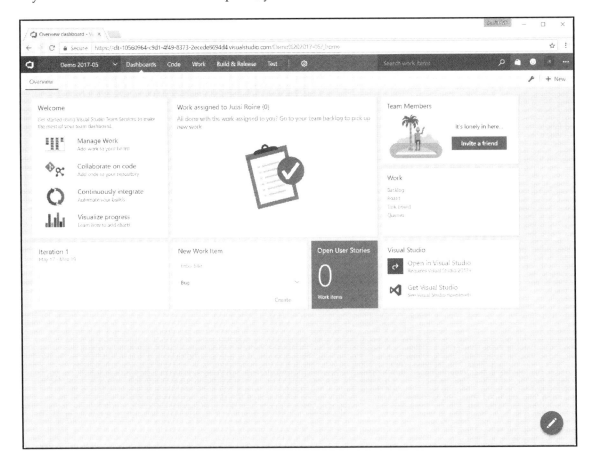

VSTS has an amazing selection of tools and services, which can be easily configured to support your ALM process, big or tiny.

Initially, you can just use VSTS as a place to store your code and not worry about much else. Later, when your project grows larger, you can involve additional aspects of VSTS, such as automated testing, user load testing, and automatic builds and deployments. This is essentially useful when you have multiple developers, and possibly a project manager, working towards a common goal. Several manual steps can be automated, thus project resources can focus on other aspects than the mundane tasks of building and deploying code that more or less remain the same throughout the project.

You can configure Visual Studio Code, where you create your code, to synchronize directly with a VSTS or GitHub repository. When you implement changes, add and remove files, and test your code, you can now always commit changes directly to either service.

The method for moving files back and forth between your local development environment, and your preferred repository service (VSTS, GitHub, or similar), is called Git. Git is a distributed version control system created by Linus Torvalds (of Linux fame). GitHub is a Git hosting service. This in itself is a version control system used to track changes to your projects, and the very same system can be used to push data from your local folders to a cloud-based versioning system.

Deploying, retracting, and managing solutions

Now that you have your code managed through VSTS or GitHub, you'll need a way to manage your SharePoint Framework customizations in SharePoint. Once again, there are multiple approaches to this task and you're free to choose the one that most fits your own development workflow and experience.

As all the SharePoint Framework solutions are packaged with Gulp to a separate package, it's very easy to move one or more files to SharePoint for testing and deploying to production. Each SharePoint Framework package is a file with the extension `.sppkg`, and they work distantly, similarly to SharePoint add-ins.

A centralized approach for this would imply you would use the application catalog, which is a special type of SharePoint site that includes the mechanisms for storing add-ins and SharePoint Framework Packages, and then deploying those through your SharePoint via site collections.

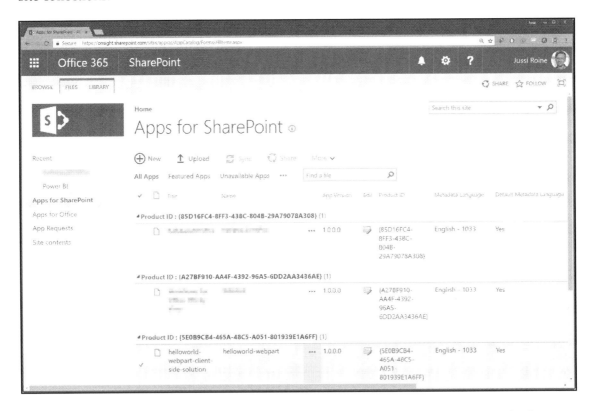

You can have multiple solutions in the application catalog, and choose where to deploy each. This allows the SharePoint admin to pre-approve solutions, as opposed to users simply downloading solutions from the internet and deploying them as they see fit. Management of solutions happens through the application catalog, as only tenant or farm admins will have access to upload, approve, and deploy new solutions. It's worth noting that Microsoft still often uses apps as a moniker for add-ins. As the SharePoint Framework uses the add-in packaging mechanism, you're bound to see apps or add-ins mentioned in several places within SharePoint.

In the following screenshot, an admin has selected the SharePoint Framework package, and the relevant management buttons light up in the ribbon.

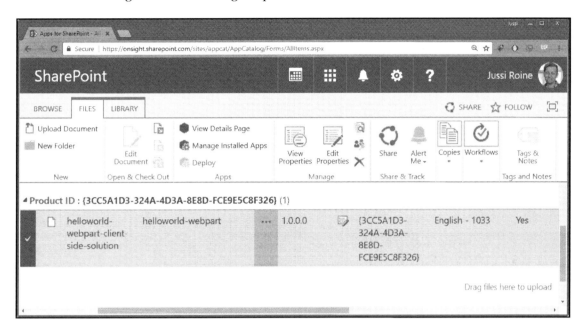

All the SharePoint Framework solutions are always deployed as tenant wide. This means that a single solution that targets a single site collection will still be visible for all other site collections within the same tenant.

Summary

In this chapter, we took an initial look at the SharePoint Framework and its capabilities. As we saw, the framework is constantly evolving and currently supports several core features SharePoint developers are used to having when implementing solutions for SharePoint and SharePoint Online. We can expect the SharePoint Framework to rapidly evolve, and extend beyond client-side web parts and basic extensions.

For writing code, Visual Studio Code is the recommended editor, as it is lightweight, free, and has native support for the SharePoint Framework solutions. The majority of the orchestration for the SharePoint Framework project is done outside Visual Studio Code, from Command Prompt, or via an embedded command window within Visual Studio Code.

The toolchain includes npm, for managing packaging, Yeoman for generating the necessary project structures and templates, and Gulp for packaging and serving the actual project. Additional tools that we recommend include browser developer tools, which are typically built-in to browsers, such as Google Chrome, Internet Explorer, and Microsoft Edge.

Finally, we had a look at ALM approaches, as it relates to the SharePoint Framework. Developers typically either use GitHub-hosted repositories, or Visual Studio Team Services (VSTS) team projects. Both support Git as the engine for moving files and changes between your development box and the source code versioning system. In the end, developers can use whichever source control system they are comfortable with and SharePoint Framework development does not require you to use GitHub or VSTS.

In the next chapter, we finally start the actual coding and creation of SharePoint Framework-based projects! This allows us to install the necessary bits and pieces, code the first solution, and deploy it manually to SharePoint. During this process, we will go through all the tools mentioned in the toolchain, including npm, Yeoman, and Gulp.

3
Getting Started with the SharePoint Framework

In this chapter, we are going to get started with creating solutions with the SharePoint Framework. We do this by first setting up our development environment using a step-by-step approach to ensure everything is working as it should before writing some real code. Then we'll test the environment and get more familiar with the toolchain by generating a simple hello world web part. Finally, we'll examine the anatomy of the generated project by looking in more detail at what's inside and how the solution works.

During this chapter, we'll:

- Learn to set up our development environment
- Deploy the necessary tools for our development needs
- Test the toolchain to see that everything works correctly

Setting up your development environment

Setting up the SharePoint Framework development environment is not a difficult task. In fact, it is straightforward and downright easy, but on the other hand, it is completely different from what a SharePoint developer has experienced before. First of all, you don't need to install the SharePoint farm to your local machine. That is a big change. You can set up the development environment on a computer with the SharePoint farm installed, but you don't benefit from having it. The second major difference is that you don't need a licensed version of Visual Studio anymore; in fact, you do better currently with free Visual Studio Code or some other editor of your choice.

You can set up your development environment on Windows, Mac, or Linux. In the following sections, we will go through how to set up your environment on Windows.

Step 1 - Installing Node.js

We start by downloading and installing Node.js Long Term Support (LTS) from this site: `https://nodejs.org/en/`.

At the time of writing, the LTS version is v6.10.3 LTS. Don't select the newest version with the latest features because the SharePoint Framework elements currently don't work on that:

If you are unsure whether you have you already installed Node.js on your computer, you can check by accessing the installed applications on the computer and searching for Node.js:

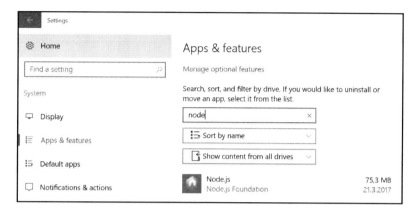

If you don't have Node.js installed, download it and run the installation, which is pretty straightforward:

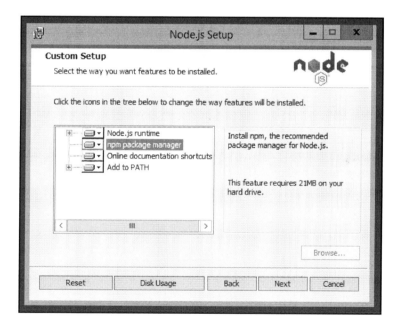

In the **Custom Setup** page of the installation wizard, ensure that **Node.js runtime**, **npm package manager**, and **Add to PATH** are all selected to be included in the installation. The installation requires administrative privileges to the computer.

After installation is complete, you can check the version of Node.js by starting Command Prompt or the PowerShell window and typing in the following command:

```
node -v
```

If you get a result such as the following, you know that you are good to go:

Step 2 - Node package manager

The next step is to ensure that npm is up to date. This is done by updating npm with the following command on Command Prompt or the PowerShell window:

```
npm install -g npm
```

Node package manager is used in the SharePoint Framework development environment in the same way that NuGet is used in Visual Studio. Basically, with npm, we are fetching and using lots of different packages. Installing Node.js installed npm for us, but the version we got with Node.js might not be the latest, so in the command line, we are actually telling npm to update itself. On my computer, the original version of npm (command line: npm -v) after Node.js installation was 3.10.10, but after I updated it, it is 4.5.0.

Step 3 - Installing Yeoman and Gulp

The next step is to use npm to install two important tools, Yeoman and Gulp, to our SharePoint Framework development environment. This is done with two commands in Command Prompt or PowerShell:

```
npm install -g yo
npm install -g gulp
```

When you are installing packages with `npm`, you can use the lower-case letter i instead of `install`. Also, you can install multiple packages in a single line, such as yo (for Yeoman) and `gulp`:

```
npm i -g yo gulp
```

As you can see, npm will also install other packages, based on the dependencies of the packages we are installing. Warnings are common and, for now, we can safely ignore them:

The installation will take a while as npm is going to download all the necessary packages and their dependencies during installation. When this is done, you will see something like this:

If something goes wrong, you can uninstall packages using npm as well; simply replace the `install` command with `uninstall` to do that. In npm, the parameter `-g` (or `-global`) means that the current working directory will function as a global package.

Step 4 - Installing the Yeoman SharePoint generator

As the final part of the command line installation, we will install the Yeoman SharePoint generator:

```
npm install -g @microsoft/generator-sharepoint
```

This command will fetch the Yeoman SharePoint generator from Microsoft. Again, it will take a while, but then we are ready to develop the SharePoint Framework web parts. However, because Notepad is not a very developer-friendly editor, we are going to install Visual Studio Code next.

You could, of course, use any code editor you feel most comfortable with, as SharePoint Framework does not have a requirement for strictly using Visual Studio Code.

Step 5 - Install Visual Studio Code

As with Node.js, npm, Yeoman, and Gulp, Visual Studio Code works on Linux, Mac, and Windows PCs. Visual Studio Code is based on the Electron framework, thus providing support for multiple platforms.

Download Visual Studio Code from the following website: `https://code.visualstudio.com/`.

When installing **Visual Studio Code**, there are few options to choose from:

What you actually choose is a personal preference. I like **Open with Code** on Windows Explorer and to have **Add to PATH** (available after the restart) selected.

We do recommend you restart your computer first, even if technically it is not needed. This will add Visual Studio Code to PATH so that in Command Prompt you can simply type the following command to start Visual Studio Code opening the project from the current folder:

```
code .
```

Testing your SharePoint Framework development environment

To test that everything works, we are going to create a `HelloWorld` web part.

Step 1 - Creating a folder for the web part

First, start Command Prompt or PowerShell. A quick way to do this anywhere in Windows is to press the Windows key with *R* (Run), and type `cmd` in the **Run** prompt. An alternative way is to navigate to your project folder in Windows File Explorer and to right-click within the folder while pressing the *Shift* key and selecting **Open Command Prompt here**.

Type the following commands to create a folder called `helloworld-webpart` and then navigate the Command Prompt to that folder:

```
md helloworld-webpart
cd helloworld-webpart
```

Step 2 - Running the Yeoman SharePoint generator

Next, type in the following command to start the Yeoman SharePoint generator:

```
yo @microsoft/sharepoint
```

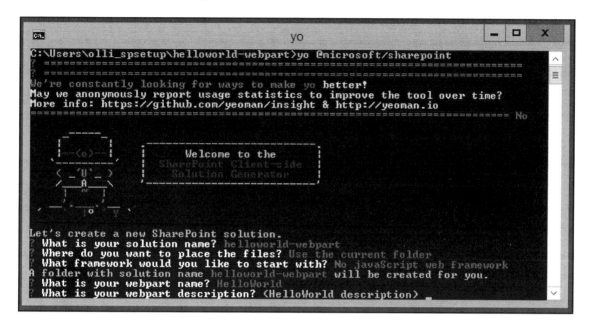

Click *Enter* to accept the solution name to be `helloworld-webpart` (based on the folder we are in), and again to accept the current folder to hold the files. For the framework selection, select **No JavaScript web framework**. Accept `HelloWorld` as the web part name and `HelloWorld description` as web part description.

Yeoman will now scaffold the file structure for your project, and this typically takes several seconds. Then Yeoman will resolve dependencies within your project and this process typically takes several minutes:

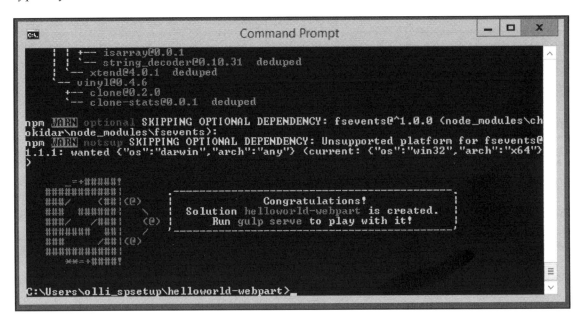

Looks good with the ASCII art SharePoint logo and everything.

Step 3 - Installing the developer certificate

Instead of the proposed `gulp serve`, type in the following command. This is something you need to do only once per development environment, as it avoids an annoying browser security message later on during your development cycle:

```
gulp trust-dev-cert
```

Accept the security warning by clicking **Yes**.

Step 4 - Running the web part on a local workbench

Now, type the following command to instruct Gulp to start the Node.js server and open the browser with a local copy of SharePoint Workbench, a page you will see a lot when doing the SharePoint Framework development:

```
gulp serve
```

Your default browser will open and navigate to `https://localhost:4321`, a well-known address for SharePoint Workbench:

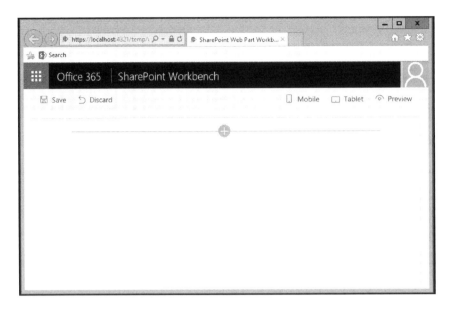

In this page, click the plus icon to add your **HelloWorld** web part to the page. The page looks like SharePoint Online, but the app menu (waffle menu in the top-left corner) is fake:

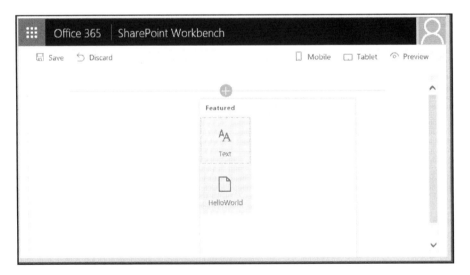

And you will see the web part in the action:

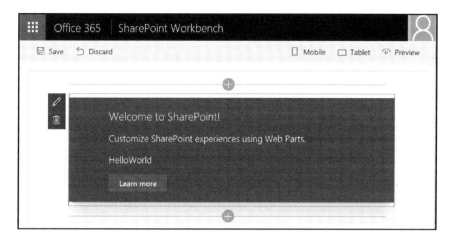

Click the pen icon to modify web part properties and change the **Description** property to your liking:

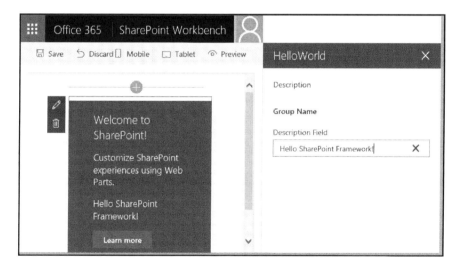

Next, we are going to do some investigation work on the code the Yeoman SharePoint generator created for us.

Anatomy of the SharePoint Framework web part project

At this point, you can open Visual Studio Code using the `helloworld-webpart` folder as the starting point. If you are unfamiliar with Visual Studio Code, you should know that there are two main ways to do this. On Command Prompt or PowerShell, you can always open Visual Studio Code from the current folder by typing in the following command, as long as Visual Studio Code is in the PATH environmental variable:

```
code.
```

The other way is to open Visual Studio Code from the desktop icon or from the Windows start menu and then select **File | Open Folder... (Ctrl+K Ctrl+O)**:

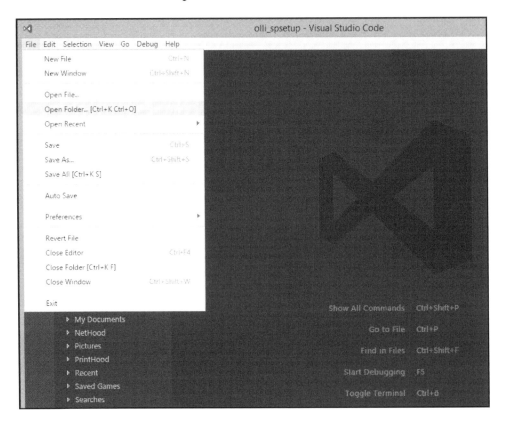

This command lets you navigate to the folder you created the web part in. Now you have the Visual Studio Code open from the correct location and we can start to examine the project files and folders:

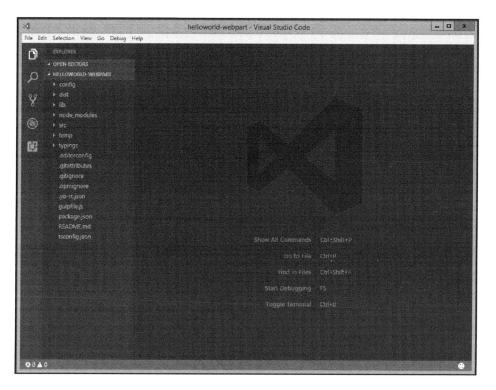

As you can see, there is a bunch of folders and some files visible.

Main folders and root level configuration files

The folders are detailed in the following table:

Folder	Contents
config	Configuration files; you will need to modify a few of these later.
dist	Distributable files; for example TypeScript files compiled into a bundled JavaScript file.
lib	Compile time files, which you don't modify yourself, but instead modify in the src folder.

node_modules	This contains all the dependencies, literally tens of thousands of files and thousands of folders. It looks ugly and downloading all these files will take a while when you are running the Yeoman SharePoint generator, but they are required for the SharePoint Framework development environment to work.
src	An import folder with the source files that you will modify when building real-life web parts.
temp	Temporary files used by the SharePoint Framework development environment.
typings	TypeScript typing information. No need to modify these.

The files in the project root folder are described in the following table. Apart from README.md, you usually don't need to modify these files:

File	Description
.editorconfig	A Visual Studio Code configuration file defining how the editor works in this folder. It contains information such as if an indent style is based on a tab or space, and how many characters are used to indent with one *Tab* click. You can modify the file to your liking or use it as it is.
.gitattributes	Attributes for Git (source code repository). The following line means that in Git, all line endings are normalized in all text files. * text=auto
.gitignore	This file instructs Git to ignore certain files. For example, build generated files and log files are ignored when pushing changes to the Git repository.
.npmignore	As per .gitignore, but this time instructing npm to ignore certain files.
.yo-rc.json	A JSON file detailing information on the Yeoman generator used in this project.
gulpfile.js	This is a Gulp configuration file. Basically, it is executed using Node.js when we are using gulp commands in this folder.
package.json	This is a configuration file for dependencies and their versions used by node package manager.

README.md	A web part documentation file for Git repositories. Modify this file to get your documentation up to date.
tsconcfig.json	A TypeScript configuration file. Modify this file if you need to configure TypeScript compilation options.

That is the basic structure of the web part project created by the Yeoman SharePoint generator. Before diving into all the important files, we are going to take a short interlude and see how TypeScript works in the SharePoint Framework web part project.

TypeScript basics in the SharePoint Framework

Open `HelloWorldWebPart.ts` located in the `src\webparts\helloWorld` folder:

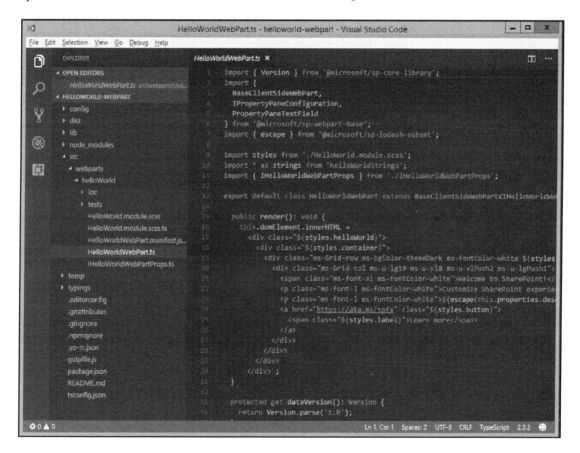

If you are unfamiliar with TypeScript, the contents of this file might look a bit scary at first, but believe me, after you get familiar with TypeScript, the contents make more sense than pure JavaScript. TypeScript adds typing information and more expressive notations of ECMAScript 6 that can be used because of how TypeScript can actually compile the JavaScript to follow ECMAScript 5, which in turn can be interpreted by most browsers used today. The main motivation for developers to learn TypeScript is to make JavaScript more accessible, especially for developers coming from a .NET background.

The main program in this web part is actually the `render()` function, which you might be familiar with if you've previously created classic SharePoint web parts as full-trust solutions.

Let's begin with the `import` statements.

In TypeScript, `import` is used to import other modules and their parts in the context of the current module. For example, in line 1, the declaration of `Version` is imported from a module called `@microsoft/sp-core-library`. In line 2, three declarations are imported from another module. In line 10, all declarations (`*`) are imported from `helloWorldStrings` with an alias called `strings`.

If you have experience of C#, you can see how `import` works a bit like the `using` statement. But with TypeScript `import`, you combine the information of the actual imported module with more detailed information on the declarations you want to use from that module.

The counterpart of `import` is `export`, as can be seen in line 13. In TypeScript, you can only import declarations that are exported at the module level. So, in this module, we are actually exporting a class called `HelloWorldWebPart` and the other files in our project could actually use it by importing it from this module.

`HelloWorldWebPart` is a class that extends another class which is called `BaseClientSideWebPart`, defined in `@microsoft/sp-webpart-base`. This parent class is defined to implement the `IHelloWorldWebPartProps` interface declared in `'./IHelloWorldWebPartProps'`--a TypeScript file located in the same folder as the file we are currently examining.

Classes and interfaces are key concepts in object-oriented programming. JavaScript is also an object-oriented programming language but doesn't use classes (not yet, at least). By defining the `BaseClientSideWebPart`, Microsoft gave us a starting point--a class which has all the basic elements needed in client-side web parts running on the SharePoint page.

In Visual Studio Code, if you right click the `BaseClientSideWebPart` class name when you select **Go to definition**, you can see the actual module, `BaseClientSideWebPart.d.ts`, which resides in the location `hello-spfx\node_modules\@microsoft\sp-webpart-base\lib\core \BaseClientSideWebPart.d.ts`. In case you find yourself wondering what a specific function or property should do or how it should be used, look at this file:

`BaseClientSideWebPart` is an abstract class, which in TypeScript, as in other class-based languages, is intended to be extended and used by other classes, such as our `HelloWorld` web part.

If you return to the `HelloWorldWebPart.ts` file, you can right click `IHelloWorldWebPartProps` and select **Go to Definition**. You will see `IHelloWorldWebPartProps.ts` opening:

It is a simple file which exports an interface which only defines one property for our web part. When you are implementing interfaces in your code, you need to fulfill what is agreed on the interface definition. In this case, the web part needs to have a description property. That is how interfaces work, and the role of TypeScript is to ensure that you do implement the interfacesbecause as JavaScript doesn't really require anything, it would just let the code fail. By the way, in Chapter 4, *Building Your First Web Part*, you will learn more of the web part properties, and in Chapter 8, *Working With the Web Part Property Pane*, we will take a deep dive into property pane configuration.

Open `HelloWorldWebPart.ts` again and look at the TypeScript in the declaration of the `render` function:

```
public render(): void {
  this.domElement.innerHTML = `
    <div class="${styles.helloWorld}">
      <div class="${styles.container}">
        <div class="ms-Grid-row ms-bgColor-themeDark ms-fontColor-white ${styles.row}">
          <div class="ms-Grid-col ms-u-lg10 ms-u-xl8 ms-u-xlPush2 ms-u-lgPush1">
            <span class="ms-font-xl ms-fontColor-white">Welcome to SharePoint!</span>
            <p class="ms-font-l ms-fontColor-white">Customize SharePoint experiences using Web Parts.</p>
            <p class="ms-font-l ms-fontColor-white">${escape(this.properties.description)}</p>
            <a href="https://aka.ms/spfx" class="${styles.button}">
              <span class="${styles.label}">Learn more</span>
            </a>
          </div>
        </div>
      </div>
    </div>`;
```

From the TypeScript perspective, there are two important things to point out--visibility modifiers in classes and type declaration.

The modifier `public` is placed in front of the function name. Inside the class declarations, functions and properties have visibility modifiers. In TypeScript, the default visibility modifier is `public`. It means that this function or property can be referenced everywhere when an instance of this class is used. Other visibility options are `private` and `protected`. The private function or property can't be accessed from outside of its class. The difference between protected and private is that a protected member can also be accessed by instances of deriving classes. In `BaseClientSideWebPart` there are a lot of protected members so that your derived web part can use them.

Please note that visibility modifiers only exist in compile time. They are there to help us to write better code; they don't offer any protection to member functions and properties when the code is compiled to JavaScript.

In TypeScript, variables and functions are typed. The type of `render` function is `void`, so TypeScript will raise an error if you try to return a value from this function. Unlike most programming languages, the type definition is expressed after the name variable or function, separated by a colon.

Here is how you declare variables in TypeScript, and some of the error checking which helps us to write better code:

```
let animal: string = "Cat";
let x: number;
const pi: number = 3.141592653589793;
var untypedVariable: any = (pi > 3) ? "Whatever" : x;
var untypedVariable: any = 3;
let y: number;
let y: number = 3;        // Can't redeclare block-scoped variable 'y'.

x = 10;
pi = 3.14;                // Can't assign to 'pi' because is a constant or readonly property

console.log(x*pi);
console.log(x*animal);   // The right-hand side of an arichmetic operation must be of type
                         // 'any', 'number' or an enum type.
```

In the first line, the variable `animal` of the type string is declared and assigned a value. In this statement, `let` is used in front of the variable name instead of `var`. `let` declares a block scoped variable and it is not actually TypeScript but ECMAScript 6, which gives us better variable scoping.

In line 2, a variable, x, is declared to be typed as a number. No initial value is given this time, but instead, the value is assigned to line 9.

In line 3, a constant variable is declared. You can't change constant variables in your code, so line 10 raises an error. The modifier `readonly` is used instead of `const` if you want to declare a constant inside a class.

In lines 4 and 5, `var` is used to declare a variable. Using `var`, you can declare the same variable again, so usually, you really should be using `le` as in lines 6 and 7, where an error is raised because of redeclaration of the same variable. In lines 4 and 5, type `any` is used. This allows you to assign the value of any type into a variable. Usually, we don't want that, but it is good to know that this untyped use of a variable or function can be allowed when needed.

Lines 12 and 13 show that TypeScript is checking that arithmetic operations have only variables of allowed types used.

The general thinking is that loose typing works well for quick scripts and customizations, but makes it difficult to write larger projects with pure JavaScript. TypeScript and its type system introduce a big advantage with more complex code because it catches errors and typos and allows us to have method signatures.

Next, we are going to look deeper inside the files that make the SharePoint Framework web parts work.

Key files of the SharePoint Framework web part projects

Let's open `HelloWorldWebPart.ts` again. As said before, the main program of `HelloWorld` web part is the `render` function in this file:

```
public render(): void {
  this.domElement.innerHTML = `
    <div class="${styles.helloWorld}">
      <div class="${styles.container}">
        <div class="ms-Grid-row ms-bgColor-themeDark ms-fontColor-white ${styles.row}">
          <div class="ms-Grid-col ms-u-lg10 ms-u-xl8 ms-u-xlPush2 ms-u-lgPush1">
            <span class="ms-font-xl ms-fontColor-white">Welcome to SharePoint!</span>
            <p class="ms-font-l ms-fontColor-white">Customize SharePoint experiences using Web Parts.</p>
            <p class="ms-font-l ms-fontColor-white">${escape(this.properties.description)}</p>
            <a href="https://aka.ms/spfx" class="${styles.button}">
              <span class="${styles.label}">Learn more</span>
            </a>
          </div>
        </div>
      </div>
    </div>`;
```

This function shows one way of building web part content. Instead of using any JavaScript framework or library, such as Angular, React, or Knockout, we are simply assigning the HTML value inside the inner HTML property of our web parts DOM element.

Using the special character ` (backtick operator) to start and end the string, HTML can be divided into multiple lines with ease. We have simple templating to use with our `${statement}` placeholders. In the code, it puts the class names in place as well as writing a `description` web part property value to the page.

Note that the `escape` function from the `lodash` library is used to ensure that any JavaScript injected by this property is sanitized (and not executed) in the page. An old saying of security experts is that all user input is evil.

If you scroll down to lines 37-57, you will see a glimpse of how property panes work:

```
       protected getPropertyPaneConfiguration(): IPropertyPaneConfiguration {
         return {
           pages: [
             {
               header: {
                 description: strings.PropertyPaneDescription
               },
               groups: [
                 {
                   groupName: strings.BasicGroupName,
                   groupFields: [
                     PropertyPaneTextField('description', {
                       label: strings.DescriptionFieldLabel
                     })
                   ]
                 }
               ]
             }
           ]
         };
       }
```

We shall focus on this later in `Chapter 8`, *Working with the Web Part Property Pane*, but for now, note that we need to have the `getPropertyPaneConfiguration` function inside our web part. The property pane consists of pages--we only have one here, which in turn have a `header` and `groups` of property fields. One thing to point out here is the use of the `strings` object. For example, the description text of the `header` is assigned a value from `strings.PropertyPaneDescription`. This is important if you are working with multilingual web parts, although it does introduce quite a bit of extra complexity. The `strings` object is declared in the `helloWorldStrings` module, which is defined in `loc\mystrings.d.ts`, as shown here:

```
declare interface IHelloWorldStrings {
    PropertyPaneDescription: string;
    BasicGroupName: string;
    DescriptionFieldLabel: string;
}

declare module 'helloWorldStrings' {
    const strings: IHelloWorldStrings;
    export = strings;
}
```

This file declares an interface called `IHelloWorldString` and the `helloWorldStrings` module, which basically includes the strings declared in the interface. The actual values are in the same `loc` folder, in language-specific JavaScript files. If you open `en-us.js`, you can see and modify the actual strings that are used when using the English user interface language:

When you are building multilingual web parts, use this method to declare all UI language-specific values and create JavaScript files to enable localization. For example, I could do a `fi-fi.js` file to support Finnish like this:

Next, open `HelloWorldWebPart.manifest.json`:

The web part manifests control how web parts are deployed. This file contains information about our `HelloWorld` web part that SharePoint needs to run it. You can see identifying information as well as information that is used in the user interface when the web part is added to the page. Inside `preconfiguredEntries`, there is group information which is used in so-called classic pages to group this web part in a collection of web parts. There is also the title and description information as well as the default value for our description property.

Next, open `HelloWorld.module.scss`:

SCSS stands for Sassy CSS, and it is an extension to CSS that will be processed by the **SASS** (**Syntactically Awesome Style Sheets**) processors. SASS allows you to have variables and code in your style sheets. The SharePoint Framework utilizes SASS CSS, the pre-processor which allows us to use advanced CSS syntax. One of the advantages is that there can be nested CSS rules for both classes and properties. For example, all other classes in our files are actually nested inside the `helloWorld` class to help us to make simpler selectors. In addition, we can also write SassScript to perform calculations.

Next, open `HelloWorld.module.scss.ts`:

This file defines the `styles` object that was used in `render` function. One thing to note is that the actual style names include random hash effectively making the style names unique so that we can define our button and not worry about other web parts or SharePoint page elements using the same style name.

Now, open `package.json` from the `helloworld-webpart` folder:

```
EXPLORER                          package.json  ×

▲ OPEN EDITORS                  1  {
    package.json                2    "name": "helloworld-webpart",
▲ HELLOWORLD-WEBPART            3    "version": "0.0.1",
  ▶ config                      4    "private": true,
  ▶ dist                        5    "engines": {
  ▶ lib                         6      "node": ">=0.10.0"
  ▶ node_modules               7    },
  ▲ src                         8    "dependencies": {
    ▶ webparts                 9      "@microsoft/sp-client-base": "~1.0.0",
  ▲ temp                       10      "@microsoft/sp-core-library": "~1.0.0",
    ▶ stats                    11      "@microsoft/sp-webpart-base": "~1.0.0",
      manifests.js             12      "@types/webpack-env": ">=1.12.1 <1.14.0"
      manifests.json           13    },
      tslint.json              14    "devDependencies": {
      workbench.html           15      "@microsoft/sp-build-web": "~1.0.1",
  ▶ typings                    16      "@microsoft/sp-module-interfaces": "~1.0.0",
    .editorconfig              17      "@microsoft/sp-webpart-workbench": "~1.0.0",
    .gitattributes             18      "gulp": "~3.9.1",
    .gitignore                 19      "@types/chai": ">=3.4.34 <3.6.0",
    .npmignore                 20      "@types/mocha": ">=2.2.33 <2.6.0"
    .yo-rc.json                21    },
    gulpfile.js                22    "scripts": {
    package.json               23      "build": "gulp bundle",
    README.md                  24      "clean": "gulp clean",
    tsconfig.json              25      "test": "gulp test"
                               26    }
                               27  }
```

This information is used by the node package **manager (npm)**. There is basic information about our web part and lots of version information **about depend**encies. First, we require node version **0.10.0** or later. Version **~1.0.0** means **that we ask npm** to use approximately the equivalent version. This is called semantic versioning and it **has many uses** within your project. In some cases, the version range is given, at other **times you might** prefer an operator such as >= to tell npm that a greater than or equal to version is required. The scripts section instructs npm to run specific commands at various times in the life cycle of our package.

The TypeScript configuration is inside `tsconfig.json`:

This file includes an object, `compilerOptions`, with a few interesting options, some of which are described in the following table:

Parameter	Description
target	Specifies ECMAScript target version; that is, the version of JavaScript to compile TypeScript. This is one of the clear advantages of TypeScript: it allows you to use features of new ECMAScript versions but still compiles JavaScript to work with older browser versions. A major impact in most cases is the use of Internet Explorer 11 in many organizations. It supports ECMAScript 5 but not 6.
module	Module code generation. SharePoint Framework uses CommonJS.
sourceMap	If this property is set to `true`, TypeScript will generate the `.map` file, which relates the TypeScript sources to the generated JavaScript. This, in turn, allows developers to debug `.ts` files instead of debugging `.js` files.

types	Type declaration files to be included in compilation. `es6-promise` refers to ECMAScript 6 type of promises. Promises give us a way to handle asynchronous processing in what looks like a synchronous fashion. In addition to promises, there are ECMAScript 6 collections (for example, sets and maps).

Next, open the `README.md` file in the `helloworld-webpart` folder:

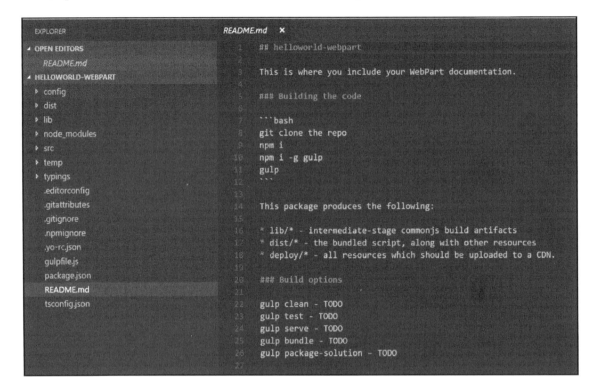

This is the starting point for your web part documentation. We therefore strongly recommend you use this file. The file uses markdown syntax, which is a lightweight and easy syntax for authoring HTML documents. If you use GitHub, it will render markdown nicely to HTML.

Here is a quick cheat sheet for your markdown use:

- Headers:

    ```
    # This is <H1>
    ## This is <H2>
    ```

This is <H4>

- Emphasis:

  ```
  *italic* and _also italic_
  **bold** and __also bold__
  _And you **can** combine_
  ```

- Images:

  ```
  ![Alt text for image](/images/image1.png)
  ```

- Links:

  ```
  https://www.contoso.com works automatically
  [Contoso](https://www.contoso.com)
  ```

- Unordered list:

  ```
  * Item 1
  * Item 2
  * Sub Item 2a
  ```

- Ordered list:

  ```
  1. Item 1
  ```

  ```
  2. Item 2
  ```

  ```
      1. Sub Item 2a
  ```

- Blockquotes:

  ```
  The security expert said:
  >> All user input is evil!
  ```

- Inline code:

  ```
  Avoid using `<script>` elements here.
  ```

There is a bash section in README.md:

```bash
```bash
git clone the repo
npm i
npm i -g gulp
gulp
```
```

This section will render into something like this:

Building the code

```
git clone the repo

npm i

npm i -g gulp

gulp
```

The folders dist and temp can be erased by the following command. The temp folder is for temporary files that are created when you build your code, and dist holds your debug build. The command will basically remove anything created by gulp serve or gulp package-solution:

```
gulp clean
```

If you now type in the following command:

```
gulp serve --nobrowser
```

It will start the service again, but this time it will not open a browser. We can, however, see that the `dist` and `temp` folders both include interesting files.

Open `dist\hello-world.bundle.js`:

This is the actual code that runs on the server. The SharePoint Framework uses bundling generated by a tool called Webpack--putting all the resources together so that all JavaScript code and CSS is in this file. Take a moment to examine the file, and also note that next to this file is `HelloWorld.budle.js.map`, which includes the mapping information needed in debugging of the original TypeScript source.

Next, open `temp/workbench.html`:

```
workbench.html  ×
    <!doctype html>
    <html dir="ltr">
    <head>
      <meta http-equiv="Content-Type" content="text/html; charset=utf-8" />
      <meta http-equiv="X-UA-Compatible" content="IE=edge" />
      <meta name="viewport" content="width=device-width, initial-scale=1" />

      <title>SharePoint Web Part Workbench</title>

      <link rel="shortcut icon" href="https://localhost:4321/node_modules/@microsoft/sp-webpart-workbench/dist/assets/server-icon.png" />

      <script type="text/javascript" src="https://localhost:4321/temp/manifests.js"></script>
      <script type="text/javascript" src="https://localhost:4321/node_modules/@microsoft/sp-loader/dist/sp-loader_en-us.js"></script>
      <script type="text/javascript" src="https://localhost:4321/node_modules/@microsoft/sp-webpart-workbench/lib/api/workbenchInit.js"></script>
    </head>
    <body>

      <script type="text/javascript">
        window.spModuleLoader.start(window.preloadedData);
      </script>
    </body>
    </html>
```

This file is our local SharePoint Workbench, with nice and clean HTML. Usually, you don't need to care about this file, but it is good to know that it is there.

Finally, we are going to look inside the `config` folder. Start by opening the `config.json` file:

```
config.json    ×
    {
      "entries": [
        {
          "entry": "./lib/webparts/helloWorld/HelloWorldWebPart.js",
          "manifest": "./src/webparts/helloWorld/HelloWorldWebPart.manifest.json",
          "outputPath": "./dist/hello-world.bundle.js"
        }
      ],
      "externals": {},
      "localizedResources": {
        "helloWorldStrings": "webparts/helloWorld/loc/{locale}.js"
      }
    }
```

As you can see, there is an entry pointing to the compiled `HelloWorldWebPart.js` file in the `/lib/webparts/helloWorld` folder. The `manifest` is pointing to the manifest file in the `src` folder, and the `outputPath` is pointing to the bundled JavaScript file in the `dist` folder. Inside the `localizedResources,` there is`helloWorldStrings`, which basically tells where to look for different locale files.

Open the `deploy-azure-storage.json` file:

This file contains information you need to set up if you are deploying the bundled JavaScript to Azure Storage. Usually, you do this if you are using Azure CDN to serve the resources. We will take a closer look at this later.

Open the `package-solution.json` file:

This file is used in solution packaging. In the paths, there is the `zippedPackage` property pointing to `solution/helloworld-webpart.sppkg`. This file will be created if you run the following command:

```
gulp package-solution
```

If you now open Windows Explorer and navigate to the `helloworld-webpart\sharepoint\solution\` folder, you will find `helloworld-webpart.sppkg` there. By renaming the file to a ZIP file, you can see its contents. The package is also unpacked in an adjacent folder called `debug`.

These files are for SharePoint, and they are all XML files: the bundled JavaScript code is not included in the package. Instead, there is a link in one of the files that point SharePoint to load the bundled JavaScript. This is the same way that SharePoint add-ins are packaged.

Summary

In this chapter, we took a deeper look into working with the SharePoint Framework through a simple hello world project. As part of this work, we installed and configured Node.js and verified that we're using the correct version of the runtime. Next, we configured npm, the node package manager, and ensured it was up to date. This guarantees we can run the SharePoint Framework-based code in our own development environment locally. Finally, we installed Yeoman and Gulp, the two core tools for generating the SharePoint Framework projects and resources and serving the code for local testing.

We used Visual Studio Code to view and test the generated project, and served the code to a local SharePoint Workbench with Gulp.

Finally, we took an in-depth look into the source files and project structure of the generated project.

Next, in Chapter 4, *Building your First Web Part*, we go beyond hello world and develop a real SharePoint Framework web part.

4
Building Your First Web Part

In this chapter, we will build a real web part. The web part will collect user feedback on the page where it is added. The implementation will be simple; we are just going to collect some text from the user and write that, along with page URL information, to a SharePoint list. If you want, you can enrich the experience later; maybe you will create a rating field as well, or create a Microsoft Flow that will kick off when feedback has been given.

This chapter will show you how to:

- Create a feedback web part project
- Set web part basics
- Build the user experience for the web part
- Localize the web part

In addition to working with SharePoint data, which is covered in much greater detail in Chapter 7, *Working with SharePoint Content*, we are going to use the property pane to create a modifiable prompt for the feedback web part.

If you need more detailed information about how to work with property panes, see Chapter 8, *Working with the Web Part Property Pane*.

Creating a feedback list

In order to collect data, we need a list to save it in. This is a very basic SharePoint task for solution designers. To keep things simple and focused on the web part design, we are going to create the list using the user interface.

1. First, open the SharePoint site or Office 365 Group you want to test using a browser. Select **Add an app**, as detailed in the following screenshot:

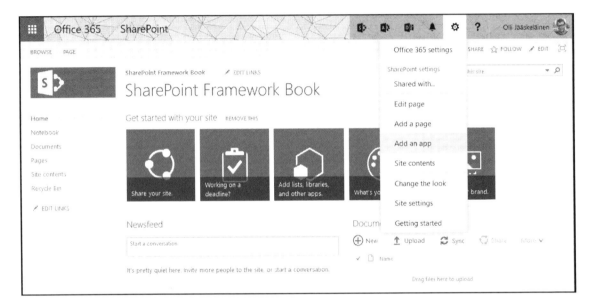

2. Select **Custom List** as the app you want to add, and name it `Feedback`.

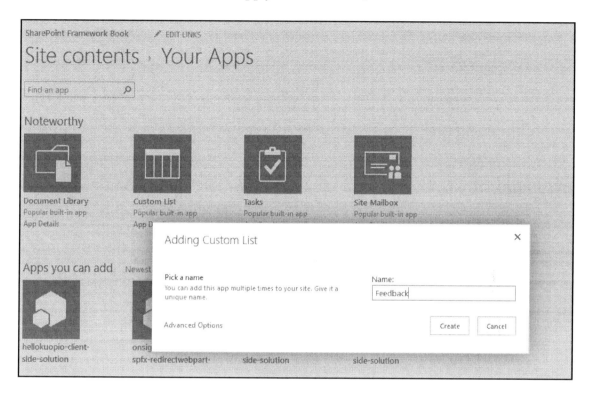

3. Navigate to the new list, and add a new column with the type of **Single line of text**, as shown in the following screenshot:

4. Name the new column URL and click **Create button**. It is important that you use a single word without white space while creating the column because it will simplify the internal name of the field. When referring to this field from our code, we must know the internal name.

The list is now created. As stated before, you can later decide to add a Microsoft Flow or other fields to the list.

Creating the feedback web part project

Now that the list of our data has been created and configured, we are ready to start building the web part. Our web part will provide a simple input form for gathering feedback and will save inputted feedback to a SharePoint list.

The use of Command Prompt and the Yeoman generator is almost the same as in the HelloWorld web part we created in `Chapter 3`, *Getting Started with the SharePoint Framework*.

First, start Command Prompt, create a new folder, go into the new folder, and start the Yeoman generator using the following commands:

```
md feedback-webpart
cd feedback-webpart
yo @microsoft/sharepoint
```

Use the following parameters to create the web part. Don't worry if your Yeoman experience looks slightly different. The tool evolves quite rapidly, and certain aspects of the interface, including the questions it asks, might change over time.

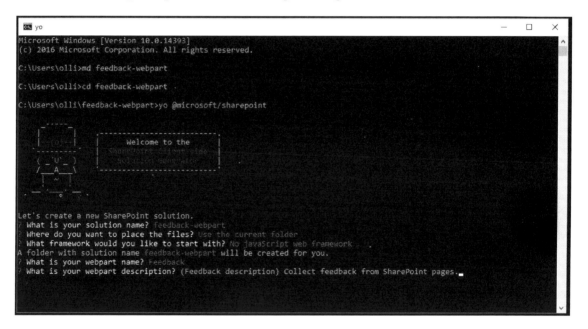

Setting web part basics

Wait until the generator finishes, and then start Visual Studio Code with the following command.

```
code .
```

Documentation is one of the key components when you are building stable, reliable solutions. So, let's open README.md from the root folder of the web part project and document what we are doing.

Find the following section:

```
## feedback-webpart

This is where you include your WebPart documentation.
```

Replace the following and save the file:

```
## Feedback web part

This web part allows the user to type in a comment concerning the current
page. The comment is saved to Feedback list on the site collection root
along with URL information of the page the comment is concerning.
```

Next, we open config\package-solution.json and replace the solution name with proper language. Remember to save the file after the modification.

```
"name": "Feedback web part",
```

The name is visible in the app catalog. Open the manifest file located in src\webparts\feedback\FeedbackWebPart.manifest.json. We are interested in modifying a few values in preconfiguredEntries object. Note that it is an array, and you could insert multiple different pre-configured entries objects on that array if you have a very configurable web part which can be used in multiple ways. Each configuration will appear as its own web part when the user is adding web parts to the page.

The group is, by default, **Under Development**, so we change that to a more meaningful and professional value. The group is used in classic pages and there are plenty of existing groups to choose from or you can create a new one:

```
"group": { "default": "SharePoint Framework web parts" },
```

The next change is the mystical officeFabricIconFontName property.

```
"officeFabricIconFontName": "NoteForward",
```

This will be the icon of the web part. Go through https://dev.office.com/fabric#/styles/icons to find the one you like.

Finally, we change the `properties` object's default values and save the file. We replace `description` with `hintText` here and will also make similar changes in other files as well.

```
"properties": {
      "hintText": "Type in feedback concerning the page"
}
```

`preconfiguredEntries` in our file should now look something like this:

```
"preconfiguredEntries": [{
"groupId": "0d59b068-2924-4a95-a63c-332026d92b16",
"group": {
"default": "SharePoint Framework web parts"
},
"title": {
"default": "Feedback"
},
"description": {
"default": "Collect feedback from SharePoint pages."
},
"officeFabricIconFontName": "NoteForward",
"properties": {
"hintText": "Type in feedback concerning the page"
}
}]
```

Open `IFeedbackWebPartProps.ts` in the same folder and make the following changes `description` to `hintText`.

```
export interface IFeedbackWebPartProps {
  hintText: string;
}
```

Open the `src\webparts\feedback\loc\mystrings.d.ts` file and replace the `IFeedbackStrings` declaration with the following. Remember to save the file after the changes:

```
declare interface IFeedbackStrings {
  PropertyPaneDescription: string;
  BasicGroupName: string;
  HintTextFieldLabel: string;
}
```

Open `src\webparts\feedback\loc\en-us.js` file and replace its contents with the following:

```
define([], function() {
  return {
    "PropertyPaneDescription": "Modify web part properties",
    "BasicGroupName": "Fields",
    "HintTextFieldLabel": "Hint Text"
  }
});
```

After you have saved the changes, open `FeedbackWebPart.ts` and locate the `getPropertyPaneConfiguration` function. To reflect the changes we have made to the other files, we are going to replace the `groupsFields` section with the following:

```
groupFields: [
            PropertyPaneTextField('hintText', {
              label: strings.HintTextFieldLabel
            })
        ]
```

Building feedback web part user experience

The `FeedbackWebPart.ts` file has the `render` method, which is at the core of user experience. We want there to be an icon, a text field with hint text, and a button. There are many ways to do that. This time we are building DOM elements by first inserting some HTML and then binding event handlers, and so on. In Chapter 9, *Using React and Office UI Fabric React Components*, and Chapter 10, *Working with Different JavaScript Frameworks and 3rd Party Frameworks*, you will see different approaches, such as React and various JavaScript libraries.

We start from the `src\webparts\feedback\Feedback.module.scss` file. Replace the contents of the file with the following simple CSS definition and save the file.

```
.input {
    border: 1px solid gray;
    width: 50%;
    margin: 0px 10px 0px 10px;
}
.successIndicator {
    border: 0px;
}
```

The reason we can get away with such simple CSS is that we are using classes from Office UI Fabric.

Next, open `FeedbackWebPart.ts` again and replace the `render` function with the following.

```
public render(): void {
    this.domElement.innerHTML =
        `<div>
            <i class='ms-Icon ms-Icon--NoteForward' aria-hidden='true'></i>
            <input type='text' class='${styles.input}' maxlenght='255'
placeholder='${escape(this.properties.hintText)}' />
            <button type='button' class='ms-Button'><span class='ms-Button-
label'>Send</span></button>
            <p class='${styles.successIndicator}'></p>
        </div>`;
    this.setComment = this.setComment.bind(this);
    const textInput: HTMLInputElement =
this.domElement.getElementsByTagName("INPUT")[0] as HTMLInputElement;
    textInput.addEventListener("keyup", this.setComment);
    this.sendFeedback = this.sendFeedback.bind(this);
    const button: HTMLButtonElement =
this.domElement.getElementsByTagName("BUTTON")[0] as HTMLButtonElement;
    button.onclick = this.sendFeedback;
}
```

Before diving into details, insert the following code fragment after the `render` method:

```
private _commentText : string; // used to store comment text
private setComment(event: Event): void {
    let srcElement: HTMLInputElement = event.srcElement as
HTMLInputElement;
    this._commentText = escape(srcElement.value);
}
private sendFeedback(): void {
    alert("Input Text Value: "+ this._commentText);
}
```

The `render` function starts by setting `innerHTML` of the web part to include a number of child elements.

```
public render(): void {
    this.domElement.innerHTML =
      `<div>
        <i class='ms-Icon ms-Icon--NoteForward' aria-hidden='true'></i>
        <input type='text' class='${styles.input}' maxlenght='255' placeholder='${escape(this.properties.hintText)}' />
        <button type='button' class='ms-Button'><span class='ms-Button-label'>Send</span></button>
        <p class='${styles.successIndicator}'></p>
      </div>`;
```

It is important to know that the `render` function can be called multiple times during the life cycle of the page for example, when a user switches to or from edit mode, so we need to be careful not to create the elements multiple times. This version of the code does not try to keep track of whether the elements already exist or not. Because of this, if the user types something into the text field and then switches the page mode, the text field will be recreated. We let it be, because it is unlikely that it will cause any harm and, if it does, the user can use our web part to give us feedback on that!

The first element is the icon. As you can see, we are using the `i` tag to create it, so the magic lies in the class definition, which relies on Office UI Fabric.

```
<i class='ms-Icon ms-Icon--NoteForward' aria-hidden='true'></i>
```

The second element is the text field. This time we are using our own class. The maximum length is set to `255` because that is maximum that the **Title** column in the `Feedback` list can hold. The placeholder is read from `hintText` web part property. Remember to use the `escape` function, because this is user input.

```
<input type='text' class='${styles.input}' maxlength='255'
placeholder='${escape(this.properties.hintText)}' />
```

For the button, we are using the Office UI `Fabric Button` component (`https://dev.office.com/fabric-js/Components/Button/Button.html`). It will look like a button in Office 365.

```
<button type='button' class='ms-Button'><span class='ms-Button-
label'>Send</span></button>
```

The last element is a paragraph element, which we are using to show a message after the feedback has been successfully saved. We don't use it for error messages because SharePoint Framework has built-in functions for that, as you will soon see.

```
<p class='${styles.successIndicator}'></p>
```

The next section of the code binds this to our `setComment` function. The syntax of the operation looks weird, but what it does is ensure that *this* in `setComment` and `render` functions refer to same object--which is our web part. Then, we create an event listener to call `setComment` whenever a user types in this input field.

```
this.setComment = this.setComment.bind(this);
const textInput: HTMLInputElement = this.domElement.getElementsByTagName("INPUT")[0] as HTMLInputElement;
textInput.addEventListener("keyup", this.setComment);
```

The binding in the `sendFeedback` function is done the same way as with `setComment`. We are assigning the `this.sendFeedback` function to an `onclick` event:

```
this.sendFeedback = this.sendFeedback.bind(this);
const button: HTMLButtonElement =  this.domElement.getElementsByTagName("BUTTON")[0] as HTMLButtonElement;
button.onclick = this.sendFeedback;
```

In addition to the `render` function, we made one private property for the web part object. It is called `_commentText` and is via the `setComment` function, which is called whenever the user types into the input field. In `setComment`, we get a reference to the input element by using an event parameter, so that we can read its value and assign it to `_commentText`. Instead of using `event.srcElement` we could have used the same `getElementsByTagName` function as we did previously. At this point, the `sendFeedback` function simply sets the text on our success indicator paragraph.

```
private _commentText : string; // used to store comment text
private setComment(event: Event): void {
  let srcElement: HTMLInputElement = event.srcElement as HTMLInputElement;
  this._commentText = escape(srcElement.value);
}
private sendFeedback(): void {
  this.domElement.getElementsByClassName(styles.successIndicator)[0]
        .innerHTML = "<i class='ms-Icon ms-Icon--Accept' aria-hidden='true'> Thank you for the feedback!</i>";
}
```

Testing the user interface

At this point, return to the Command Prompt and type the following command to test the web part in the local workbench:

```
gulp serve
```

The local workbench will load and insert the web part to the page.

At this point, we can test the web part to see if everything looks as expected. While testing web parts, it is good practice to insert multiple instances in the same page to see if they mess each other up.

You can also test the web part using SharePoint Workbench. The styles of SharePoint Workbench and a locally hosted Workbench look a little different. You might also see some minor changes when you try out the web part with different browsers.

Saving the feedback

Now we are ready to save the data to the SharePoint list. We are going to do it using REST API but, to help us out, we are using `SPHttpClient` class. If we are running on a local workbench, that will not work, so we need to know the environment type before trying to save the data and act accordingly. Open `FeedbackWebPart.ts` and insert the following `import` statement after the other `import` statements at the start of the file:

```
import { SPHttpClient, ISPHttpClientOptions, SPHttpClientResponse } from
'@microsoft/sp-http';
import { Environment, EnvironmentType } from '@microsoft/sp-core-library';
```

Replace the `sendFeedback` function with the following code.

```
private sendFeedback(): void {
    this.context.statusRenderer.clearError(this.domElement);
    const paragraphElement: HTMLParagraphElement =
```

```
        this.domElement.getElementsByClassName(styles.successIndicator)[0] as
HTMLParagraphElement;
    paragraphElement.innerHTML = "";

    if (this._commentText === undefined || this._commentText.length === 0)
{
      this.context.statusRenderer.renderError(this.domElement, "Please type
in a comment or suggestion.");
      return;
    }

    if (Environment.type === EnvironmentType.Local) {
      this.context.statusRenderer.renderError(this.domElement, "Feedback
can't be saved when running in local workbech.");
      return;
    }

    const url: string =
this.context.pageContext.site.absoluteUrl+"/_api/web/lists/getbytitle('Feed
back')/items";
    const item : any = {
        "Title": this._commentText,
        "URL": window.location.href
    };
    const spHttpClientOptions: ISPHttpClientOptions = {
      "body": JSON.stringify(item)
    };
    this.context.statusRenderer
      .displayLoadingIndicator(paragraphElement, "- Sending feedback");
    this.context.spHttpClient.post(url,SPHttpClient.configurations.v1,
spHttpClientOptions)
      .then((response: SPHttpClientResponse) => {
this.context.statusRenderer.clearLoadingIndicator(paragraphElement);
        if (response.status === 201) {
this.domElement.getElementsByClassName(styles.successIndicator)[0]
          .innerHTML = "<i class='ms-Icon ms-Icon--Accept' aria-
hidden='true'> Thank you for the feedback!</i>";
        } else {
          this.context.statusRenderer.renderError(this.domElement,
            `Failed to save feedback. Error code: ${response.statusText}
(${response.status})`);
        }
      });
  }
```

At the start of the function, there are few lines of codes that will clear messages that may be present.

```
private sendFeedback(): void {
  this.context.statusRenderer.clearError(this.domElement);
  const paragraphElement: HTMLParagraphElement =
    this.domElement.getElementsByClassName(styles.successIndicator)[0] as HTMLParagraphElement;
  paragraphElement.innerHTML = "";
```

The first one uses `statusRenderer`, which is available via the SharePoint Framework. Later in the function, we use it to show an error message, but here we are clearing that error message. The `clearMessage` function takes one parameter, which points to the DOM element the possible error message has been added to previously. The second part at the start of the function finds our success indicator paragraph element and clears the HTML contents of the element.

Next, we check if the feedback message is valid. It is `undefined` if no `keyup` events have happened or the length of the string is `0` if there is no text. An error message is shown and the `return` statements exit the function.

```
if (this._commentText === undefined || this._commentText.length === 0) {
  this.context.statusRenderer.renderError(this.domElement, "Please type in a comment or suggestion.");
  return;
}
```

This is what the error message looks like in the local workbench:

However, this is what it looks like in SharePoint Workbench:

In SharePoint Workbench the actual error message is only shown when you click **TECHNICAL DETAILS** link. There is nothing wrong with the error message's behavior, but in real life, we would probably like to show it like this in real error situations. The better functionality here would be to keep the **Send** button disabled until the message is valid on the text field.

The next part of the code checks if we are running on local SharePoint Workbench as opposed to running in the context of SharePoint.The environment is defined for us as a property of the base web part. In that case, we are not going to save the feedback.

```
if (Environment.type === EnvironmentType.local) {
  this.context.statusRenderer.renderError(this.domElement, "Feedback can't be saved when running in local workbech.");
  return;
}
```

In the next code segment, we take the URL of the site collection root web (`this.context.pageContext.site.absoluteUrl`) and add the SharePoint REST API there. We are using root web instead of the current web because we only created one list to collect feedback. If we want to access the current web, we can find the information inside `this.context.pageContext.web`.

Page context in SharePoint provides us a clean way to retrieve common data about the current page including contents, URL, navigation menu, and so on.

```
const url: string = this.context.pageContext.site.absoluteUrl+"/_api/web/lists/getbytitle('Feedback')/items";
const item : any = {
      "Title": this._commentText,
      "URL": window.location.href
};
const spHttpClientOptions: ISPHttpClientOptions = {
  "body": JSON.stringify(item)
};
```

SharePoint REST API has been available since SharePoint Server 2013 was published. However, most of the client-side coding has been made through **client-side object model (CSOM)**, or **JavaScript object model (JSOM)**, which is an object model instead of a RESTful API. We believe this is because the SharePoint developers were used to using a server-side object model which has many similarities to the client-side object model. In addition, CSOM was designed to be similar to the **server-side object model (SSOM)**, to lower the learning curve for SharePoint developers moving from server-side to client-side. REST, however, evolved at the same time and it uses a much simpler approach to HTTP verbs and URI structure and has been widely adopted, along with open standards like **OData** and **OAuth**.

In the code, we are building a JSON presentation of the new list item. JSON stands for JavaScript Object Notation, and it's a simple, open standard for data exchange. For the value of the `Title` property, we set the message from the text field, and for the URL property we use the link to the current page which is available via the standard JavaScript `window.location.href`. This item is added to a body of our `spHttpClientOptions` object.

Before sending the message, we call `statusRenderer.displayLoadingIndicator` for the duration of the operation with two parameters.The first is the element to render the loading indicator and the second is the message we want to show to the user.

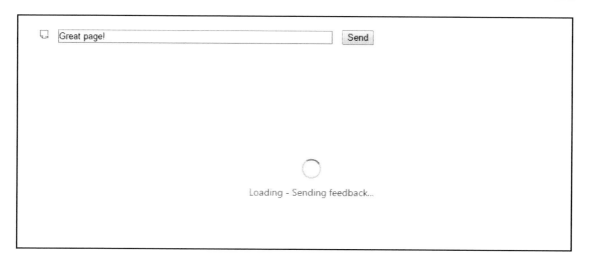

Usually, the loading indicator doesn't even appear on the page before the response has been received. If for example, you're accessing SharePoint while your mobile device is in flight mode (and thus offline), you can see not only your message is present; there is also the word Loading at the start of the message. That's why we added – as a separator between the words.

```
this.context.statusRenderer.displayLoadingIndicator(paragraphElement, "- Sending feedback");
this.context.spHttpClient.post(url,SPHttpClient.configurations.v1, spHttpClientOptions)
  .then((response: SPHttpClientResponse) => {
    this.context.statusRenderer.clearLoadingIndicator(paragraphElement);
    if (response.status === 201) {
      this.domElement.getElementsByClassName(styles.successIndicator)[0]
        .innerHTML = "<i class='ms-Icon ms-Icon--Accept' aria-hidden='true'> Thank you for the feedback!</i>";
    } else {
      this.context.statusRenderer.renderError(this.domElement,
        `Failed to save feedback. Error code: ${response.statusText} (${response.status})`);
    }
  });
```

The actual call of the spHttpClient.post is rather simple. We supply three parameters: The first is the URL, the second is a configuration version (currently only v1 is available), and the final one is the spHttpClientOptions object which holds our new list item for the feedback list.

In REST APIs the URL points to the resource (the collection of list items) and the verb (POST) tells the system what needs to be done. In this example, POST means that we want to create a new list item. If we would like to update an item, the URL should point to that specific item, for example;
`https://yourtenant.sharepoint.com/_api/web/lists/getbytitle('Feedback')`
`/items(1)` would point to the list item with an ID of 1.

The call is asynchronous, taking usually a few hundred milliseconds or less. The way `then` operate, is that it returns a `Promise` object, which is part of ECMAScript 2015. Promises is an API style for dealing with asynchronous calls without needing very deep nesting of callbacks, which looks ugly and is often difficult to follow.

We are using a lambda or arrow function, which is also part of new ECMAScript, to state that when we get the result from the post call, we receive a `SPHttpClientResponse` object. Despite using these new JavaScript features, it will run in older browsers because TypeScript will transpile the code to older versions of JavaScript. At that moment, we clear the loading indicator and examine the return value. The HTTP return code *201* stands for *created*. If we get that one, we know that the item has been successfully created and we can present the good news for the user. If we get something else as the return code, then something went wrong and we render the error message.

Testing and troubleshooting the web part

Now we are ready to test the web part. Save the web part file and type the following commands to the Command Prompt. If you are developing your web parts and have a feeling that not all of your modifications are present on the workbench, it is a good idea to use `gulp clean` and start fresh.

```
gulp clean
gulp serve
```

After you have tested that everything works as expected on the local SharePoint Workbench, open a hosted SharePoint Workbench from your SharePoint site. This is found under `https://{site}/_layouts/workbench.aspx`.

One possible error you might find is that the web part can't find the list. This is what it will look like:

You can easily test this by modifying the URL of the `spHttpClient.post` call. Alternatively, you can create the feedback list so that the name of the URL field is `Url` instead of URL. This will give you an error message that is less clear.

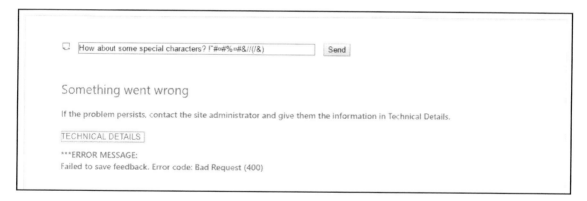

When troubleshooting this kind of situation, you need more information than the HTTP error code. One of the best tools for the job is **Fiddler**, a tool for monitoring the HTTP traffic between your computer and the SharePoint servers. The only problem is that HTTP traffic might seem overwhelming and difficult to interpret. You can download Fiddler from `https://www.telerik.com/download/fiddler`. You can also use built-in browser developer tools, although they are not as powerful as Fiddler.

When Fiddler is running, try to send feedback using the web part. You can find the failed REST call in the midst of other traffic:

This allows us to examine both the request and the response objects. If you look at the response in JSON view, you can see the actual error:

Of course, you can also access this information on the response object as well, but then you need to write the code to examine the error object.

So, when sending data to the SharePoint list, you must specify the so-called internal name of the field in question. Note that the internal name is case sensitive.

When you get all of the errors sorted out, you will see that our web part actually works and saved data to the feedback list.

If you examine the special characters, you can see that the `escape` function changed the ampersand `&` to `&amp;`.

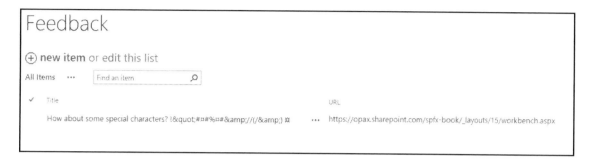

In `Chapter 11`, *Troubleshooting and Debugging SharePoint Framework Solutions*, we will take a deeper look at Fiddler and other troubleshooting techniques.

Ideas for fine tuning the web part for production use

At this point, we are ready; our web part can be packaged and deployed to test and production site collections, following the instructions in `Chapter 6`, *Packaging and Deploying Solutions*. But we are going to go through some ideas how to make this web part even better.

Using Office 365 to build better business process

One aspect of making this web part better is to take care that site (or page) owners are aware of the feedback they are getting.The traditional approach is to create an alert for the owners on the feedback list or have some sort of logic within the web part that executes. Another, even more useful approach is to use SharePoint Workflows. The modern way is to use **Microsoft Flow**. With Microsoft Flow, we can easily create a flow that will trigger when a new item is added to the feedback list, and then maybe send emails to owners. The email could include the link to the page in question and our feedback list could have additional fields like status and owner's comment. The flow could also send an email back to the original user because we know him as the creator of the feedback list item.

The flow would benefit from additional information about the page the feedback concerns. For example, information which will allow it to open the page as a list item and read or even modify its properties.

The way to do this is to access this information on our web part and save it as part of the feedback. We already know the URL and we can easily access other information via the `this.context.pageContext` object.

Property	Description
web.absoluteUrl	The URL of the web where the page is.
web.id	The GUID of the web object.
list.id	The GUID of the list, or actually the library, containing either Site pages or Pages.
list.serverRelativeUrl	A URL pointing to the list.
list.title	The title of the list.
listitem.id	The ID of the list item in question.

With that information, either the flow or our TypeScript code can query and retrieve more information. In TypeScript, you can make another query to get all the properties of the current page:

```
const url: string = this.context.pageContext.web.absoluteUrl
    +"/_api/web/lists/getbytitle('"+this.context.pageContext.list.title
    +"')/items("+this.context.pageContext.listItem.id+")/FieldValuesAsHtml";
```

With the `get` method, you are interested in the actual data that is returned from the `spHttpClient` call. It will be available through `response.json()`.

```
this.context.spHttpClient.get(url,SPHttpClient.configurations.v1)
.then((response: SPHttpClientResponse) => {
  this.context.statusRenderer.clearLoadingIndicator(paragraphElement);
  if (response.status === 200) {
    return response.json();
  } else {
    this.context.statusRenderer.renderError(this.domElement,
      `Failed retrieve information. Error code: ${response.statusText} (${response.status})`)
  }
});
```

We can use this approach to read the page owner's information from the page properties. It could be the author of the page or a custom field used to indicate the ownership. If the owner information is not on the page, it can be read from web properties. We just need to remember that our code can only access information using the user's permissions.

Building smarter controls

In simple web parts like this, we should keep the JavaScript payload low. This means that, when you are building a web part with a few fields and simple communication needs, we don't need Angular or React or even jQuery, as you can see. However, as business requirements for the user experience grow, the need for third-party frameworks and libraries increases. The subject is covered in detail in Chapter 9, *Using React and Office UI Fabric React Components*, and Chapter 10, *Working with Different JavaScript Frameworks and 3rd Party Frameworks*.

Simple requirements can be addressed with simple solutions. For example, if we want to change the behavior of our web part so that it doesn't allow clicking of the **Send** button when there is no text in the text field, we can make the following changes.

In the render function, just before the function ends, add the following line:

```
button.disabled = true;
```

Then, replace the setComment function with the following:

```
private setComment(event: Event): void {
    let srcElement: HTMLInputElement = event.srcElement as
HTMLInputElement;
    this._commentText = escape(srcElement.value);
    const button: HTMLButtonElement =
this.domElement.getElementsByTagName("BUTTON")[0] as HTMLButtonElement;
    button.disabled = (this._commentText.length === 0);
}
```

Now, the button will be disabled when there is no text in the text field. For a SharePoint developer, it is good to know that various JavaScript libraries and frameworks are not always needed. Of course, there is a point after which it becomes less expensive and error-prone to use third party libraries to build web parts more effectively. A good indicator that you have reached this point is when you find that the logic to keep the UI elements consistent is becoming complex and difficult to follow.

Provisioning of the Feedback list and other resources

At the beginning of the chapter, we created the feedback list at the root of a SharePoint Online site collection. We did this using the user interface. There is nothing wrong with that, unless you need to create dozens or even hundreds of lists. In that case, the provisioning of the required SharePoint resources should be automated. Many SharePoint professionals will script the creation of lists even when they only need a few them. It is good practice because it is less error-prone and you can easily delete everything and recreate it while developing the solution.

Currently, the main approach to provisioning is called remote provisioning, as mentioned in the first chapters. In remote provisioning, a code, which is usually a PowerShell script but can be also native C# application of any type, creates the required lists and other resources when the administrator wants them to be created, or in scheduled manner, or as part of another provisioning operation. For example, whenever site collection is created via remote provisioning, we could hook the creation of our feedback list generation onto the provisioning code as well.

Instead of remote provisioning, our code in the web part could check if the feedback list has already been created and if not, it could create the list and the custom columns. It is not bad practice, but it requires that the user who is the first to write feedback has permissions to create the list on root site level. That might be the case anyway, as the web part is usually added to the page by the site owner. Even if it added by a normal user and the list creation fails, we could simply instruct the user to contact an administrator.

Localization

What about building web parts which take into account the fact that Office 365 is global, and many of the organizations that use Office 365 services operate in many different languages? In Chapter 3, *Getting Started with the SharePoint Framework*, we already looked at the files that make supporting multiple languages possible. It is very nice that those files are built into Microsoft's Yeoman SharePoint scaffolding, but it is down to us as the developers to use them.

If you know that the web part you are building doesn't need to support multiple cultures, then you can ignore the following. You can write all text in English, French, or whatever language you want. However, if you have reasons to believe that the web part needs to support more than one language, you should build it to do that from the beginning.

This doesn't mean that you need to have translations for all of your text from the start. At the start, you probably don't even know what to translate. Instead, develop the web part in one language, but always create all the texts inside the strings object by using the files in `loc` folder.

There are three different parts of localizing a web part. These are: localizing the web part manifest, localizing text, and taking other cultural aspects like currency and calendar into account.

Localizing web part manifest

Our nonlocalized web part manifest (`FeedbackWebPart.manifest.json`) looks like this:

```json
"preconfiguredEntries": [{
  "groupId": "0d59b068-2924-4a95-a63c-332026d92b16",
  "group": { "default": "SharePoint Framework web parts" },
  "title": { "default": "Feedback" },
  "description": { "default": "Collect feedback from SharePoint pages." },
  "officeFabricIconFontName": "NoteForward",
  "properties": {
    "hintText": "Type in feedback concerning the page"
  }
}]
```

The language dependent parts have default properties. If you want to translate those parts to other languages, you do it by adding new language-specific properties and values.

```
"preconfiguredEntries": [{
  "groupId": "0d59b068-2924-4a95-a63c-332026d92b16",
  "group": {
    "default": "SharePoint Framework web parts",
    "fi-fi": "SharePoint Framework verkko-osat"
  },
  "title": {
    "default": "Feedback",
    "fi-fi": "Palaute"
  },
  "description": {
    "default": "Collect feedback from SharePoint pages.",
    "f-fi": "Kerää palautetta SharePoint-sivuilta."
  },
  "officeFabricIconFontName": "NoteForward",
  "properties": {
    "hintText": "Type in feedback concerning the page"
  }
}]
```

There is one problem in the web part manifest. You can't localize the default values for the properties as easily as other values. There are two ways to do it: either you create multiple `preconfiguredEntries` objects to support multiple languages or you handle default property values in your code using the strings object as you do with the other language dependent text. The problem with multiple `preconfiguredEntries` objects is that you usually only want to show the web part to the user once, when he or she is adding it to the page.

Localizing texts

To localize text, we use the strings object like our code does in `getPropertyPaneConfiguration` function:

```
header: {
  description: strings.PropertyPaneDescription
},
```

We just need to add all of the language dependent strings into the two files in the `loc` folder. Insert all of the text in the declaration of the `IFeedbackStrings` interface in `loc\mystrings.d.ts` and all values inside language specific files such as `loc\en-us.js`.

Calendar and currency

Localization is not just text. For example, for some people the first day of the week is Sunday, but for others it is Monday. The date is also displayed differently in different parts of the world.

In the SharePoint Framework, you can access the `this.context.pageContext.cultureInfo` object to find out what culture you should support. The object has three properties like `currentCultureName` and `currentUICultureName`. In TypeScript, you can, for example, use the following notation to present the current date in a specific culture's format:

```
let today : Date = new Date();
let todayStr : string = today.toLocaleDateString(this.context.pageContext.cultureInfo.currentCultureName);
```

Summary

In this chapter, we built a real web part using the SharePoint Framework. This went beyond a simple Hello World web part like we made earlier and actually walked you through the steps in provisioning the necessary data structures, and building the user interface for the solution. We also had a look at some additional ideas for building smarter controls for the web part, including a model for not showing a **Send** button unless there's a value in a text field, by using a JavaScript-based approach in the web part.

In the next chapter, we'll learn how to use Visual Studio Code more productively when working with the SharePoint Framework projects.

5
Using Visual Studio Code and Other Editors

This chapter provides an introduction and a deeper look at Visual Studio Code and how it works for you as a developer. It's widely used, and it is also the chosen code editor that Microsoft uses for the SharePoint Framework guidance and sample code. You are free to use any text or code editor you're most familiar with, as the SharePoint Framework does not require you to specifically use Visual Studio Code.

During this chapter, we'll install Visual Studio Code, if you did not install it during `Chapter 3`, *Getting Started with the SharePoint Framework*. We'll take a tour of the features, including VS Code Extensions, configuration, and the Command Palette, which is a central utility for navigating and finding functionality within VS Code.

In addition, a community-driven project released the first version of SPFx project template for Visual Studio 2015 and 2017. This is an extension to Visual Studio allowing you work with SPFx-based projects in Visual Studio, rather than VS Code. We'll walk through installing and using the extension if you are more familiar with Visual Studio already.

After completing this chapter, you should be:

- Familiar with using VS Code in your projects
- Confident to continue working with SPFx-based projects
- Able to install extensions and configure VS Code to your liking

Introducing Visual Studio Code

Visual Studio Code (or VS Code for short) is a lightweight code editor and debugging tool, that derives from the familiar features and look and feel of Visual Studio. It was first released in April 2015 and has since evolved to a stable 1.x release. It evolves consistently and constantly, and since it's open source, the source codes can be viewed on GitHub at `https://github.com/Microsoft/vscode`.

The thinking behind VS Code is that while Visual Studio, the real version of development tooling on the Windows platform, evolves quite slowly, VS Code could evolve on a monthly basis. Thus, it's much more lightweight and also cross-platform, as it was written using the Electron Framework. Installation takes just a minute or two. Compare this to Visual Studio 2017 installation, which often takes an hour depending on the features chosen.

VS Code is cross-platform, and it runs natively on Windows, Linux, and Mac platforms.

You can also sign up for daily releases by signing up to the **Insiders** version of VS Code. See `https://code.visualstudio.com/insiders` for details.

VS Code can be considered as a powerful text editor rather than a full IDE but it includes source control and debugging support, which makes it close to an IDE. When developing the SharePoint Framework solutions, you are not enforced to use VS Code; in fact, you could use any type of text editor, such as Notepad++, to create your solution, but you would typically need to make more manual steps as the editor of your choosing might not have SPFx-specific tooling. We recommend you learn the basics of VS Code, as it's a highly useful tool, and fully free.

VS Code can be used to write code for JavaScript, TypeScript, and Node.js. In addition, VS Code supports - through extensions - writing code for other languages, including C++, C#, Python, PHP, and Go, as well as Unity and .NET runtimes. There is also an extension for writing PowerShell in VS Code.

Installing Visual Studio Code

The installation of VS Code was shown in `Chapter 3`, *Getting Started with the SharePoint Framework*. Just in case you have not installed VS Code yet, take a few moments to perform the installation now:

1. On your development workstation, navigate to `http://code.visualstudio.com/`. If you are planning to use Windows, select **Download for Windows** on the left.

2. In case you need a different platform, select **Other platforms and Insiders Edition** to choose between Linux versions (Debian, Ubuntu, Red Hat, Fedora, SUSE) and a Mac-version (macOS 10.9+ required).

3. On Windows, double-click the installation package and walk through the installation wizard.

4. Select **Next**, and then accept the **License Agreement**.

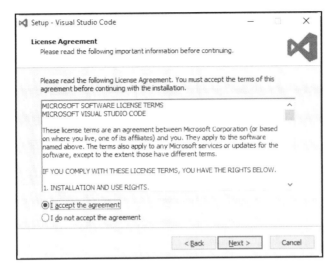

5. The default path is usually fine, so just accept the defaults.

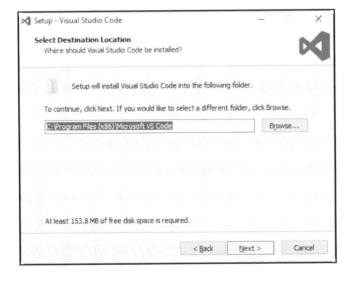

6. The **Start Menu Folder** dictates what to call the folder in your Windows start menu. You can safely accept the default value.

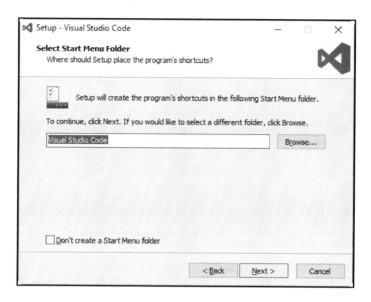

7. If you need, select additional properties for installation, such as integrating **Open with Code** selection in your Windows File Explorer for a shorthand.

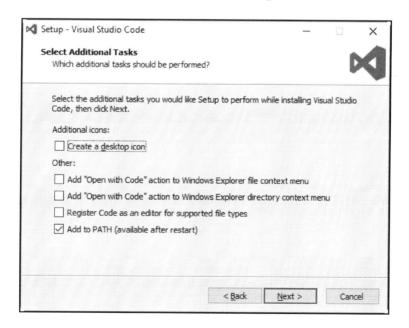

8. Click **Next**, and then **Install**.

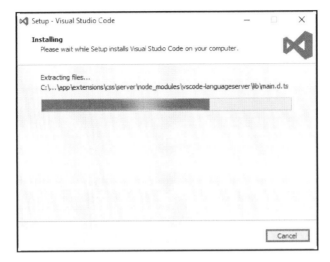

9. Installation takes a minute or two, after which you can choose to launch Visual Studio Code.

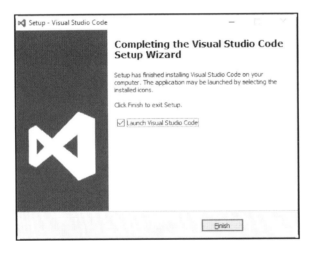

10. Congratulations, Visual Studio Code should now have installed and you are ready to start diving deeper into the features of the tool!

Getting to know Visual Studio Code

Upon opening VS Code, you are shown a dark-themed editor without any files open.

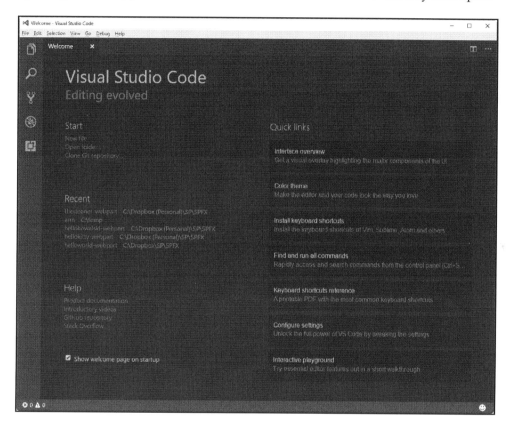

On top, you have a few menu items with the usual tools including file and folder management, editing, and debugging. We'll get to these in a bit.

On the left-hand side, you have five icons that act as quick links to your most used tools.

The first one will open **EXPLORER**, which allows you to navigate between the files and folders of your project. If you are familiar with Visual Studio, this might seem familiar to you. The main difference is that you will not be working with solution files, but directly with file and folder structures. The shortcut key for opening **EXPLORER** is *Ctrl + Shift + E*.

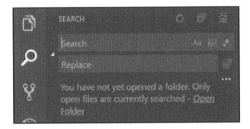

The next one is **SEARCH**, for searching content across files and folders. The shortcut key is *Ctrl + Shift + F*.

The third one, which looks a bit like a crossroad, is **SOURCE CONTROL** access. The shortcut key is *Ctrl + Shift + G*, and this is used when you need to commit your code to a local repository and possibly push those changes to another copy of the repo or a central repo, such as Visual Studio Team Services or `Github.com`.

The fourth one, **DEBUG**, is about squashing bugs; debugging. You'll get the usual watch window, call stack, breakpoints, and variables. The shortcut key is *Ctrl + Shift + D.*

The fifth and last one is **EXTENSIONS**. You can freely install any extensions you feel are useful and give you more productivity. Some good to know extensions are:

- PowerShell, for editing PowerShell scripts and getting Intellisense support
- **vscode-icons**, for proper Visual Studio Code icons for files
- XML Tools, for formatting XML-based files
- Office UI Fabric Snippets, for quick snippets to insert Office UI Fabric elements in HTML files

We'll take a deeper look into extensions later in this chapter.

Changing the color theme

Let's start our journey with VS Code by trying to change the color theme. By default, VS Code ships in a very dark theme, which is a stark contrast from Visual Studio's light and clean white theme.

In order to access settings, and modify VS Code behavior, we need to use the Command Palette. It's not visible by default, and it automatically hides when you click outside the Command Palette if it's visible. To make it visible, press *Ctrl + Shift + P* or click **View | Command Palette**.

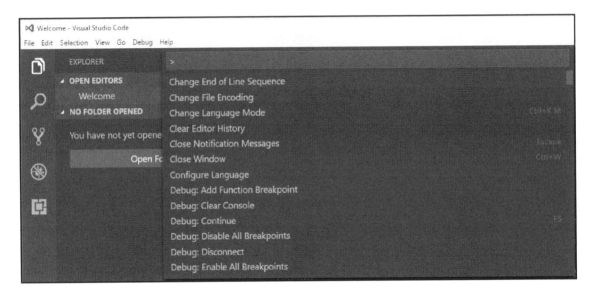

The **Command Palette** has IntelliSense, so you can just start typing characters from a command or setting you need to find. Type `theme` and you should get a shorter list of settings to access.

From here, we can see that changing the color theme can quickly be accessed via the *Ctrl + K, Ctrl +T* Keyboard combination. Select the middle one, **Preferences: Color Theme**.

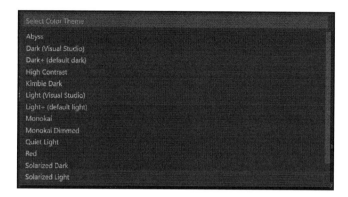

We get a long list of pre-defined themes. Choose any theme you feel might be good for your use. As an example, we'll select **Light (Visual Studio)** to mimic Visual Studio's look and feel. When you hover over the options, the theme is updated in real time.

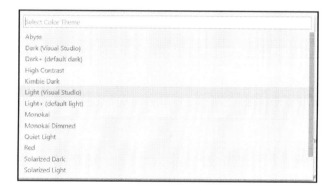

You can now switch back to **Dark+ (default dark)**, which is the default, or experiment with the other alternatives.

Click anywhere outside the Command Palette, and you're back to the initial welcome screen.

Whenever you need to find a tool or a setting, keep the Command Palette in your mind, as in VS Code it's a great little utility to help you navigate around. Developers coming from a Visual Studio experience might find the ribbon or toolbar more convenient. The approach in VS Code is more extensible and often less cluttered.

Working with files

As you might recall, VS Code works by working with files and folders directly, as they are located on your workstation. Thus it is up to you, as a developer, to choose the base path for your projects. Each project will be a directory underneath your base path. A typical development file hierarchy could be as follows:

- Basepath: `C:\Projects\`
- Intranet-project: `C:\Projects\Intranet`
- Extranet-project: `C:\Projects\Extranet`

You can now select **File** | **Open Folder** in VS Code to select `C:\Projects\Intranet` as your working folder if you're working on that particular project.

As you'll see, since the folder is still empty, we just get a placeholder for the `INTRANET` folder. You can add a new file by clicking the small icon with a green plus-icon.

We'll add a simple HTML file, called `hello.html`. VS Code recognizes this is a file for HTML content, and provides you with IntelliSense supports automatically in the editor.

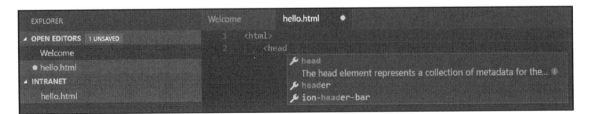

If we add a second file, such as a text file, to the folder, we can work with multiple files through the tabbed navigation.

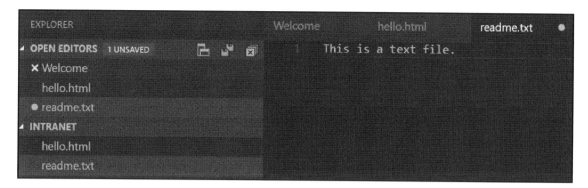

As you can see, working with multiple files in a modern editor such as VS Code makes developing solutions much easier to work with. When working with larger projects with dozens of files, you'll find that using search in VS Code helps immensely in navigating between multiple files.

Extensions

Extensions allow you to extend VS Code with powerful new features, such as support for new programming languages and frameworks. To view available extensions on the VS Code Extension Marketplace, press *Ctrl + Shift + X* or click on the *Tab*.

By default, extensions are sorted in descending order based on total installations. Let's start by installing the vscode-icons.

1. If it's not visible on the list, simply type the extension name in the search box.

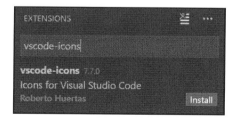

2. Click **Install**, and the button changes briefly to *Installing*. After the installation is complete, you need to reload the VS Code window by clicking **Reload**.

3. Verify the extension was installed by clicking **EXTENSIONS** on the left-hand bar or pressing *Ctrl + Shift + X*.

4. You can also uninstall the extension by clicking on the gear icon and selecting **Uninstall**.

5. Extensions do not automatically update themselves and require either manual updating or changing the auto-update setting to true. You can change the auto-update setting as follows:

6. Select **File | Preferences | Settings** from the top toolbar.

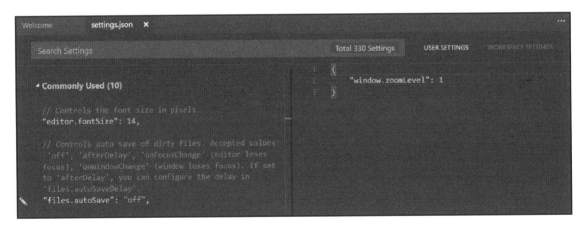

7. A `settings.json` configuration file opens in the editor. By changing values in this file, you can parametrize VS Code to perform additional tasks, such as automatically updating extensions or automatically saving open files on certain events.

8. Press *Ctrl + F* to initiate a search, and type autoupdate in the search toolbar.

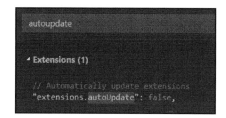

9. You can now verify that extensions are not automatically being updated. Hover your mouse on the line, and press the pencil icon on the left to modify the line. Change the value to true from false. The changed line of text should now be shown on the right, as it is now a user setting:

10. Commit the changes by selecting **File | Save All**.

Working with the SharePoint Framework in Visual Studio Code

When you start working with SPFx-based projects, you often navigate through the folders through Windows' Command Prompt. You can then quickly open Visual Studio Code in the current folder by typing:

```
code .
```

This is the equivalent of first opening VS Code, pressing *Ctrl + K, Ctrl + O*, and finding the correct folder to work with.

Running commands with the Integrated Terminal

When developing SPFx-projects, you often need to run specific commands on a command line, such as instructing Gulp to do certain things. You can use the Integrated Terminal in VS Code to run them directly, instead of hopping between two different windows.

To open the Integrated Terminal, from the top toolbar select **View | Integrated Terminal**. You can also show it by first opening Command Palette (*Ctrl + Shift + P*) and typing `integrated`:

This opens a smaller terminal window in the lower right area of VS Code and places the current path to the same that your project is in. You can now run commands directly here, such as `gulp serve` to start up your project in a local SharePoint Workbench.

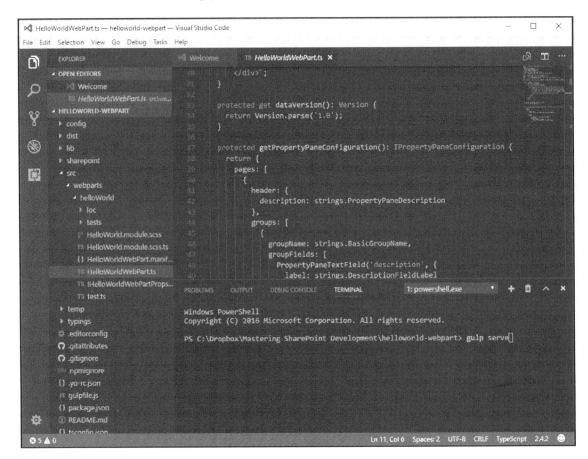

Using Visual Studio instead of Visual Studio Code

Visual Studio Code has always been the recommended code editing tool for the SharePoint Framework projects. Up until recently, it was also the only one for which Microsoft provided guidance and documentation.

Developers, especially those coming from a SharePoint full-trust solution background, are still using Visual Studio, not VS Code. Several developers have asked us why they cannot use Visual Studio 2015 or Visual Studio 2017 and are forced to use VS Code. The thinking here is that Visual Studio could have had a new project template for the SharePoint Framework, instead of having to learn a new tool. One reason might be the speed of development for SPFx, as new features and functionality are being rapidly introduced and the Visual Studio release cycle has often been much slower.

This also proves non-productive if most code is written in Visual Studio and only SharePoint Framework-related elements have to be written in VS Code. Having to learn multiple editors and their intricacies is time-consuming, but then again, developing solutions is a journey of learning new things.

The community stepped up to this and through the work of several people a native Visual Studio extension (a `.VSIX` file) that allows developing SPFx projects within Visual Studio 2015/2017 was created.

You can download the extension to Visual Studio 2015 or 2017 from the Visual Studio Marketplace, by searching for `SPFx project template` at `https://marketplace.visualstudio.com`.

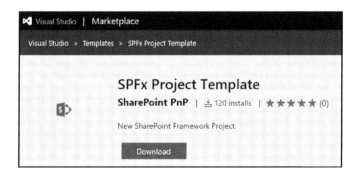

As the extension is community-driven, there are bound to be issues and bugs that might force you to move to VS Code for SPFx development. In the context of this book, we'll aim to use VS Code, and occasionally mention if something works (or doesn't work) within the SPFx Project Template extension in Visual Studio 2015/2017.

Installing the extension is easy, as you only need to double-click the installation file.

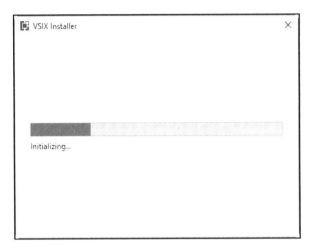

If you have multiple versions of Visual Studio installed, you can choose the targets-- normally you would choose both 2015 and 2017 versions.

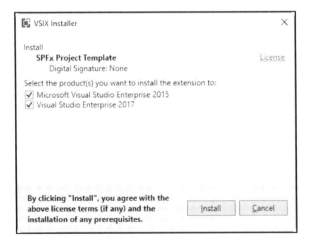

Successful installation takes about a minute, and then you're ready to run Visual Studio.

In Visual Studio, select **File | New Project**. The extension has installed a new project template under **Visual C# | Office/SharePoint | SharePoint | SharePoint Framework** called `SPFx Web Part Project`.

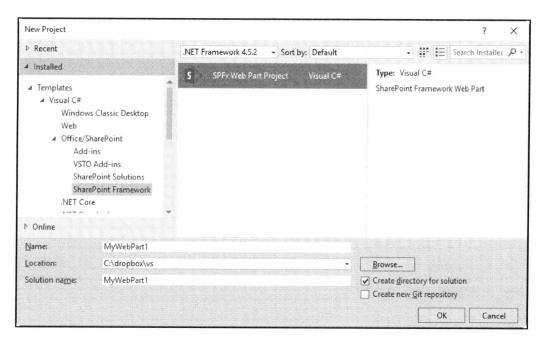

When we choose a name for the project and click **OK**, the new SPFx Web Part Project template starts to show its benefits. Instead of running several command-line tools, like in a VS Code-based project scenario, Visual Studio gives us a nice wizard that queries for the values and runs the tools behind the scenes for us.

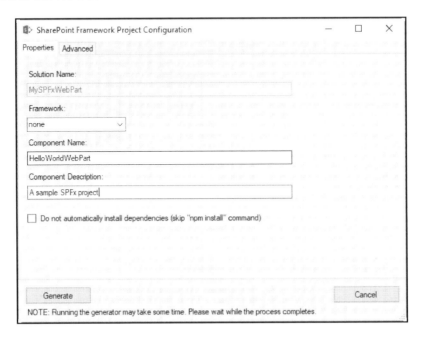

We can choose the desired framework from between **none**, **React** and **Knockout**. If you're not sure, you typically choose **none** and add the necessary framework later during your development cycle.

By clicking **Generate**, Visual Studio will try to run the Yeoman generator (yo @microsoft/sharepoint).

In our experience, this takes time, both when executed manually in a VS Code-scenario and here. This is because the extension is actually running the same command-line tools behind the scenes. Be patient.

After the generator is done, you should be seeing a log file with the output from Yeoman.

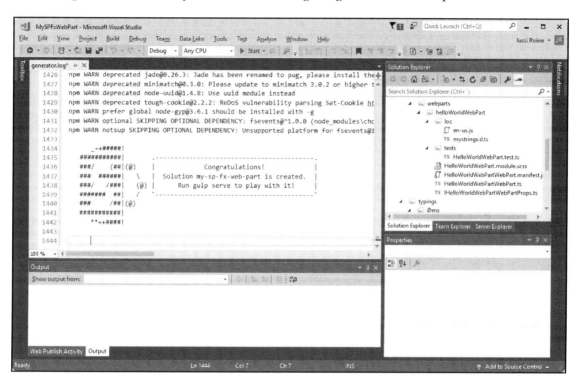

In **Solution Explorer**, we can now see that all the necessary SPFx project files are available, and we can edit them just like in VS Code. The template has also generated a Visual Studio project.

Running code in Visual Studio works just like in any other project--you press *F5* to build and run the code. This runs `gulp serve`, just like you would run it manually, and opens a browser to load the SharePoint Workbench from the localhost.

You can even edit files in your project while your code is running, and reload SharePoint Workbench to see the changes.

```
15   public render(): void {
16     this.domElement.innerHTML = `
17       <div class="${styles.helloWorld}">
18         <div class="${styles.container}">
19           <div class="ms-Grid-row ms-bgColor-themeDark ms-fontColor-white ${styles.row}">
20             <div class="ms-Grid-col ms-u-lg10 ms-u-xl8 ms-u-xlPush2 ms-u-lgPush1">
21               <span class="ms-font-xl ms-fontColor-white">Welcome to SharePoint!</span>
22               <p class="ms-font-l ms-fontColor-white">Hello! SharePoint experiences using Web Parts.</p>
23               <p class="ms-font-l ms-fontColor-white">${escape(this.properties.description)}</p>
24               <a href="https://aka.ms/spfx" class="${styles.button}">
25                 <span class="${styles.label}">Learn more</span>
26               </a>
```

In this example, we've changed the introduction text in the sample SPFx Web Part to include **Hello!**. SharePoint Workbench should automatically refresh (with help from `gulp serve`) and immediately show the change.

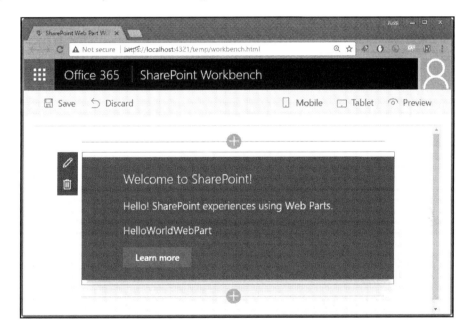

For now, though we foresee that the SPFx Project Template will evolve rapidly in the coming months, most sample code is still written in VS Code. Therefore, sample code you find will typically not have a Visual Studio project file. You can choose to use either development tool (or any other code editor), but we recommend you also be familiar with VS Code, as it's a highly useful code editor and already widely in use.

Summary

In this chapter, we took a look at Visual Studio Code more closely. As you've seen, it's a powerful code editor and available free of charge for all major platforms, including Windows, Linux, and Mac. The main difference between VS Code and Visual Studio is that the latter has project templates, and a whole integrated development environment built-in. VS Code is mainly an editor and a good one at that, but it lacks the majority of the more enterprise-focused features you might find in Visual Studio 2015 and 2017.

VS Code is currently the best tool you have for writing code for an SPFx project. Microsoft recently released the stable version of an extension for Visual Studio that allows projects based on SPFx. This seems like a good alternative, but developers will still need to be comfortable with VS Code, as it's a tool that is widely used and Microsoft is heavily supporting VS Code-based documentation and extensions.

6
Packaging and Deploying Solutions

Now that we're getting more familiar with SharePoint Framework and Visual Studio Code, it's time to start deploying our code more properly to SharePoint. The difference between running your code against a local SharePoint Workbench, a hosted SharePoint Workbench and deploying it to SharePoint is important to understand. For this, we need to learn to package our customization into a neat package and install the packages through SharePoint's App Catalog service. In addition, SharePoint Framework supports the use of **Content Delivery Networks (CDN)** that greatly optimize the client-side behavior for your users, so we'll take a look at how to configure CDN properly either through SharePoint Online or Microsoft Azure. You could use an on-premises SharePoint also, but typically this is either not needed or is handled in another device (such as a proxy server).

After you've completed this chapter you will have learned:

- A lot about using Gulp to instruct and orchestrate your packages
- How and where to configure SharePoint to correctly serve your code for clients
- How and when to use Content Delivery Networks to provide a more performant solution

Overview of packaging and deploying

As discussed in `Chapter 1`, *Introducing SharePoint Online for Developers*, packaging and deploying of SharePoint solutions has always been slightly too complex and error-prone.

With SharePoint 2007, 2010, and 2013, full-trust based solutions were the standard of the time for packaging customization. These files would hold a single XML-based manifesto that would say what is in the package, and it was left up to SharePoint to figure out just how to deploy assets and artifacts correctly.

In situations where SharePoint failed the deployment, it was left up to the developer, or even worse, the IT professional performing the deployment to clean up whatever was left behind. This produced all types of utilities, tools, and best practices on deployment order, and how to update your existing packages in production in order not to break anything else.

With SharePoint Framework, we're finally moving beyond this problematic approach, as each SharePoint Framework asset is packaged automatically for us and deployment is now much easier and less error-prone. We often feel that SharePoint customizations should be deployed with the same ease as regular users deploy mobile apps on their smartphones: select an app, deploy, and use. Remove at will, and it will clean up automatically. With SPFx, we are inching closer to this model, although everything is not yet perfect.

Packaging SharePoint Framework solutions

Each SharePoint Framework solution will be packaged in order to deploy them to the SharePoint. As we want to deploy solutions in a clean and simple way, the tool we will use to build and package code is **Gulp**. This is the same command-line utility you've used to build and package code in earlier chapters before running a locally hosted copy of SharePoint Workbench.

Using Gulp to package a project

Gulp is accessible in VS Code using the Integrated Terminal, that you can access from **View | Integrated Terminal**. By typing gulp without any extra parameters, Gulp will run a default task. You can also run gulp from a Command Prompt or PowerShell window.

Tasks are described in a separate configuration file within the project folder called gulpfile.js. It is rather small in the SPFx default project, as a lot of work is done through SPFx tooling (sp-build-web, for example), but it is more than sufficient for your typical needs as a developer:

```
1    'use strict';
2
3    const gulp = require('gulp');
4    const build = require('@microsoft/sp-build-web');
5
6    build.initialize(gulp);
7
```

Line 6 is key here; it runs initialization for `gulp` as part of the build process. To understand what's going on here, we need to locate `@microsoft/sp-build-web`, which is one of the packages we installed earlier. By initializing the package, we automatically import and configure the necessary build tasks for a web browser-based (SharePoint Workbench in this case) build target.

To see what we can do with Gulp in a SharePoint Framework project, we need to peek at a file called `package.json`, which is also in the same directory as the project. This file describes our project, project dependencies, and also the Gulp tasks that are equivalent to our project tasks:

```
22    "scripts": {
23        "build": "gulp bundle",
24        "clean": "gulp clean",
25        "test": "gulp test"
```

As we can see, we have the following Gulp tasks pre-configured for us:

- `bundle`: Bundles the entry point client-side file, and the required dependent files to a single JavaScript file.
- `clean`: Cleans up build files left over from previous builds
- `test`: Runs all tests against the current project

But why is it that we do not have `gulp serve` here, as that is something we've been using to run our projects? The reason lies in another package, the `@microsoft/sp-build-core-tasks`, that is being referenced as a Node.js module. This lists the following additional tasks for Gulp:

- `build`: Builds the project
- `serve`: Runs SharePoint Workbench locally

- `nuke`: Cleans everything within the project, including build artifacts, and build target directories
- `package-solution`: Packages the solution to a SharePoint package
- `deploy-azure-storage`: Deploys assets to Microsoft Azure-hosted storage

To find all Gulp tasks, you can run `gulp --tasks`.

As is evident, Gulp as a tool is critical but, at the same time, it's quite simplistic to use. Besides `gulp serve`, you will be using `gulp package-solution` quite a bit when you choose to test your code in a real SharePoint environment tenant outside SharePoint Workbench.

To package a project for our next phase, we'll start with `gulp bundle`to put everything together first. We can append the `--ship` parameter to create a mini version of all assets, essentially optimizing the solution:

```
C:\Dropbox\Mastering SharePoint Development\helloworld-webpart>gulp bundle --ship
Build target: SHIP
[13:46:51] Using gulpfile C:\Dropbox\Mastering SharePoint Development\helloworld-webpart\gulpfile.js
[13:46:51] Starting gulp
[13:46:51] Starting 'bundle'...
[13:46:51] Starting subtask 'pre-copy'...
[13:46:51] Finished subtask 'pre-copy' after 7.76 ms
[13:46:51] Starting subtask 'copy-static-assets'...
[13:46:51] Starting subtask 'sass'...
[13:46:52] Finished subtask 'sass' after 589 ms
[13:46:52] Starting subtask 'tslint'...
[13:46:52] Starting subtask 'typescript'...
[13:46:52] [typescript] TypeScript version: 2.1.6
[13:46:52] Finished subtask 'copy-static-assets' after 654 ms
[13:46:52] Warning - tslint - src\webparts\helloWorld\HelloWorldWebPart.ts(7,10): error no-unused-imports: unused import: 'escape'
[13:46:52] Warning - tslint - src\webparts\helloWorld\test.ts(5,5): error no-duplicate-variable: Duplicate variable: 'untypedVariable'
[13:46:54] Finished subtask 'tslint' after 1.74 s
```

This produces the minified files, with localization support under `/temp/deploy` of our project folder structure:

```
    Directory: C:\Dropbox (Personal)\Mastering SharePoint Development\helloworld-webpart\helloworld-webpart\temp\deploy

Mode                LastWriteTime         Length Name
----                -------------         ------ ----
-a----        24/05/2017     13:36           1191 fba70b52-a501-4995-bf8e-fd4f7e187954.json
-a----        24/05/2017     13:36           6160 hello-world.bundle_09e704a8341751e14e72756decf58286.js
-a----        24/05/2017     13:36            179 helloworld-webpart-helloworldstrings_en-us_536e65149b0acf4d52c0043073b9fc59.js
-a----        24/05/2017     13:36            175 helloworld-webpart-helloworldstrings_fi-fi_bd3ea395f25b16f376857e1688e9cda8.js
```

Next, we need to produce a deployment package with `gulp package-solution`:

```
PS C:\Dropbox (Personal)\Mastering SharePoint Development\helloworld-webpart\helloworld-webpart> gulp package-solution
Build target: DEBUG
[15:24:59] Using gulpfile C:\Dropbox (Personal)\Mastering SharePoint Development\helloworld-webpart\helloworld-webpart\gulpfile.js
[15:24:59] Starting gulp
[15:24:59] Starting 'package-solution'...
[15:24:59] Starting subtask 'package-solution'...
[15:24:59] [package-solution] Found manifest: C:\Dropbox (Personal)\Mastering SharePoint Development\helloworld-webpart\helloworld-webpa
rt\dist\fba70b52-a501-4995-bf8e-fd4f7e187954.manifest.json
[15:24:59] Verifying configuration...
[15:24:59] Done!

[15:24:59] Normalizing solution information...
[15:24:59] Attempting creating component definitions for {1} manifests
[15:24:59] Created component definitions for {1} manifests
```

This will create a file with the `.sppkg` extension, that is a package SharePoint Framework project. It is stored under a sub-directory of the project folder at `/sharepoint/solution`:

```
    Directory: C:\Dropbox (Personal)\Mastering SharePoint Development\helloworld-webpart\helloworld-webpart\sharepoint\solution

Mode                LastWriteTime         Length Name
----                -------------         ------ ----
da----        24/05/2017     13:24                debug
-a----        24/05/2017     13:24           3413 helloworld-webpart.sppkg
-a----        17/05/2017     04:55           3413 helloworld-webpart.sppkg.zip
-a----        17/05/2017     04:55           1807 WebPart_fba70b52-a501-4995-bf8e-fd4f7e187954.xml
```

If we take a copy of the `.sppkg` file and rename the copy with the new file extension `.zip`, we can easily open the compiled package to reveal its content:

It looks very similar to a SharePoint add-in package, with a special `AppManifest.xml` file to instruct SharePoint what to do upon installation. In order to view the XML-file in VS Code, we can simply open the file, but for easier reading, we need an extension that helps us to format the XML properly. One such would be XML Tools:

Now we can open `AppManifest.xml` to reveal its logic:

```
<?xml version="1.0" encoding="utf 8"?>
<App
    xmlns="http://schemas.microsoft.com/sharepoint/2012/app/manifest" Name="helloworld-webpart-client-side-solution"
    ProductID="3cc5a1d3-324a-4d3a-8e8d-fce9e5c8f326" Version="1.0.0.0" SharePointMinVersion="16.0.0.0" IsClientSideSolution="true">
    <Properties>
        <Title>helloworld-webpart-client-side-solution</Title>
    </Properties>
</App>
```

This is a client-side solution, as all SharePoint Framework solutions are, and it also requires at least version 16.0.0.0 for SharePoint. In the package, we also have a separate XML for individual SharePoint Features, which act as the provisioning engine for SharePoint Framework-based web parts. These are identical to classic SharePoint Feature Framework-type customizations but they are now autogenerated for us.

Now that we have a package, we can clean up the temporary files from the previous build by running `gulp clean`.

Next, we'll actually deploy the package to SharePoint.

Deploying SharePoint Framework solutions

Deploying is often a manual task, as you'll need to be certain you are deploying things correctly and that there are no issues with your solution. As things are bound to be different in SharePoint compared to a local debug run, this phase might also produce additional things you'll need to fix in your code.

App Catalog

Deploying SharePoint Framework packages happens through a special site called the App Catalog in SharePoint.

Verify that you have App Catalog correctly provisioned before moving on to installing your app:

1. Navigate to your **SharePoint admin center** as a global admin or a SharePoint admin of your tenant. The direct link is `https://{tenant}-admin.sharepoint.com/`, where `{tenant}` is obviously your chosen tenant name, such as `CompanyA`. If you're deploying code to a locally hosted SharePoint, you need to create the App Catalog manually through central admin first.

2. From the left-hand navigation, choose **apps** and then choose **App Catalog:**

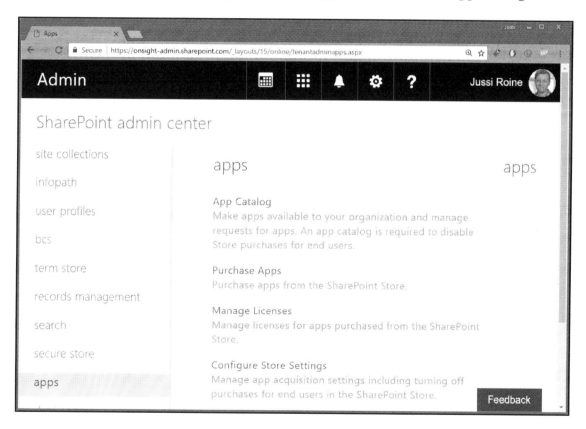

3. If you haven't already created an App Catalog, you are now prompted to create a new site collection that will be your App Catalog:

4. After creating the site collection, you can navigate to the **App Catalog** the same way through **Apps** | **App Catalog**, and it now points to your **App Catalog** site:

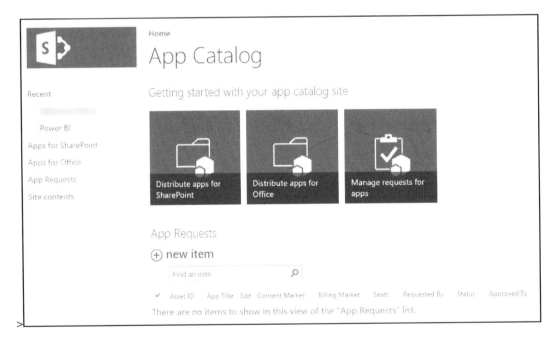

This is a site that end-users do not visit, and its purpose is to serve as a repository and deployment tool for your customizations, including SharePoint Framework-based packages.

Installing the app

In order to install the app, we need to upload it first to the App Catalog:

1. Click **Apps for SharePoint** and upload your .sppkg file here. You can simply drag and drop the file from Windows file explorer directly to the Apps for SharePoint document library:

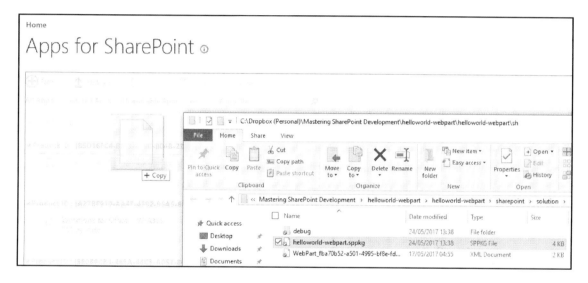

2. After the upload finishes, SharePoint will present you with a consent dialog. In this case you are deploying the solution to yourself, but in general, an administrator sees this and must make a decision whether to trust this solution or not:

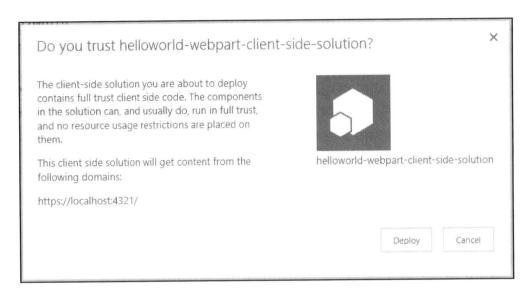

3. Your app should now be listed in the library:

4. The app is now deployed to the tenant and listed in the App Catalog, but you also need to deploy it to the site where you intend to use it. To deploy the app, navigate to the SharePoint site where you want to deploy the app, typically under /sites/, such as
https://{tenant}.sharepoint.com/sites/{your-site}. In the site, select **Site contents** from the gear menu (top right):

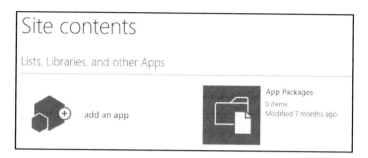

5. Then select **Add an app** to get a list of all available apps built-in, and custom apps:

6. Select your app and it will start deploying itself to the site:

7. After the app has been deployed, it shows like any other app in your site:

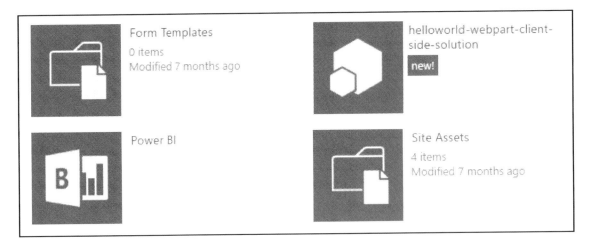

One last thing to do is to actually try out the app. As this is a SharePoint Framework-based app and it consists of a web part, we can simply add the new web part on a SharePoint page. In SharePoint, we can have modern and classic pages, and while SharePoint Workbench is designed to behave like a modern page, you can also use classic SharePoint pages to host your web parts.

1. Navigate to the root of the site where you deployed the app. Click **Edit** on the top-right to edit the page:

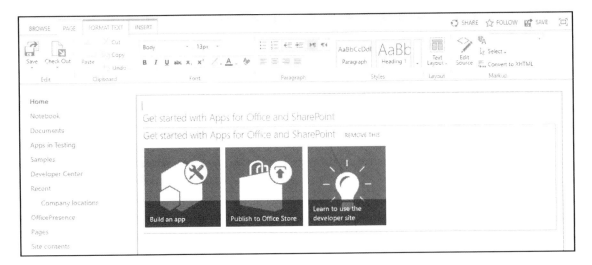

2. Select a place on the page where you would like to add the web part--such as at the top or directly beneath existing content. Then click the **Insert** tab. From here, select **Web Part**, and by default all SPFx-based web parts are in **Under Development** category:

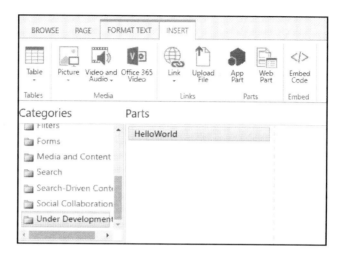

3. Select the **HelloWorld** web part, and click **Add**. It will be added on the page and start loading:

4. The loading takes a while, and you should get an error. Under **technical details** of the error, you should be able to debug the issue further:

```
***ERROR MESSAGE: ***Failed to load component "fba70b52-
a501-4995-bf8e-fd4f7e187954" (HelloWorldWebPart). Original
error: ***Failed to load URL
'https://localhost:4321/lib/webparts/helloWorld/loc/en-us.js'
for resource 'helloWorldStrings' in component 'fba70b52-
a501-4995-bf8e-fd4f7e187954' (HelloWorldWebPart). There was a
network problem. Make sure that you have run 'gulp trust-dev-
cert'.
```

5. It's evident that the solution is trying to load our code from `https://localhost:4321`, and not from SharePoint. The reason for this behavior, which might seem erratic, is that we haven't yet deployed our assets anywhere. We've simply uploaded a package that describes the solution, but this does not deploy the JavaScript bundle or other assets. If you were still running `gulp serve` for the solution, you would not see the error and everything might seem fine even if it wasn't!

6. To fix this issue for testing, hop back to Visual Studio Code and in Integrated Terminal, type `gulp serve`. This will launch locally hosted SharePoint Workbench, but it will also provide the bits of your solution back to SharePoint!:

```
PS C:\Dropbox (Personal)\Mastering SharePoint Development\helloworld-webpart\helloworld-webpart\sharepoint\solution> gulp serve
[14:32:03] Working directory changed to C:\Dropbox (Personal)\Mastering SharePoint Development\helloworld-webpart\helloworld-webpart
Build target: DEBUG
[14:32:05] Using gulpfile C:\Dropbox (Personal)\Mastering SharePoint Development\helloworld-webpart\helloworld-webpart\gulpfile.js
[14:32:05] Starting gulp
[14:32:05] Starting 'serve'...
[14:32:05] Starting subtask 'pre-copy'...
[14:32:05] Finished subtask 'pre-copy' after 6.57 ms
[14:32:05] Starting subtask 'copy-static-assets'...
[14:32:05] Starting subtask 'sass'...
```

7. When `gulp serve` is running, go back to your SharePoint browser window and reload the window. The web part should now load normally:

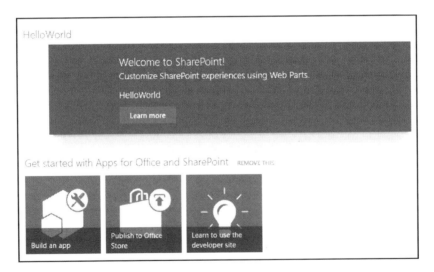

As you've seen, implementing a SharePoint Framework-based web part and deploying it to SharePoint has a few additional steps besides just building the deployment package. Next, we'll deploy the missing assets to a centralized location, so that we are not reliant on a locally executed `gulp serve` anymore. We can't expect all our users to set up a development environment and run `gulp serve`, so we need a way of making these assets available to end users.

Deploying assets

Assets that belong to our project, including images and JavaScript files, should be centrally hosted somewhere so that clients (web browsers) can access them. In our previous deployment, the assets were sitting on a developer workstation and server with Gulp.

SharePoint Online CDN and Microsoft Azure CDN

We could host these assets anywhere that we can be sure that our users will be able to access them, for example, a public website. But best practice is to use a Content Delivery Network or CDN. These are commercial hosting services that ensure that users download files from servers that are physically close to them and have high bandwidth Internet connections. In some cases, for example, popular JavaScript libraries, the user's browser may already have a cached version of the file avoiding the need to download it altogether.

We'll start with the SharePoint Online-based CDN, as it's probably easier to set up for developers, and often a common approach for serving assets.

Configuring a SharePoint Online CDN

First, we need to provide a folder for our asset files. This is a special library that will typically be hosted on Microsoft Azure datacenter infrastructure or a similar globally available infrastructure.

1. Start by finding your Site Assets document library in the SharePoint Online site you wish to use. The usual address is
   `https://{tenant}.sharepoint.com/sites/{your-site}/Site Assets/`.

2. Create a new folder named `cdn` in this document library:

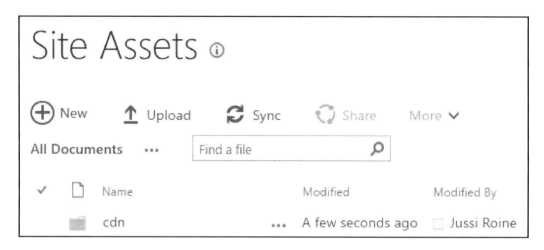

3. Now, we need to tell SharePoint Online that this particular folder in this particular document library should be enabled for CDN purposes. As CDN carries some additional infrastructure changes on Office 365, we need to instruct SharePoint Online via PowerShell to enable CDN functionality.

4. For this task, we will need the **SharePoint Online Management Shell**, which is a PowerShell-enabled shell for configuring SharePoint Online. Start by downloading the package from `https://www.microsoft.com/en-us/download/details.aspx?id=35588`, and running through the installation wizard.

5. After installing the package, you can search for `SharePoint` in your start menu to find a shortcut to the tool:

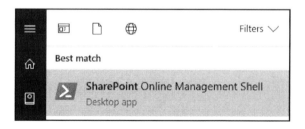

6. Next, we need to authenticate against SharePoint Online in order to start configuring our CDN. Start by capturing your credentials in a variable with the following PowerShell command: `$credentials = get-credential`.

7. Enter your email address and password for an account that has SharePoint Admin privileges:

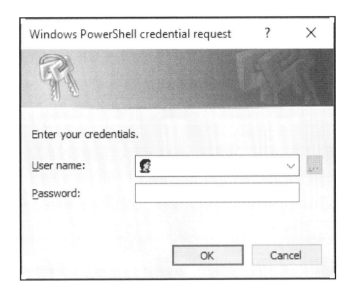

8. Next, `Connect` with SharePoint Online with the following command:

```
Connect-SPOService -Url https://{tenant}-admin.sharepoint.com -
Credential $credentials
```

And just like before, replace `{tenant}` with your Office 365 tenant name, such as CompanyA. Now, query the SPO Tenant settings whether or not Public CDN endpoints are enabled:

```
Get-SPOTenant | select PublicCdnEnabled
```

This should return a value of `true`.

9. Next, query the SPO Tenant settings for which file types are allowed within the CDN: `Get-SPOTenant | select PublicCdnAllowedFileTypes`. This should produce a list with the following values: `CSS`, `EOT`, `GIF`, `ICO`, `JPEG`, `JPG`, `JS`, `MAP`, `PNG`, `SVG`, `TTF`, `WOFF`, `TXT`. If the listing is incomplete or empty, update the settings with the following command:

```
Set-SPOTenant -PublicCdnAllowedFileTypes
"CSS,EOT,GIF,ICO,JPEG,JPG,JS,MAP,PNG,SVG,TTF,WOFF,TXT"
```

Then make sure the values are updated by querying again with `Get-SPOTenant`.

10. Finally, we'll add a new CDN endpoint that points to our `cdn` folder that we created earlier:

```
New-SPOPublicCdnOrigin -Url
https://{tenant}.sharepoint.com/sites/{site}/SiteAssets/cdn
```

11. This produces a warning that all files stored in the CDN will be anonymously accessible. For us, this is fine but it's a good thing to keep in mind when implementing functionality that needs to be secured.

12. And lastly, query for the CDN endpoint to make sure it was configured successfully.

```
Get-SPOPublicCdnOrigins | Format-List
```

Format-List produces a more readable list for us. The output should resemble the following listing:

Id : 13200052f97a4dd249b6768527c2d4bf49dfb4dbec0eff57a88a7ef9dfede4d01883a44

Url : HTTPS://TENANT.SHAREPOINT.COM/SITES/SITE/SITEASSETS.

Id : 12390061f758b807354244dd12e9808aba5c97058384a46b61b43861da5e600492d2947

Url : HTTPS://TENANT.SHAREPOINT.COM/SITES/SITE2/SITEASSETS/CDN.

Updating the project to support a SharePoint Online CDN

For now, our CDN endpoint is ready, but the folder is still empty. We need to instruct our SharePoint Framework project to start using the CDN path next. Before changing anything in the configuration, we have to construct a publicly accessible URL that points to our CDN.

The base address is always `https://publiccdn.sharepointonline.com/{tenant-name}.sharepoint.com/{cdn-origin-id}`. We need to replace the `{tenant-name}` to point to our Office 365 tenant, and then replace the CDN origin ID with a real ID. This is the ID you got from `Get-SPOPublicCdnOrigins` commands.

A base address with our tenant name and modifications might look like this: `https://publiccdn.sharepointonline.com/tenant.sharepoint.com/12390061f758b807354244dd12e9808aba5c97058384a46b61b43861da5e600492d2947`. Write this down, as you'll need it next.

Now, let's update the project:

1. Go back to Visual Studio Code and find the `write-manifests.json` file in the `/config` folder of the project. It only contains a placeholder that we now need to fill:

   ```
   {
       "cdnBasePath": "<!-- PATH TO CDN -->"
   }
   ```

2. Replace the value of `cdnBasePath` to the URL you crafted previously:

   ```
   {
       "cdnBasePath":
   "https://publiccdn.sharepointonline.com/tenant.sharepoint.com/12390061f758b807354244dd12e9808aba5c97058384a46b61b43861da5e600492d2947"
   }
   ```

3. Next, package the solution again. Use `gulp bundle -ship` first to minify and bundle everything together, and then use `gulp package-solution -ship` to re-package the solution. The `--ship` parameter will generate optimized bundles and copy them to the `/temp/deploy` folder of your project:

```
C:\Dropbox\Mastering SharePoint Development\helloworld-webpart>gulp package-solution --ship
Build target: SHIP
[13:49:10] Using gulpfile C:\Dropbox\Mastering SharePoint Development\helloworld-webpart\gulpfil
e.js
[13:49:10] Starting gulp
[13:49:10] Starting 'package-solution'...
[13:49:10] Starting subtask 'package-solution'...
[13:49:10] [package-solution] Found manifest: C:\Dropbox\Mastering SharePoint Development\hellow
orld-webpart\temp\deploy\fba70b52-a501-4995-bf8e-fd4f7e187954.json
[13:49:10] Verifying configuration...
[13:49:10] Done!

[13:49:10] Normalizing solution information...
[13:49:10] Attempting creating component definitions for {1} manifests
[13:49:10] Created component definitions for {1} manifests
[13:49:10] config.solution.features not set! Instead generating a feature for each component.
[13:49:10] Creating feature for HelloWorld...
[13:49:10] Done!

[13:49:10] Reading custom Feature XML...
```

4. You should now have a new `.sppkg` file:

```
Mode                LastWriteTime         Length Name
----                -------------         ------ ----
da----       24/05/2017     15:18                debug
-a----       24/05/2017     15:18           3574 helloworld-webpart.sppkg
-a----       17/05/2017     04:55           1807 WebPart_fba70b52-a501-4995-bf8e-fd4f7e187954.xml
```

5. And also new minified asset files under `/temp/deploy`:

```
Mode                LastWriteTime         Length Name
----                -------------         ------ ----
-a----       24/05/2017     15:18           1305 fba70b52-a501-4995-bf8e-fd4f7e187954.json
-a----       24/05/2017     15:18           6160 hello-world.bundle_09e704a8341751e14e7256decf58286.js
-a----       24/05/2017     15:18            179 helloworld-webpart-helloworldstrings_en-us_536e65149b0acf4d52c0043073b9fc59.js
-a----       24/05/2017     15:18            175 helloworld-webpart-helloworldstrings_fi-fi_bd3ea395f25b16f376857e1688e9cda8.js
```

Deploying assets to a SharePoint Online CDN

Now we are ready to deploy our bundled assets to SharePoint Online-based CDN. Upload all the `.js`-files from your `/temp/deploy` folder to the `Site Assets/cdn` folder in your SharePoint Online Site:

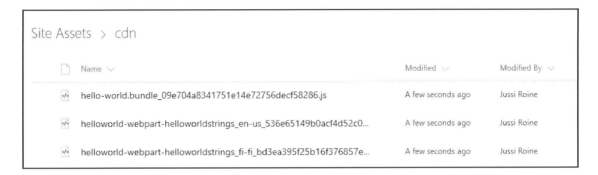

Note that you do not need to upload any assets that will not be used by your solution.

We still have to update our old previously deployed SharePoint Framework package. In order to do this, navigate back to your App Catalog site and re-upload the new `.sppkg` file to replace the old version (which did not use CDN).

Upon completing the upload, you'll get the dialog for deploying the solution just like before. Note that it now takes into consideration the CDN path and shows you the full URL where content will be served:

If you still have the web part on the page, navigate to your SharePoint Online site where the previous deployment took place. When you reload the page, content should be served correctly, without `gulp serve` running in your localhost.

To verify that everything is working, you can press *F12* in your browser to open up developer tools. In Internet Explorer, you will have multiple tabs visible in the new pane. Select **Network** and click the green play icon next to it. When you reload the page, developer tools capture the network traffic and visually shows a list of files that are being loaded.

Use search (*Ctrl* + *F*) to find `publiccdn`:

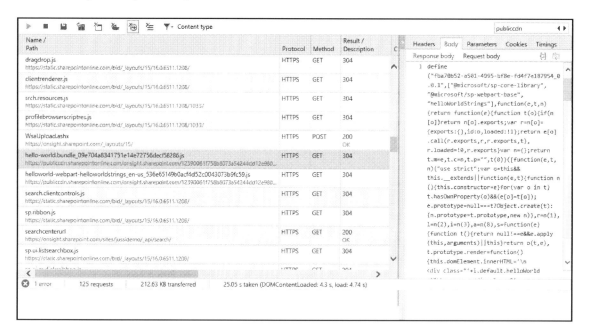

You have now verified that your SharePoint Framework web part is loading correctly, and all JavaScript assets are loaded from a SharePoint Online-based CDN!

Configuring Microsoft Azure Storage CDN

Normally, you can use a SharePoint Online-based CDN for most projects. As you've just seen it's far from a simple configuration setting to set up. Luckily it only needs to be done once, as you can later reuse the same CDN as long as assets do not overlap between each deployment.

An alternative to using a SharePoint Online CDN is to use storage from Microsoft Azure.

The difference between a SharePoint Online CDN and a Microsoft Azure CDN is that the former is easier to configure and has fewer options for fine-tuning the CDN. The latter will cost you extra, as services within Azure will incur fees based on consumption. SharePoint Online-based CDN is factored into the monthly fees you pay for user licenses, so there will be no extra cost for that option.

Sometimes it will be challenging to estimate in advance how much consumption your solution will create. If you're unsure which one to use, opt for the SharePoint Online-based CDN. You can always change it to Azure-based CDN later if you need certain options that Azure provides.

To configure Microsoft Azure Storage-based CDN, we'll need a Microsoft Azure subscription.

- If you don't already have a subscription, you can sign up for a free trial subscription at `https://azure.microsoft.com/en-us/offers/ms-azr-0044p/`.

Once you have a Microsoft Azure subscription ready and accessible, start with the following steps:

1. Navigate to Azure Portal at `https://portal.azure.com` and log in with an account that has permissions to provision new services in Microsoft Azure. Note that this subscription does not have to be tied to an Office 365 subscription, as there is no fixed link between the two when using a CDN from Azure.

2. Press the green plus icon on the top-left corner, and then select **Storage** from the list of available services in the marketplace:

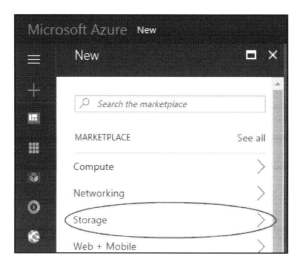

3. From the submenu, select **Storage account - blob, file, table, queue**. The naming changes somewhat regularly, so this might be named just slightly differently, but regardless, select the normal Storage account service here.

4. Now, when you provision services within Microsoft Azure, based on services and their features, pricing differs a bit. For a CDN, we need to select the following options, as they are the most cost-effective at the same time:

- **Name**: choose any name here, no whitespaces or special characters
- **Deployment model**: **Resource manager**
- **Account kind**: **General purpose**
- **Performance**: **Standard**
- **Replication**: **Read-access geo-redundant storage (RA-GRS)**
- **Storage service encryption**: **Disabled**
- **Subscription**: Select your subscription
- **Resource group**: Create a new one, and name it as you like
- **Location**: Choose the nearest geographical location to your intended users; in Europe, you can choose **West Europe**, and in the US, you can choose either **East**, **Central** or **West US**.

An example of the selections would look like this:

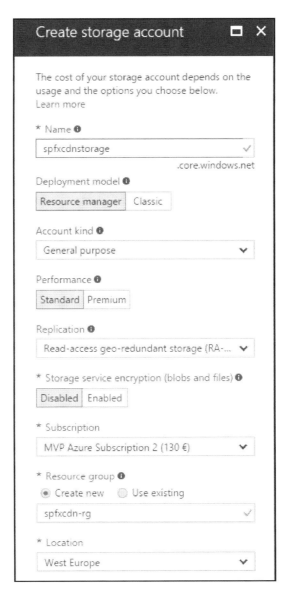

5. Click **Create** to provision the storage account. This will take about a minute, and you can verify progress by clicking on the small bell icon in the top-left corner:

6. In order for us to store assets in this storage account, we need to create a Blob container that acts as a type of special folder for our needs. When provisioning is complete, Azure Portal should redirect you directly to the Storage account management blade. If it doesn't, click **Storage accounts** on the left-most navigation in Azure Portal, and then select your newly-created Storage account from the list.

7. In the Storage account management blade, click **Blobs** and then click **+ Container** from the top menu:

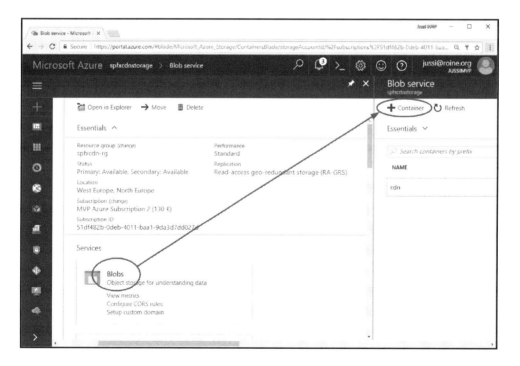

8. Enter a name for your blob, such as cdn, and click **OK**.

9. Go back to the Storage account management blade, and select **Access keys** from the menu under **Settings**:

10. Copy the **Storage account name**, and **key1** to a text file, as you will need this later:

11. Next, now that we have a CDN storage created, we need to create a CDN profile within Azure. For this, click the green + -icon from the top-left, and select **Web + Mobile** under the Marketplace categories. Under this menu, select **CDN**:

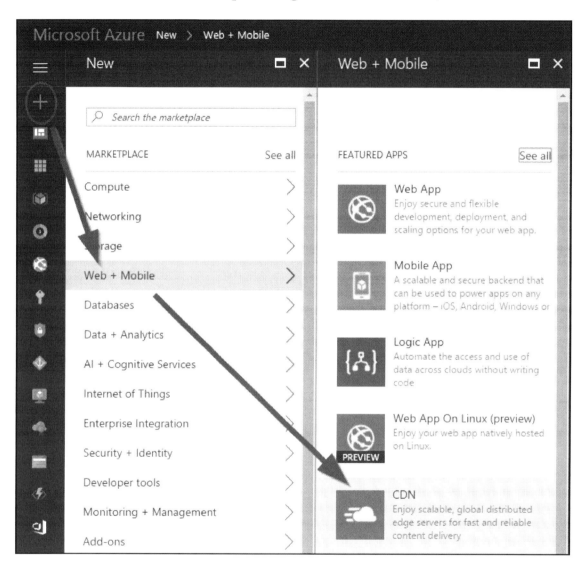

12. Fill out the necessary fields here:

- **Name**: Use any descriptive name, such as `spfxcdn`
- **Subscription**: Choose the same subscription as you chose for storage account
- **Resource group**: Choose the same Resource group as for the storage account
- **Pricing tier**: You have three options: a Premium Verizon, and two Standard options for Verizon and Akamai. You can click on the small blue link above the field to reveal pricing details. We recommend choosing either Standard option for now, as the pricing is identical between the two:

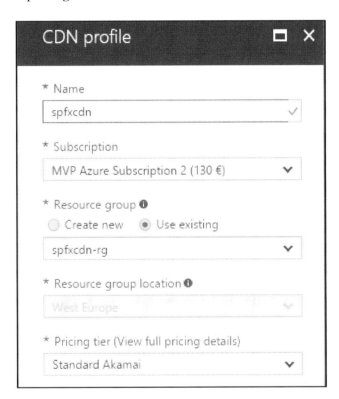

13. Click **Create** to provision the CDN profile. Once provisioning is ready, navigate to the CDN management blade--either through the left-most navigation or through the bell icon on the top right.

14. In the CDN management blade, click **+ Endpoint** in the top menu, and fill in the values for creating an endpoint:

- **Name**: Use any available name
- **Origin type**: **Storage**
- **Origin hostname**: Select the Storage account hostname you created earlier
- **Origin path**: Leave empty
- **Origin host header**: Accept the default value
- **Protocol**: Leave defaults that allow ports 80 and 443 (HTTP and HTTPS)
- **Optimized for**: **General web delivery**

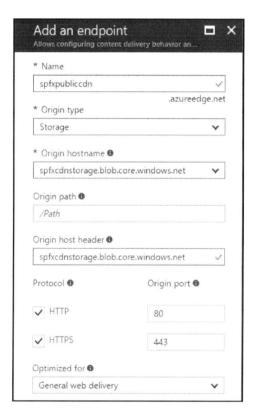

15. Click **Add** to add the endpoint.

Microsoft Azure is now configured to support CDN use from SharePoint Framework and SharePoint Online. You could, naturally, use this CDN to support your assets in an on-premises SharePoint installation.

Next, we need to update the project to use this CDN endpoint.

Updating the project to support Microsoft Azure CDN

Now, let's update the project:

1. Go back to Visual Studio Code and find the `deploy-azure-storage.json` file in the `/config` folder of the project. It contains a placeholder that we now need to fill:

   ```
   {
     "workingDir": "./temp/deploy/",
     "account": "<!-- STORAGE ACCOUNT NAME -->",
     "container": "helloworld-webpart",
     "accessKey": "<!-- ACCESS KEY -->"
   }
   ```

Replace the value of account, container, and accessKey with the following values:

- `account`: The Storage account name that you created in Microsoft Azure
- `container`: The container name you created in the Storage account, such as cdn
- `accessKey`: The Storage account access key you recorded earlier (key1)

The updated `deploy-azure-storage-json` file should look like this:

```
{
  "workingDir": "./temp/deploy/",
  "account": "spfxcdnstorage",
  "container": "cdn",
  "accessKey":
"ubwLikM1FKFGzxKg2wkjf2ZotlxHmW1ecRjksIszK7voaOfgoJ+yS7G4c24D9X
K0B6hcx3X8QqbuPQRzQ=="
}
```

2. You might recall that we changed the same project earlier in Visual Studio Code to employ the SharePoint Online document library as a CDN. We need to update the value in the`write-manifests.json` file to map to the Azure Storage-based CDN.

3. Open the `write-manifests.json` file from `/config`, and update the value to point to the Storage account path with the container name. Remember to add the container name the end so that the format of the URL is `https://{storage-account-name}.blob.core.windows.net/{container -name}`. The updated file might now look like this:

```
{
  "cdnBasePath":
"https://spfxcdnstorage.blob.core.windows.net/cdn"
}
```

4. Save both files (`deploy-azure-storage.json` and `write-manifests.json`).

5. In the Integrated Terminal, bundle the package with `gulp bundle -ship`:

```
PS C:\Dropbox (Personal)\Mastering SharePoint Development\helloworld-webpart\helloworld-webpart> gulp bundle --ship
Build target: SHIP
[17:08:38] Using gulpfile C:\Dropbox (Personal)\Mastering SharePoint Development\helloworld-webpart\helloworld-webpart\gulpfile.js
[17:08:38] Starting gulp
[17:08:38] Starting 'bundle'...
[17:08:38] Starting subtask 'pre-copy'...
[17:08:38] Finished subtask 'pre-copy' after 11 ms
[17:08:38] Starting subtask 'copy-static-assets'...
```

6. Then package the solution with `gulp package-solution -ship`:

```
PS C:\Dropbox (Personal)\Mastering SharePoint Development\helloworld-webpart\helloworld-webpart> gulp package-solution --ship
Build target: SHIP
[17:09:17] Using gulpfile C:\Dropbox (Personal)\Mastering SharePoint Development\helloworld-webpart\helloworld-webpart\gulpfile.js
[17:09:17] Starting gulp
[17:09:17] Starting 'package-solution'...
[17:09:17] Starting subtask 'package-solution'...
[17:09:17] [package-solution] Found manifest: C:\Dropbox (Personal)\Mastering SharePoint Development\helloworld-webpart\helloworld-webpart\temp\deploy\fba70b52-a501-4995-bf8e-fd4f7e187954.json
[17:09:17] Verifying configuration...
[17:09:17] Done!
```

7. You should now have the updated `.sppkg` package in `/sharepoint/solution/`:

```
Mode              LastWriteTime        Length Name
----              -------------        ------ ----
da----     25/05/2017     17:09               debug
-a----     25/05/2017     17:09          3523 helloworld-webpart.sppkg
-a----     17/05/2017     04:55          1807 WebPart_fba70b52-a501-4995-bf8e-fd4f7e187954.xml
```

8. And the updated bundled (and minified) assets in `/temp/deploy`:

```
Mode           LastWriteTime        Length Name
----           -------------        ------ ----
-a----      25/05/2017    17:08       1219 fba70b52-a501-4995-bf8e-fd4f7e187954.json
-a----      25/05/2017    17:08       6160 hello-world.bundle_09e704a8341751e14e72756decf58286.js
-a----      25/05/2017    17:08        179 helloworld-webpart-helloworldstrings_en-us_536e65149b0acf4d52c0043073b9fc59.js
-a----      25/05/2017    17:08        175 helloworld-webpart-helloworldstrings_fi-fi_bd3ea395f25b16f376857e1688e9cda8.js
```

Our project is now updated to support Microsoft Azure-based CDN, and the package is once again ready for deployment to SharePoint Online. We still need to upload our assets to Azure Storage, as we cannot simply upload them to SharePoint Online's document library anymore.

Deploying assets to Microsoft Azure CDN

We need to upload all assets from `/temp/deploy/` to our Azure Storage account. Microsoft has built a handy Gulp task for this, called **deploy-azure-storage** that we can simply execute. It reads through the configuration file and automatically uploads our assets to Azure Storage. This is also a handy but crude test to see if our Storage account is accessible and correctly configured within the project.

1. In the Integrated Terminal, run `gulp deploy-azure-storage`:

```
[17:15:49] [deploy-azure-storage] Uploading files '**/*.*' from directory './temp/deploy/' to Azure
[17:15:49] [deploy-azure-storage] Created container: cdn
[17:15:49] [deploy-azure-storage] Uploading [4] files...
[17:15:50] [deploy-azure-storage] Uploaded file: fba70b52-a501-4995-bf8e-fd4f7e187954.json
[17:15:50] [deploy-azure-storage] Uploaded file: hello-world.bundle_09e704a8341751e14e72756decf58286.js
[17:15:50] [deploy-azure-storage] Uploaded file: helloworld-webpart-helloworldstrings_en-us_536e65149b0acf4d52c0043073b9fc59.js
[17:15:50] [deploy-azure-storage] Uploaded file: helloworld-webpart-helloworldstrings_fi-fi_bd3ea395f25b16f376857e1688e9cda8.js
[17:15:50] [deploy-azure-storage] Upload complete!
[17:15:50] [deploy-azure-storage] Access your files at: https://spfxcdnstorage.blob.core.windows.net/cdn
```

2. You should see from the output of the task that the upload completes. You can also verify that the files have been uploaded by opening the **Blob Container** from Azure Storage, and the files should be visible there:

NAME
fba70b52-a501-4995-bf8e-fd4f7e187954.json
hello-world.bundle_09e704a8341751e14e72756decf58286.js
helloworld-webpart-helloworldstrings_en-us_536e65149b0acf4d52c0043073b9fc59.js
helloworld-webpart-helloworldstrings_fi-fi_bd3ea395f25b16f376857e1688e9cda8.js

We still have to update our old previously deployed SharePoint Framework package. In order to do this, navigate back to your App Catalog site, and re-upload the new .sppkg file to replace the old version (which did not use CDN).

Upon completing the upload, you'll get the dialog for deploying the solution just like before. Note that it now takes into consideration the CDN path and shows you the full URL where content will be served:

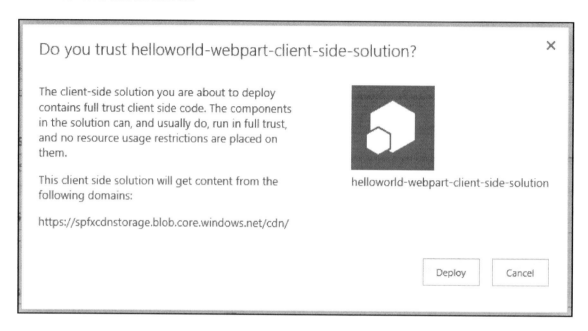

If you still have the web part on the page, navigate to your SharePoint Online site where the previous deployment took place. When you reload the page, content should be served correctly, without gulp serve running in your localhost.

As before, we can verify that the assets are being downloaded from the CDN. Press *F12* in your browser to open up developer tools. In Internet Explorer, you will have multiple tabs visible in the new pane. Select Network and click the green Play icon next to it. When you reload the page, developer tools capture the network traffic and visually show a list of files that are being loaded.

Use search (*Ctrl + F*) to find `akamai` or `Verizon` depending on which CDN provider you chose in Azure:

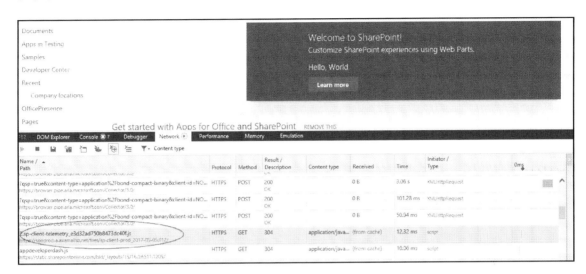

You have now verified that your SharePoint Framework web part is loading correctly, and all JavaScript assets are loaded from a Microsoft Azure Storage-based CDN!

Summary

This chapter took you through deploying and packaging code so that it can be deployed to test and production environments. To speed up serving content, we used CDN-services through SharePoint Online and Microsoft Azure. Normally you would choose either one based on your requirements and user base. Most often you'll resort to using SharePoint Online-based CDN's, as it's slightly easier to configure and will not incur additional costs. For on-premises SharePoint environments, a logical CDN location would be either Azure Storage or an on-premises service, such as a proxy server.

In `Chapter 7`, *Working with SharePoint Content*, we'll learn how to use mock data when developing solutions locally, as well as accessing real SharePoint-based data from within your code.

7
Working with SharePoint Content

In this chapter, we are focusing on working with SharePoint content. First, there is a high-level overview, and then we are going to learn how to use mock data in our web parts when you are running them from the local workbench. Then we are going to focus on how to work with SharePoint content using `SPHttpClient`; first, we will be accessing lists and then we will perform basic operations with list items.

During this chapter, we'll cover the following:

- Learn to access and work directly with SharePoint content
- Understand how we can use mock data while developing a solution and then later change it to real data
- Start using SPHttpClient to access SharePoint lists and do basic operations

Overview of working with SharePoint content

When you build solutions for SharePoint, you will inevitably run into scenarios where you need some sort of data and content. This might be a situation where you are creating a web part that lists news items that are saved in a SharePoint list. Or this might be a scenario where you'll show the latest modified documents, and based on that, provide additional information for users. In most scenarios, you'll find it more helpful if you have data and content within SharePoint that you can access, view, and use.

With previous development models for SharePoint, it was customary to mock up data. This could be garbage, or classic *lorem ipsum* content scattered around to help a developer mimic a real-world service when developing, testing, and troubleshooting code. For, on-premises SharePoint (and to a certain degree SharePoint Online), there have been several tools that generate content that looks and acts real.

You might still, at times, need to resort to this approach. But as a SharePoint Framework developer, you might also expect things to be more agile, smoother and a bit more dynamic. For starters, you will often not have a real SharePoint Online tenant in use when you are fleshing out your solution. Thus, there will be no place to host your content as most of the time your code is running in a local copy of SharePoint Workbench. Eventually, when you'll move to test your code in SharePoint Online (against the hosted SharePoint Workbench) content and data are needed. But then, troubleshooting will become much slower if that is the first time you are really seeing if you can access data and render it correctly in your solution.

Mocking data when building the SharePoint Framework solutions is finally now a valid approach, and Microsoft went to great lengths in providing you a pattern for this.

Using mock data

The purpose of mock data is to simulate data that feels dynamic and real. It could be mock data that looks as if it's originating from SharePoint, or from an external data source such as an API or a database.

Local SharePoint Workbench does not have a connection to SharePoint, as it simply mimics the canvas to host SharePoint Framework solutions. This makes developing solutions much quicker, as you can catch typical access issues early in the development cycle. It also makes the end to end development effort much more civilized as developers can be more confident that accessing data when moving to SharePoint Online-based testing is less error-prone, as code can be quickly tested against mock data first.

Using mock data with locally hosted SharePoint Workbench

In order to use mock data, you'll need to create a simple data model. This will mimic things such as the contents of a SharePoint list, so you can design the data model to include the necessary site columns and corresponding data types for these columns.

To learn this, create a new `HelloWorld` web part or use an existing one.

Step 1 - create data model

To create a data model, in Visual Studio Code we first create an `interface` to describe it. It is good practice to put this file into a separate file, for example, `ISPListItem.ts`.

```
export interface ISPListItem {
    Id: string;
    Title: string;
}
```

The preceding code assumes that you save the file in the same folder than the web part is located. This isn't necessary, you can place all data model files to separate folder as well, but then you need to adjust import statements accordingly.

Step 2 - create MockSharePointClient

Create another file, called `MockSharePointClient.ts` in the same folder where the web part is located.

```
import { ISPListItem } from "./ISPListItem";

export default class MockSharePointClient {
    private static _listItems: ISPListItem[] = [
        { Id: 1, Title: "First list item" },
        { Id: 2, Title: "Second list item" },
        { Id: 3, Title: "Third list item" },
        { Id: 4, Title: "Fourth list item" },
        { Id: 5, Title: "Fifth list item" },
        { Id: 6, Title: "Sixth list item" },
        { Id: 7, Title: "Seventh list item" },
        { Id: 8, Title: "Eight list item" },
        { Id: 9, Title: "Ninth list item" },
    ];
    public static get(restUrl: string, options?: any)
        : Promise<ISPListItem[]> {
            return new Promise<ISPListItem[]>((resolve) => {
            resolve(MockSharePointClient._listItems);
        });
    }
}
```

Let's examine the code. It starts by importing the definition of a data model from
ISPListItem.ts

```
1    import { ISPListItem } from "./ISPListItem";
```

Then, in the declaration of the MockSharePointClient class, it creates the static mockup
data in a private array of ISPListItem objects.

```
3     export default class MockSharePointClient {
4         private static _listItems: ISPListItem[] = [
5           { Id: 1, Title: "First list item" },
6           { Id: 2, Title: "Second list item" },
7           { Id: 3, Title: "Third list item" },
8           { Id: 4, Title: "Fourth list item" },
9           { Id: 5, Title: "Fifth list item" },
10          { Id: 6, Title: "Sixth list item" },
11          { Id: 7, Title: "Seventh list item" },
12          { Id: 8, Title: "Eight list item" },
13          { Id: 9, Title: "Ninth list item" },
14        ];
```

Finally, it includes one public function called get, which mimics the way the actual
SPHttpClient client works. Instead of an array of ISPListItem objects, we return a
Promise of the array. The Promise is used with actual asynchronous clients to keep the
code simple and easy to read.

```
15      public static get(restUrl: string, options?: any)
16        : Promise<ISPListItem[]> {
17            return new Promise<ISPListItem[]>((resolve) => {
18            resolve(MockSharePointClient._listItems);
19        });
```

Step 3 - consume the mock data in the web part

Now, open your web part TypeScript file and insert the following import statements at the
beginning section of the file before the web part class definition.

```
import { Environment, EnvironmentType } from '@microsoft/sp-core-library';
import { ISPListItem } from "./ISPListItem";
import MockSharePointClient from "./MockSharePointClient";
```

The first line imports `Environment` and `EnvironmentType` from `sp-core-library`; we use these to find out if we are running from a local Workbench and thus need to use mock data.

Inside the web part class definition, insert the following functions.

```
private _getMockListData(): Promise<ISPListItem[]> {
  return MockSharePointClient.get("")
    .then((data: ISPListItem[]) => {
        return data;
      });
}

private _getListItems(): Promise<ISPListItem[]> {
  if (Environment.type === EnvironmentType.Local) {
    return this._getMockListData();
  } else {
    alert("TODO: Implement real thing here");
    return null;
  }
}
```

Finally, we modify the web part's `render()` function to render all the data we have acquired.

```
 public render(): void {
  let listItemsStr : string = "";
  this._getListItems().then(listItems => {
    listItems.forEach(listItem => {
      listItemsStr += `
      <li>${listItem.Id} - ${listItem.Title}</li>
      `;
    });
    this.domElement.innerHTML = `<h3>List
items</h3><ul>${listItemsStr}</li>`;
  });
}
```

Let's examine the code again to understand it perfectly. In the `render` function, we call the `_getListItems` method to get the data. Since it returns a `Promise`, we use `then` to form an `arrow` function to get the actual list items, and go through them and build a HTML list of the items to show inside the web part's DOM element. The `render` function is not concerned with where the data comes from; that is done inside `_getListItems`.

```
22    public render(): void {
23        let listItemsStr : string = "";
24        this._getListItems().then(listItems => {
25            listItems.forEach(listItem => {
26                listItemsStr += `
27                <li>${listItem.Id} - ${listItem.Title}</li>
28                `;
29            });
30            this.domElement.innerHTML = `<h3>List items</h3><ul>${listItemsStr}</li>`;
31        });
32    }
```

In `_getListItems`, we examine if the environment is a local workbench, and if it is, we call `_getMockListData` and return its value. The call to the actual `SPHttpClient` should be placed in lines 61 and 62, but we are not there yet.

```
57    private _getListItems(): Promise<ISPListItem[]> {
58        if (Environment.type === EnvironmentType.Local) {
59            return this._getMockListData();
60        } else {
61            alert("TODO: Implement real thing here");
62            return null;
63        }
64    }
```

Finally, `_getMockListData` uses the `MockSharePointClient` class and calls the `get` function to retrieve the static data. We are simply passing an empty string as a `URL` parameter since we know that our function doesn't do anything with that information.

```
50    private _getMockListData(): Promise<ISPListItem[]> {
51      return MockSharePointClient.get("")
52        .then((data: ISPListItem[]) => {
53            return data;
54        });
55    }
```

Now, it is time to start Command Prompt; go to the web part project's folder and start the local workbench with the following command.

```
gulp serve
```

When you insert the web part to the workbench, it will show a list of mock data.

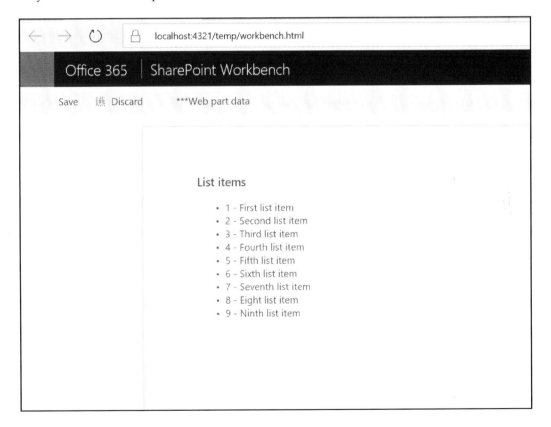

Accessing real data with SPHttpClient

The standard approach to access and perform CRUD operations (Create - Read - Update - Delete) with SharePoint data is to use SPHttpClient. We did already use SPHttpClient when working with our first real web part in Chapter 4, *Building your First Web Part*. Next, we are going to be focusing more deeply on the use of SPHttpClient, but you should know that it is not the only way to work with SharePoint data while you are using the SharePoint Framework. SPHttpClient is built into the SharePoint Framework to perform REST calls against SharePoint, but you can do the REST calls using some other framework (e.g. jQuery) or simply using JavaScript's XMLHttpRequest object. In addition to REST-based approaches, you can use SharePoint JSOM, a JavaScript Object Model which is a subset of the SharePoint client-side object model first introduced in SharePoint 2010.

Using an object model instead of REST is a habit of SharePoint old-timers. Back in the good old days, our code was running on a SharePoint server and accessing the SharePoint farm via a Server-Side Object Model. It was bad because a developer could ruin SharePoint farm performance with poorly written code. The other main reason this approach became nearly extinct is the general trend to move web development to client-side HTML5, CSS, and JavaScript. Also, SharePoint Online does not support server-side code, thus developers are forced to eventually move to a different development model.

So, SharePoint CSOM and JSOM where introduced to allow SharePoint developers a somewhat familiar ground and mindset to build client-side solutions. But under the hood client-side object models execute SOAP and XML calls against SharePoint. The client-side object model is just a covering layer which abstracts these calls from the developer. When Microsoft introduces a new feature in the client-side object model, they have to implement it in JavaScript, C#, and all other versions of the object model. At the end of the day, REST is simpler, more robust way to develop and utilize APIs when compared to the object-models. This is the reason Microsoft has shifted our focus to SPHttpClient instead of JSOM when working with SharePoint data using the SharePoint Framework.

With this introduction, we can finally dive into SPHttpClient.

Working with SharePoint lists

When we work with SharePoint data, we first try to access a SharePoint list. To access a list via REST, we need to know the title or ID of the given list. If we don't know at least one of those, we can iterate through all the lists on the site.

Open a SharePoint site in a browser and check that it is working normally. In the following picture, we are opening a site collection root site from the URL address `https://yourtenant.sharepoint.com/sites/spfx`.

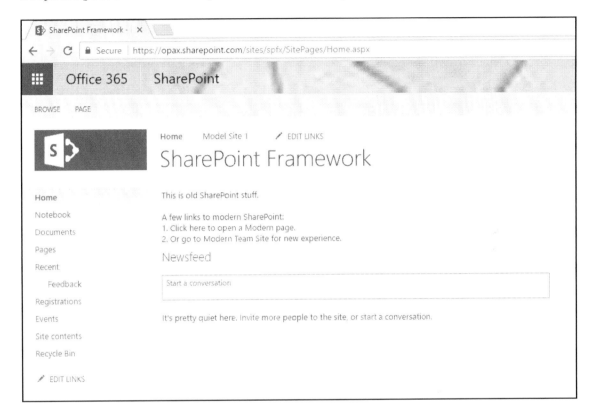

When we open a SharePoint site in a browser, we authenticate the browser, and after that, we can manually modify the URL in the browser address bar to access the API service endpoint. Change the URL address to `https://yourtenant.sharepoint.com/sites/spfx/_api/web/lists`, and what you can see is SharePoint REST API responding to a simple GET request. The default response format is XML and not JSON because of historical reasons. The word *historical* is a bit odd in the context of the Web in general, because this probably goes back only about two decades.

It is useful for us to know that we can quite easily test GET calls against SharePoint REST API, because it is fast to test that the API is actually responding to a specific request in an orderly fashion. If we want other HTTP Requests like POST or DELETE, or to get the response in JSON, we need to use more complex tooling like Fiddler or Postman.

So, in order to list the lists in a SharePoint site, we add `/_api/web/lists` at the end of the site's URL address. If we know an ID of a list, the GUID information which is actually available in the XML response--we can access the specific list like this:

```
https://yourtenant.sharepoint.com/sites/spfx/_api/web/lists(guid'c271be23-9
106-4426-a88c-938382fc734b')
```

And if we know the title of the list, we can access it by modifying the URL like this:

```
https://yourtenant.sharepoint.com/sites/spfx/_api/web/lists/GetByTitle('Fee
dback')
```

While testing these URLs with your browser, you might find the response XML a bit overwhelming to handle. With JavaScript, it is generally easier to work with JSON as it is the native data format.

Now, let's open Visual Studio Code. You can create a new web part or use one you have created before.

Requesting the list of lists with SPHttpClient

First, ensure that the SPHttpClient is imported in the web part file.

```
import { SPHttpClient } from '@microsoft/sp-http';
```

Then we need a data model of the list of lists, and we do this by adding a file, ISPList.ts, with the following content. As you can see, we are interested in the Title and Id of the list, but also we are going to retrieve a piece of information about the last change in list items and the nice image URL for the list.

```
export interface ISPList {
    Title: string;
    Id: string;
    LastItemUserModifiedDate: string;
    ImageUrl: string;
}
```

To be totally honest, we don't need the data model. We could simply use the raw JSON data that is returned from the GET request. But by using the data model, our code becomes a great deal more readable and our natural ability to create bugs is reduced by the strong typing. In case our data model includes a property that is not returned by the request, its value will be undefined.

Add another import statement in the web part file.

```
import { ISPList } from "./ISPList";
```

Then insert the following function that will get the data from SharePoint to our web part class. The URL to access is not hardcoded, as we can access the page context to dynamically retrieve the absolute URL of a page.

```
private _getSharePointLists(): Promise<ISPList[]> {
    const url: string = this.context.pageContext.web.absoluteUrl +
"/_api/web/lists";
    return this.context.spHttpClient.get(url,
SPHttpClient.configurations.v1)
        .then(response => {
          return response.json();
        })
    .then(json => {
        return json.value;
    }) as Promise<ISPList[]>;
}
```

And then we are going to modify the render method as follows:

```
public render(): void {
  let listItems : string = "";
  this._getSharePointLists().then(lists => {
    lists.forEach(list => {
      listItems += `
      <div>
        <img src='${list.ImageUrl}'/> ${list.Title}<br/>
        ID: ${list.Id}<br/>
        Last Item User Modified Date: ${list.LastItemUserModifiedDate}
      </div><hr/>`;
    });
    this.domElement.innerHTML = `<h1>List of
lists:</h1><div>${listItems}</div>`;
  });
}
```

Now, let's walk through the code:

```
17    public render(): void {
18      let listItems : string = "";
19      this._getSharePointLists().then(lists => {
20        lists.forEach(list => {
21          listItems += `
22          <div>
23            <img src='${list.ImageUrl}'/> ${list.Title}<br/>
24            ID: ${list.Id}<br/>
25            Last Item User Modified Date: ${list.LastItemUserModifiedDate}
26          </div><hr/>`;
27        });
28        this.domElement.innerHTML = `<h1>List of lists:</h1><div>${listItems}</div>`;
29      });
30    }
31
32    private _getSharePointLists(): Promise<ISPList[]> {
33      const url: string = this.context.pageContext.web.absoluteUrl + "/_api/web/lists";
34      return this.context.spHttpClient.get(url, SPHttpClient.configurations.v1)
35        .then(response => {
36          return response.json();
37        })
38      .then(json => {
39        return json.value;
40      }) as Promise<ISPList[]>;
41    }
```

The `render` function starts at line 18 by declaring a string variable `listItems` for HTML representation of the lists. Then we are calling the `_getSharePointLists` function, which will make the same query we did use the browser, but this time using the `SPHttpClient`. It is a `get` function call in line 34 with very simple parameters. What the `_getSharePointLists` does is returns an array of `ISPList` objects. Back in lines 19 and 20 we are using a function which takes the JSON return value in the `lists` variable, and then in lines 21 through 26 we are formatting the JSON information in HTML format, and finally, in line 28, we are inserting that HTML into the web part's DOM Element.

Type the following command in Command Prompt while in the web part's `root` folder to start the service. We use the `--nobrowser` parameter to avoid opening a new browser window.

```
gulp serve --nobrowser
```

Then open the hosted SharePoint Workbench (`https://yourtenant.sharepoint.com/sites/spfx/_layouts/Workbench.aspx`) and add the web part to the page. You should see something like this.

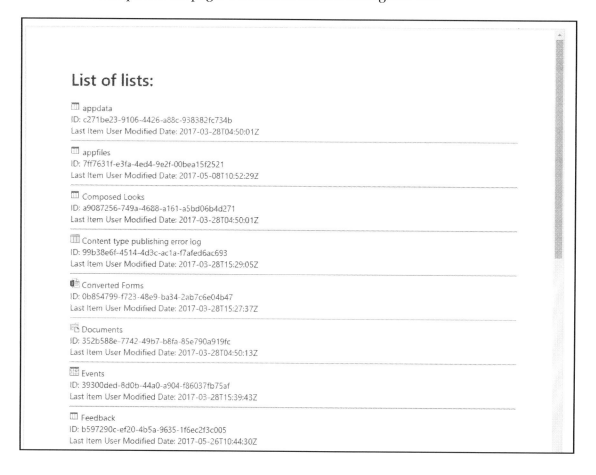

Checking if the list exists and creating lists

Now that we know how to find lists, we can change our code a bit. What we are doing next is checking if a list exists, and if it doesn't, we are going to create it.

Add the following function to your web part class.

```
private _createSharePointList(): void {
  const getListUrl: string = this.context.pageContext.web.absoluteUrl
  + "/_api/web/lists/GetByTitle('My List')";
  this.context.spHttpClient.get(getListUrl, SPHttpClient.configurations.v1)
  .then((response: SPHttpClientResponse) => {
      if (response.status === 200) {
        alert("List already exists.");
        return; // list already exists
      }
      if (response.status === 404) {
        const url: string = this.context.pageContext.web.absoluteUrl +
"/_api/web/lists";
        const listDefinition : any = {
                "Title": "My List",
                "Description": "My description",
                "AllowContentTypes": true,
                "BaseTemplate": 100,
                "ContentTypesEnabled": true,
        };
        const spHttpClientOptions: ISPHttpClientOptions = {
            "body": JSON.stringify(listDefinition)
        };
        this.context.spHttpClient.post(url, SPHttpClient.configurations.v1,
spHttpClientOptions)
            .then((response: SPHttpClientResponse) => {
              if (response.status === 201) {
                alert("List created successfully");
              } else {
                alert("Response status "+response.status+" -
"+response.statusText);
              }
            });
      } else {
        alert("Something went wrong. "+response.status+"
"+response.statusText);
      }
    });
}
```

Then replace the `render` method with the following code.

```
public render(): void {
  this.domElement.innerHTML =
        `<div>
          <button type='button' class='ms-Button'>
            <span class='ms-Button-label'>Create List</span>
          </button>
        </div>`;
      this._createSharePointList = this._createSharePointList.bind(this);
      const button: HTMLButtonElement =
this.domElement.getElementsByTagName("BUTTON")[0] as HTMLButtonElement;
      button.addEventListener("click", this._createSharePointList);
}
```

Let's examine this code. We are using the `get` function of `SPHttpClient` to retrieve list information. We first create the URL for the REST request using the `GetByTitle` method which is part of SharePoint API. In the `then` section, we are examining the response status to find out if the list already exists. If the status is `200`, then the list exists; if it is `404` (not found), then we can create it; and if the status is something else, something has gone wrong.

```
89    private _createSharePointList(): void {
90      const getListUrl: string = this.context.pageContext.web.absoluteUrl
91      + "/_api/web/lists/GetByTitle('My List')";
92      this.context.spHttpClient.get(getListUrl, SPHttpClient.configurations.v1)
93      .then((response: SPHttpClientResponse) => {
94        if (response.status === 200) {
95          alert("List already exists.");
96          return; // List already exists
97        }
```

If the list doesn't exist, we create it using the same pattern that was used in our first real web part when we created list items. The beauty of REST is that things work in similar manners. We need to form an URL, this time pointing to the lists collection and list definition, which includes `Title`, `BaseTemplate`, and other configurations concerning the new list. Again, we are putting the information about a new resource inside an object which is defined in `ISPHttpClientOptions` interface. Then, we are going to make a post-function call using the `SPHttpClient` and handle the results. Status code `201` indicates that list creation was successful.

```
 98    if (response.status === 404) {
 99        const url: string = this.context.pageContext.web.absoluteUrl +
100           "/_api/web/lists";
101        const listDefinition : any = {
102               "Title": "My List",
103               "Description": "My description",
104               "AllowContentTypes": true,
105               "BaseTemplate": 100,
106               "ContentTypesEnabled": true,
107        };
108        const spHttpClientOptions: ISPHttpClientOptions = {
109           "body": JSON.stringify(listDefinition)
110        };
111        this.context.spHttpClient.post(url, SPHttpClient.configurations.v1,
112           spHttpClientOptions)
113         .then((response: SPHttpClientResponse) => {
114           if (response.status === 201) {
115             alert("List created successfully");
116           } else {
117             alert("Response status "+response.status+" - "+response.statusText)
118           }
119         });
120    } else {
121        alert("Something went wrong. "+response.status+" "+response.statusText);
122    }
```

In the `render` function, we create a button and bind it's click event to the `_createSharePointList` function.

```
22    public render(): void {
23      this.domElement.innerHTML =
24          `<div>
25            <button type='button' class='ms-Button'>
26            <span class='ms-Button-label'>Create List</span>
27            </button>
28          </div>`;
29        this._createSharePointList = this._createSharePointList.bind(this);
30        const button: HTMLButtonElement = this.domElement.
31          getElementsByTagName("BUTTON")[0] as HTMLButtonElement;
32        button.addEventListener("click", this._createSharePointList);
33    }
```

If you are using this kind of pattern to provision lists and other artifacts to SharePoint sites, you need to remember that it works with user's permissions. If the user doesn't have the permission to create lists, the code doesn't work. In this case, adding the web part is the site owner's task.

Now that we know how to access and create lists, let's start working with the actual data, the list items.

Working with SharePoint list items

To work with list items, we are first creating a list using the normal user interface. To make things a bit different this time, we are not going to put our list in a normal SharePoint site; we are using Office 365 Group's Team site instead. If you are not familiar with Office 365 Groups yet, you'll find that they are very easy to create. However, the code works just as well with regular SharePoint sites as it does with Office 365 Group's Team site.

Creating an Office 365 Group and new SharePoint list

There are multiple ways to create Office 365 Groups; you can do it from the SharePoint Home, as we are going to do next, from Outlook (both Web Access and Outlook 2016 client work just nicely), or you can create a team in Microsoft Teams, which actually creates an Office 365 Group.

1. Open `https://portal.office.com` in your browser.
2. Sign-in using your developer tenant account and password.
3. From the tile, select and click your favorite; **SharePoint**.

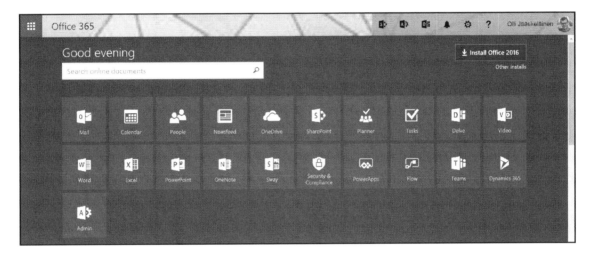

4. This will lead you to SharePoint home.
5. Click **Create site**.

6. Write in **Team site name**, for example, SPFX-testing. As you can see, the email name and **Team site address** are derived from the site name. You can also edit the email name, which in turn changes the Team site address.

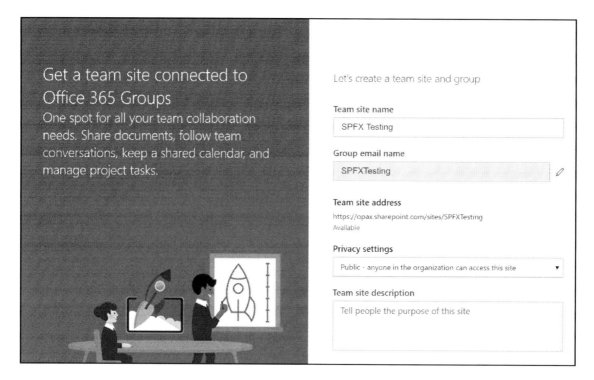

7. Click **Next**.
8. Wait a bit, then click **Finish**.
9. In a few seconds, you will be redirected to the newly created Team site, which is part of the Office 365 Group's functionality.

10. To add a new list, click **New** and **Select List**.

11. Give the list a name, such as My List and click **Create**.

12. Add a new column to the list using the type **Multiple lines of text**.

13. Name the column `Info` and click **Save**.
14. Using the **New** button, create at least three new list items to act as our sample data.

A note concerning custom columns: when you access columns from the code, you use the internal name of the column. If you are creating the columns using the UI as we did, it is best practice to create them without whitespace, and then rename then later to include whitespace. This will make column internal names simpler. Otherwise, SharePoint will generate ugly names with underscores and other extraneous information. Internal names are case sensitive, so we actually created a column with the internal name `Info`, not info.

Now let's write some code.

Basic operation with SharePoint list items using SPHttpClient

Next, we are going to create a new web part project and do all the basic operations with list items.

Step 1 - create a hello-listitems web part project

Open a command line and create a new folder for the new SharePoint Framework web part. Go to that folder, start Yeoman, and generate a new web part project with the name `hello-listitems`. Again, we are using a `No JavaScript framework` type of project.

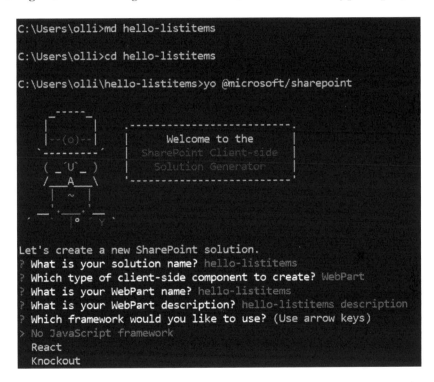

Step 2 - add a data model for list items

Open Visual Studio Code and open the folder where you created the `hello-listitems` web part project.

Add a new file called `ISPListItems.ts` to the same folder that holds the `HelloListItemsWebPart.ts` file. Define the `ISPListItems` interface and save the file.

```
export interface ISPListItem {
    Id: number;
    Title: string;
    Info: string;
}
```

Step 3 - build the user interface for the web part

We are going to make things simple here; the idea is just to show how to use basic operations, so we replace the existing `render` function with the following code.

```
public render(): void {
  this.domElement.innerHTML = `
    <div class="${styles.helloListitems}">
      <div class="${styles.container}">
        <h3>List Items</h3>
        <ul>
        </ul>
        <span class="${styles.label}">Select operation</span>
        <select>
          <option value="Create">Create</option>
          <option value="Read">Read</option>
          <option value="Update">Update</option>
          <option value="Delete">Delete</option>
        </select>
        <button type='button' class='ms-Button'>
          <span class='ms-Button-label'>Run operation</span>
        </button>
        <p>Select operation and click the button.</p>
      </div>
    </div>`;
  this._itemsList = this.domElement.getElementsByTagName("UL")[0] as
HTMLULIListElement;
  this._operationSelect =
this.domElement.getElementsByTagName("SELECT")[0] as HTMLSelectElement;
  this._runOperation = this._runOperation.bind(this);
  const button: HTMLButtonElement =
this.domElement.getElementsByTagName("BUTTON")[0] as HTMLButtonElement;
  button.onclick = this._runOperation;
```

```
    this._operationResults = this.domElement.getElementsByTagName("P")[0]
as HTMLParagraphElement;
    this._readAllItems = this._readAllItems.bind(this);
    this._readAllItems();
}
```

If you take a look at the HTML, we have created <ul> to hold the list of list items, a SELECT with different operations, a BUTTON to execute an operation and a <p> element to show operation results.

```
public render(): void {
  this.domElement.innerHTML = `
    <div class="${styles.helloListitems}">
      <div class="${styles.container}">
        <h3>List Items</h3>
        <ul>
        </ul>
        <span class="${styles.label}">Select operation</span>
        <select>
          <option value="Create">Create</option>
          <option value="Read">Read</option>
          <option value="Update">Update</option>
          <option value="Delete">Delete</option>
        </select>
        <button type='button' class='ms-Button'>
          <span class='ms-Button-label'>Run operation</span>
        </button>
        <p>Select operation and click the button.</p>
      </div>
    </div>`;
```

The latter part of the `render` function uses the `getElementsByTagName` API to get the HTML elements, saves the reference of them to the object properties, and binds the button `onclick` event to the `_runOperation` function call. At the end of the `render` function, we are calling the `_readAllItems` function.

```
38    this._itemsList = this.domElement.getElementsByTagName("UL")[0] as HTMLULListElement;
39    this._operationSelect =
40      this.domElement.getElementsByTagName("SELECT")[0] as HTMLSelectElement;
41    this._runOperation = this._runOperation.bind(this);
42    const button: HTMLButtonElement =
43      this.domElement.getElementsByTagName("BUTTON")[0] as HTMLButtonElement;
44    button.onclick = this._runOperation;
45    this._operationResults =
46      this.domElement.getElementsByTagName("P")[0] as HTMLParagraphElement;
47    this._readAllItems = this._readAllItems.bind(this);
48    this._readAllItems();
```

Next, add a few imports to the beginning of the web part file.

```
import { SPHttpClient, ISPHttpClientOptions, SPHttpClientResponse } from
'@microsoft/sp-http';
import { ISPListItem } from "./ISPListItem";
```

Add the following code after the `render` function inside the web part class. This includes our hooks for the different UI elements as well as two functions. We will implement the `_runOperation` function later but for starters, we are defining the `_readAllItems` function, which calls another function to execute the `SPHttpClient` request to read all items on the list and renders them to inside our list element. We are also using the backtick operator (`` ` ``), which is a template literal. This allows string literals as embedded expressions.

```
private _itemsList: HTMLULListElement = null;
private _operationSelect: HTMLSelectElement = null;
private _operationResults: HTMLParagraphElement = null;
private _runOperation(): void {
  alert("Not implemented!");
}
private _readAllItems(): void {
  this._getListItems().then(listItems => {
    let itemsStr: string = "";
    listItems.forEach(listItem => {
      itemsStr += `<li>${listItem.Title}</li>`;
    });
    this._itemsList.innerHTML = itemsStr;
  });
}
```

Step 4 - define the function that will make SPHttpClient request to read list items and test the web part

Add the following code after the _readAllItems function:

```
private _getListItems(): Promise<ISPListItem[]> {
  const url: string = this.context.pageContext.site.absoluteUrl+
    "/_api/web/lists/getbytitle('My List')/items";
  return this.context.spHttpClient.get(url,SPHttpClient.configurations.v1)
    .then(response => {
      return response.json();
    })
    .then(json => {
      return json.value;
    }) as Promise<ISPListItem[]>;
}
```

This function will use SharePoint API to read all list items in from the list called My List which we created in step 1.

Now it is time to test our web part. In the command line, type in the following command:

```
gulp serve --nobrowser
```

Next, switch to the browser and open the workbench from the Team site of the Office 365 Group we created in step 1. The URL is something like https://yourtenant.sharepoint.com/sites/SPFXTesting/_layouts/15/Workbench.aspx. Add the web part to the page. You should see the list items you added in the first step.

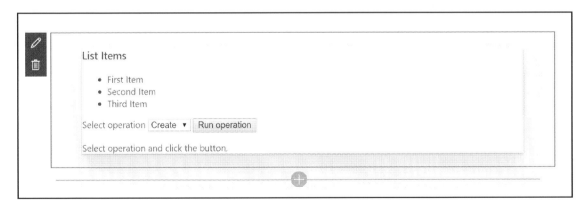

So, that is the first list item operation; we are able to list them.

Step 5 - implementing the _runOperation function and building a skeleton for CRUD operation functions

Replace the existing _runOperation function with the following code:

```
private _runOperation(): void {
  const operation: HTMLOptionElement =
    this._operationSelect[this._operationSelect.selectedIndex] as
HTMLOptionElement;
  this._createListItem = this._createListItem.bind(this);
  this._readListItem = this._readListItem.bind(this);
  this._updateListItem = this._updateListItem.bind(this);
  this._deleteListItem = this._deleteListItem.bind(this);
  switch (operation.value) {
    case "Create":
      this._createListItem();
      break;
    case "Read":
      this._readListItem();
      break;
    case "Update":
      this._updateListItem();
      break;
    case "Delete":
      this._deleteListItem();
      break;
  }
}
```

Notice that we are using a switch-case type of structure, which is supported by TypeScript and functions like you would expect if you are familiar with C#.

After that function build skeletons for our CRUD operation functions.

```
private _createListItem(): void {this._operationResults.innerHTML =
"Create: Not implemented.";}
private _readListItem(): void {this._operationResults.innerHTML = "Read:
Not implemented.";}
private _updateListItem(): void {this._operationResults.innerHTML =
"Update: Not implemented.";}
private _deleteListItem(): void {this._operationResults.innerHTML =
"Delete: Not implemented.";}
```

It is a good idea to test everything works; this can be done very quickly when using Workbench.

Step 6 - implementing the create operation

To create a list item, replace the _createListItem function with the following code:

```
private _createListItem(): void {
  const url: string = this.context.pageContext.site.absoluteUrl+
    "/_api/web/lists/getbytitle('My List')/items";
  const itemDefinition : any = {
    "Title": "SPFX created item",
    "Info": "Info column value"
  };
  const spHttpClientOptions: ISPHttpClientOptions = {
          "body": JSON.stringify(itemDefinition)
  };
  this.context.spHttpClient.post(url, SPHttpClient.configurations.v1,
spHttpClientOptions)
      .then((response: SPHttpClientResponse) => {
        if (response.status === 201) {
              this._operationResults.innerHTML = "Create: List Item created
successfully.";
              this._readAllItems();
            } else {
              this._operationResults.innerHTML = "Create: List Item
creation failed. "
                +response.status+" - "+response.statusText;
            }
      });
  }
```

As you can see, we are using the same pattern that we used when we created the SharePoint list. The only real differences here are that in line 78 we are adding the list item to the collection of items in a list, and in lines 79-82 we use a different definition of the resource we are creating. After a successful operation, we are notifying the user and calling _readAllItems to update the list of items.

```
76    private _createListItem(): void {
77      const url: string = this.context.pageContext.site.absoluteUrl+
78        "/_api/web/lists/getbytitle('My List')/items";
79      const itemDefinition : any = {
80        "Title": "SPFX created item",
81        "Info": "Info column value"
82      };
83      const spHttpClientOptions: ISPHttpClientOptions = {
84            "body": JSON.stringify(itemDefinition)
85      };
86      this.context.spHttpClient.post(url, SPHttpClient.configurations.v1, spHttpClientOptions)
87        .then((response: SPHttpClientResponse) => {
88          if (response.status === 201) {
89                this._operationResults.innerHTML = "Create: List Item created successfully.";
90                this._readAllItems();
91          } else {
92                this._operationResults.innerHTML = "Create: List Item creation failed. "
93                  +response.status+" - "+response.statusText;
94          }
95        });
96    }
```

Test your code using SharePoint Workbench again, and you should be able to see that the list item is indeed created. When creating lists, SharePoint ensures that there is no list of the same title on the site, but when you create list items, it doesn't matter if the title is already used. Only the generated ID needs to be unique.

Step 7 - implementing the read operation

For the read operation, replace the _ReadListItem function with the following code:

```
private _readListItem(): void {
  const id: number = 1;
  this._getListItem(id).then(listItem => {
    this._operationResults.innerHTML = `
      <div>
        Read list item<br/>
        Title: ${listItem.Title}<br/>
        Info: ${listItem.Info}
      </div>`;
  })
  .catch(error => {
    this._operationResults.innerHTML = "Read: Operation failed.
"+error.message;
  });
}
private _getListItem(id: number): Promise<ISPListItem> {
  const url: string = this.context.pageContext.site.absoluteUrl+
    "/_api/web/lists/getbytitle('My
List')/items?$select=Title,Id,Info&$filter=Id eq "+id;
  return this.context.spHttpClient.get(url, SPHttpClient.configurations.v1)
    .then((response: SPHttpClientResponse) => {
      return response.json();
    })
    .then( (listItems: any) => {
      const untypedItem: any = listItems.value[0];
      const listItem: ISPListItem = untypedItem as ISPListItem;
      return listItem;
    }) as Promise <ISPListItem>;
}
```

This time we have two functions, _readListItem and _getListItem. _readListItem uses _getListItem to actually read the data and formulate the results as HTML inside the _operationResults object, the paragraph.

```
98    private _readListItem(): void {
99      const id: number = 1;
100     this._getListItem(id).then(listItem => {
101       this._operationResults.innerHTML = `
102         <div>
103           Read list item<br/>
104           Title: ${listItem.Title}<br/>
105           Info: ${listItem.Info}
106         </div>`;
107     })
108     .catch(error => {
109       this._operationResults.innerHTML = "Read: Operation failed. "+error.message;
110     });
111   }
```

In _getListItem we are returning the list item data as a Promise of the object that implements the ISPListItem interface. We query the list using $select and $filter parameters. The select parameter states that we are interested in the fields Title, Id, and Info. The filter parameter is used to select just the object with a given Id. We will get the result in an array, but since list item id is unique in the list, we are handling the first list item in the result set. Using the select and filter parameters will give you much more power over the queries you want to perform. These parameters follow the OData specification, which is an open standard, instead of being SharePoint-specific like CAML queries that are typically used with Server-side and Client-side object models for SharePoint.

```
112   private _getListItem(id: number): Promise<ISPListItem> {
113     const url: string = this.context.pageContext.site.absoluteUrl+
114       "/_api/web/lists/getbytitle('My List')/items?$select=Title,Id,Info&$filter=Id eq "+id;
115     return this.context.spHttpClient.get(url, SPHttpClient.configurations.v1)
116       .then((response: SPHttpClientResponse) => {
117         return response.json();
118       })
119       .then( (listItems: any) => {
120         const untypedItem: any = listItems.value[0];
121         const listItem: ISPListItem = untypedItem as ISPListItem;
122         return listItem;
123       }) as Promise <ISPListItem>;
124   }
```

Again, test that your web part works as expected:

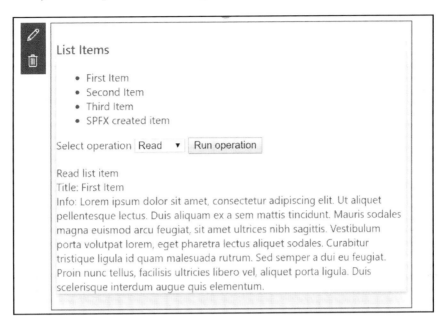

Step 8 - implementing the update operation

Updating a list item works in a similar manner to creating a new item. Replace the
_updateListItem function with the following code:

```
private _updateListItem(): void {
   const url: string = this.context.pageContext.site.absoluteUrl+
     "/_api/web/lists/getbytitle('My List')/items(1)";
   const itemDefinition : any = {
     "Title": "Modified title field value!"
   };
   const headers : any = {
     "X-HTTP-Method":"MERGE",
     "IF-MATCH": "*",
    };
   const spHttpClientOptions: ISPHttpClientOptions = {
       "headers": headers,
       "body": JSON.stringify(itemDefinition)
   };
   this.context.spHttpClient.post(url, SPHttpClient.configurations.v1,
spHttpClientOptions)
     .then((response: SPHttpClientResponse) => {
       if (response.status === 204) {
```

```
                     this._operationResults.innerHTML = "Update: List  Item  updated
  successfully.";
                     this._readAllItems();
                } else {
                     this._operationResults.innerHTML = "Update: List  Item  update
  failed. "
                        +response.status+" - "+response.statusText;
                }
         });
  }
```

The differences here are that we need to specify which list item we want to modify in the URL in line 127, where we state that this operation concerns the list item with ID 1 and that we need to specify some headers that separate this operation from the create operation. Headers are added to the object which implements the ISPHttpClientOptions in lines 131 and 133. The response code for successful action is 204.

```
125   private _updateListItem(): void {
126     const url: string = this.context.pageContext.site.absoluteUrl+
127       "/_api/web/lists/getbytitle('My List')/items(1)";
128     const itemDefinition : any = {
129       "Title": "Modified title field value!"
130     };
131     const headers : any = { "X-HTTP-Method":"MERGE", "IF-MATCH": "*" };
132     const spHttpClientOptions: ISPHttpClientOptions = {
133         "headers": headers,
134         "body": JSON.stringify(itemDefinition)
135     };
136     this.context.spHttpClient.post(url, SPHttpClient.configurations.v1, spHttpClientOptions)
137       .then((response: SPHttpClientResponse) => {
138         if (response.status === 204) {
139             this._operationResults.innerHTML = "Update: List Item updated successfully.";
140             this._readAllItems();
141         } else {
142             this._operationResults.innerHTML = "Update: List Item update failed. "
143               +response.status+" - "+response.statusText;
144         }
145     });
146   }
```

Step 9 - implementing the delete operation

Replace the _deleteListItem function with the following code:

```
private _deleteListItem(): void {
  const url: string = this.context.pageContext.site.absoluteUrl+
    "/_api/web/lists/getbytitle('My List')/items(1)";
  const headers : any = { "X-HTTP-Method":"DELETE", "IF-MATCH": "*" };
  const spHttpClientOptions: ISPHttpClientOptions = {
      "headers": headers
  };
  this.context.spHttpClient.post(url, SPHttpClient.configurations.v1,
spHttpClientOptions)
      .then((response: SPHttpClientResponse) => {
        if (response.status === 204) {
              this._operationResults.innerHTML = "Delete: List Item deleted
successfully.";
              this._readAllItems();
            } else {
              this._operationResults.innerHTML = "Delete: List Item delete
failed."
                +response.status+" - "+response.statusText;
          }
      });
  }
```

What we need to do to delete the list item is specify the ID in the URL at line 149 and headers in line 150. Again, 204 marks as a successful result.

```
147    private _deleteListItem(): void {
148      const url: string = this.context.pageContext.site.absoluteUrl+
149        "/_api/web/lists/getbytitle('My List')/items(1)";
150      const headers : any = { "X-HTTP-Method":"DELETE", "IF-MATCH": "*" };
151      const spHttpClientOptions: ISPHttpClientOptions = {
152          "headers": headers
153      };
154      this.context.spHttpClient.post(url, SPHttpClient.configurations.v1, spHttpClientOptions)
155          .then((response: SPHttpClientResponse) => {
156            if (response.status === 204) {
157                  this._operationResults.innerHTML = "Delete: List Item deleted successfully.";
158                  this._readAllItems();
159                } else {
160                  this._operationResults.innerHTML = "Delete: List Item delete failed."
161                    +response.status+" - "+response.statusText;
162              }
163          });
164    }
```

Summary

In this chapter, we focused on working with SharePoint data from your client-side web parts. We started with an overview of accessing SharePoint content, then we practiced how to work with mock data in local Workbench. After that, we covered in detail how to access lists in SharePoint sites as well as how to do all the basic operations with SharePoint list items.

In the next chapter, we'll work with SharePoint Web Parts, and especially the property pane that allows us to provide parameter values and data to our Web Parts. This is important as configuration data is often dynamic and should be easy to update when using the solution in different pages and tenants.

8
Working with the Web Part Property Pane

In this chapter, we'll focus on a single feature of SharePoint Framework, the property pane that is part of the web part model. This is especially useful when we want to allow users and content editors to provide additional choices and parameters to further configure the web part.

In this chapter, you will learn how to do the following:

- Configuring a web part within the property pane
- Adding new fields within the property pane
- Configuring between reactive and non-reactive event handling within the property pane
- Creating custom property pane fields

At the end of this chapter, you should have a clear understanding of the property pane and how to implement parameters for your web parts to allow users to better configure values within the web part.

Web part property pane

Web parts are viewed on SharePoint pages and users normally simply consume the data and features they provide. Content editors, and sometimes power users too, need a way to parametrize web parts. The property pane is an ideal way to do this, as it is a built-in feature of the web part model, and thus it is also implemented as a more modern approach within the SharePoint Framework-based web parts.

Property panes in classic web parts

Classic web parts, and also typically those that have been available in SharePoint Online for a long time, expose a classic property pane. This is readily accessible when you edit a page and hover the mouse over a web part.

In the following screenshot, a **Content Editor** Web Part has been added on a page, and in order to edit the contents, we need to click on the small down-arrow in the top-right corner:

This forces a page refresh, which also instructs the **Content Editor** Web Part to display the property pane on the right side of the page:

This has been both cumbersome and also problematic when a page consists of multiple web parts, as the property pane is in a fixed position relative to page contents. In pages with more content, the property pane is fixed in the top-right corner, while the content you're truly working on might be several page lengths lower.

Regardless of its usability, the property pane is very useful and easy to use. Developers tend to add custom properties in the property pane in custom Web Parts, which is a good way of providing a customizable UI for the user.

Property panes in SharePoint Framework web parts

Property panes in the more modern SharePoint Framework-based web parts still carry the same feel, but not the same look of the classic web part property panes.

As part of Communications Sites feature, Microsoft provided a plethora of new SPFx-based web parts in a ready-made template that can be configured. For each web part, a custom property pane is accessible.

By clicking the pencil icon of a web part, the property pane is shown:

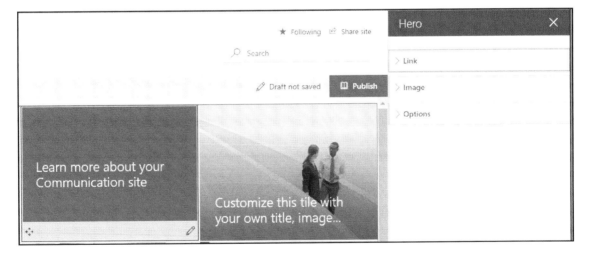

Each top-level item in the property pane reveals more configuration values and data for the content editor:

Changes performed in the property pane are immediately reflected on the page, thus providing a more fluid experience for managing page content. It also helps page editors to avoid the constant `Edit/Save/Reload-loop` when fine-tuning page content and element positioning.

Within our earlier **HelloWorld** Web Part, the property pane is accessible similarly to how it is available in classic web parts through the small menu:

Microsoft aims to provide a legacy bridge between classic and modern web parts, thus the property pane inherits the classic properties, but builds upon that to show a button to access the modern properties:

Clicking on**Configure** replaces the classic property pane with the modern one showing you the web Part properties:

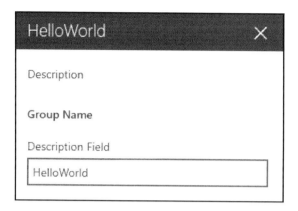

Possibly in the future, we might not have to worry that much on the classic property pane, and the currently modern property pane could be the default one.

Implementing a property pane

To get started in implementing a property pane and controlling the property values within the property pane, we must first understand the elements available in a property pane.

The property pane consists of the following three key elements:

- Pages, which are separate pages in a single property pane
- Headers, the title for the property pane
- Groups, which are sections in the property pane

Each property pane has to contain a page and at least one group. The header is always optional, as it is more or less a usability element.

In the following screenshot, 1 is the page, 2 is the header, and 3 is the group:

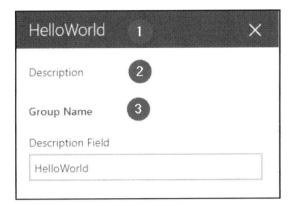

Fields in property panes

Individual properties in a property pane are shown as fields. Each field has a field type, such as textbox or link.

The allowed and currently supported field types are as follows:

- Label, for text labels
- Textbox, for a single-line text entry
- Multi-line textbox, for a multi-line text entry
- Checkbox, for a single checkable item
- Dropdown, for a drop-down list of selectable items
- Link, for clickable URLs
- Slider, for a slider for selecting a value
- Toggle, for an on/off toggle switch
- Custom, for a custom field type

You would typically use several fields to provide a number of selections within a tool pane. The custom field is something you would use when none of the built-in field types fit your purpose. We will look at custom field types later in this chapter.

Implementing headers, groups, and fields

In order to implement our own property pane, we'll need a working SPFx Web Part. You can use any of the web part samples we've created earlier or simply generate a new one with the Yeoman generator.

First, double-check that your web part and the property pane work with `gulp serve`:

Open the project with Visual Studio Code and then navigate to the `src` folder and `clickTypeScript` file open for the web part.

In our example, this file is called `PropertypaneWebPart.ts`. Locate the `getPropertyPaneConfiguration` method:

```
protected getPropertyPaneConfiguration(): IPropertyPaneConfiguration {
    return {
        pages: [
            {
                header: {
                    description: strings.PropertyPaneDescription
                },
                groups: [
                    {
                        groupName: strings.BasicGroupName,
                        groupFields: [
                            PropertyPaneTextField('description', {=
                                label: strings.DescriptionFieldLabel
                            })
                        ]
                    }
```

```
        ]
      }
    ]
  };
```

This method returns the pages, and beneath this the header and groups (one or more). The relevant piece of code here is in `groupFields`, which allows you to define the field types. By default, the Yeoman generator for a SharePoint Framework project only includes one field type, the `PropertyPaneTextField`, which is a single-line text field.

Let's start our journey with property panes by adding another group under the default header, and within that group, we'll add another text field of the same type (`PropertyPaneTextField`):

1. Add the following code under `groups`, and under the group that is already defined:

```
{
  groupName: "Custom group",
  groupFields: [
    PropertyPaneTextField('textboxField', {
      label: "Enter a custom value"
    })
  ]
}
```

2. Your `groups` code should now look like this:

```
groups: [
  {
    groupName: strings.BasicGroupName,
    groupFields: [
      PropertyPaneTextField('description', {
        label: strings.DescriptionFieldLabel
      })
    ]
  },
  {
    groupName: "Custom group",
    groupFields: [
      PropertyPaneTextField('textboxField', {
        label: "Enter a custom value"
      })
    ]
  }
]
```

3. If you still have `gulp serve` running, switch to the browser session and it should automatically refresh itself. Click on the pencil icon to reveal the updated `propertypane`:

4. Our custom group is now visible, and it allows us to add a custom value.

You can also add new fields to an existing group of fields.

5. Go back to the previous code, and add the following underneath the `textboxField` you added previously:

```
PropertyPaneTextField('textboxField2', {
        label: "Enter another custom value"
})
```

6. Your code for `Custom group` should now have two fields and look like this:

```
groupName: "Custom group",
groupFields: [
  PropertyPaneTextField('textboxField', {
    label: "Enter a custom value"
  }),
  PropertyPaneTextField('textboxField2', {
    label: "Enter another custom value"
  })
]
```

7. Once again, switch back to the browser running SharePoint Workbench and wait for a refresh. Then, click on the pencil to verify that your `propertypane` is updated with another text field within the same group:

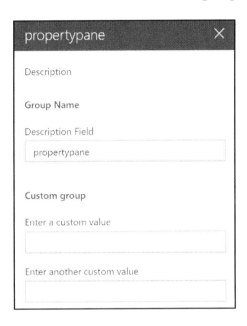

Next, we'll need to add a third field type that is of a different type. So far, we've only added a label, which allows us to get input from a single line of text. As previously listed, there are multiple other field types, but they are not included by default in the project to simplify the code.

8. To add another field type, navigate to the start of your Web Part Typescript file, where the `import` statement for `PropertyPaneTextField` is already listed. Add the `PropertyPanelLabel` in the list as follows:

```
import {
  BaseClientSideWebPart,
  IPropertyPaneConfiguration,
  PropertyPaneTextField,
  PropertyPaneLabel
} from '@microsoft/sp-webpart-base';
```

9. Now, navigate back to `groupFields` you manipulated earlier, and change the latter `PropertyPaneTextField` to `PropertyPaneLabel`. Also, change `label` to `text` under your `PropertyPaneLabel`.

Your code should now look like this:

```
groupFields: [
  PropertyPaneTextField('textboxField', {
    label: "Enter a custom value"
  }),
  PropertyPaneLabel('labelField', {
    text: "This is a custom text in PropertyPaneLabel"
  })
]
```

10. Your updated `propertypane` should now have a text label instead of a single-line textbox visible:

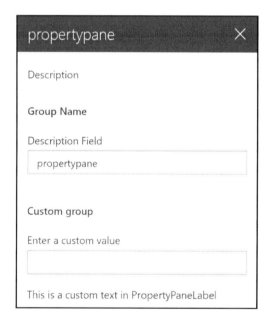

You can try out other field types, such as a link or a slider. Simply add the necessary import for the field type.

The logic follows the syntax of `PropertyPane` + `FieldType`, such as `PropertyPaneLink`, `PropertyPaneDropdown`, and so on. All field types are listed in the `sp-webpart-base` library under the `node_modules/@microsoft/sp-webpart-base` folder.

Implementing multiple pages in property panes

Another interesting aspect of the property pane is the ability to add multiple pages. SharePoint will perform automatic paging, allowing the user to flip between property pane pages. It goes without saying that developers should be careful in adding pages, as it might distract the user from performing common web part editing when they need to search through multiple pages for a setting.

As you already have one page in the property pane, you can add additional pages quite easily:

1. First, copy the existing code between the square brackets under `pages`.
2. Paste this code within the same code block as `pages`, by adding a comma before the closing curly brackets:

```
    },
    {
      header: {
        description: strings.PropertyPaneDescription
      },
      groups: [
        {
          groupName: strings.BasicGroupName,
          groupFields: [
            PropertyPaneTextField('description', {
              label: strings.DescriptionFieldLabel
            }
            )
          ]
        },
        {
          groupName: "Custom group",
          groupFields: [
            PropertyPaneTextField('textboxField', {
              label: "Enter a custom value"
            }),
            PropertyPaneLabel('labelField', {
              text: "This is a custom text in PropertyPaneLabel"
            })
          ]
```

```
        }
      ]
   }
```

3. Edit the `description` field for `header` in this new section from
   `strings.BasicGroupName` to `Group` (page 2).

4. Edit the names and labels for this new group to reflect that they are now being
   shown in page 2, instead of the default page of the property pane:

```
groups: [
  {
    groupName: "Custom group (page 2)",
    groupFields: [
      PropertyPaneTextField('descriptionPage2', {
        label: "Description"
      }
      )
    ]
  },
  {
    groupName: "Custom group 2 (page 2)",
    groupFields: [
      PropertyPaneTextField('textboxFieldPage2', {
        label: "Enter a custom value"
      }),
      PropertyPaneLabel('labelFieldPage2', {
        text: "This is a custom text in page 2"
      })
    ]
  }
```

5. Save changes and switch to SharePoint Workbench. The changes should be visible when you click the pencil icon once more:

6. By clicking on Next, we can see page 2, with the corresponding groups and fields:

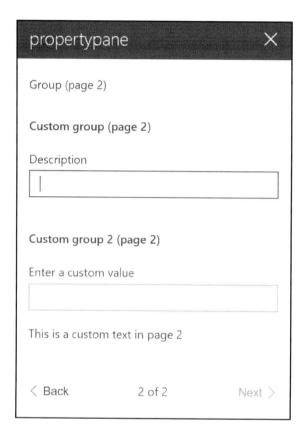

In this example, we saw how easy it is to add additional pages to a property pane and provide more functionality within the web part.

Handling property field events

By now you've probably seen that typing in values within fields fires off a field event. This is evident in fields that are shown in the web part, as each update to the field text forces an update on the text being displayed.

By changing the **Description Field** in our sample, the same text is being reflected within the web part canvas on the left:

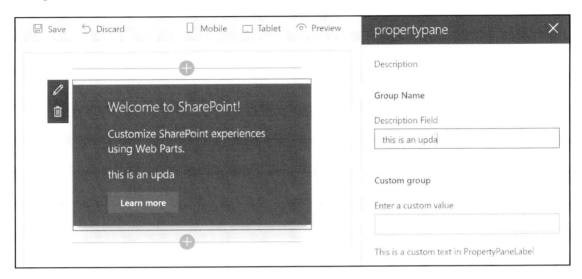

This is called a **reactive mode**, and it simply forces the web part to update the user interface whenever the property field values are updated.

An alternative to this is the **non-reactive mode**, which might be useful in certain scenarios.

Reactive mode is especially useful for text-based data, but might be problematic if a change fires off a chain of events that might be time-consuming. Updating a simple field value would take a longer time if our code insists on updating content after each key click.

As the property pane is in reactive mode by default, changing to the non-reactive mode is simple. All you need to do is add a method called `disableReactivePropertyChanges()` that returns a boolean value of `true` within your code:

```
protected get disableReactivePropertyChanges(): boolean {
  return true;
}
```

What happens now in your web part is that changes to a field value do not automatically update, but you'll get an **Apply** button to commit the changes.

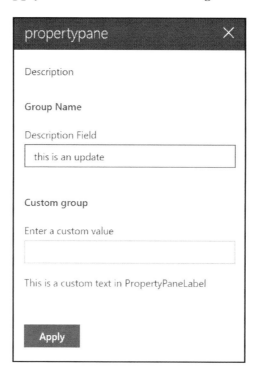

Clicking on Apply updates the web part canvas. The **propertypane** will still remain open, so this is similar to applying changes without clicking on**OK** in traditional Windows user experience.

Implementing custom properties in a property pane

Besides the built-in property pane field types, you might have a need for custom field types within the property pane. Usually, you should suffice quite well with the default field types, but at times you might find yourself in a situation that is best resolved with a custom field type. These are primarily used to render custom HTML.

Building a custom field type is not trivial, so consider for a moment before building your own. This tends to complicate your code and might bring future issues if or when Microsoft should update the collection of available field types. These changes might, in turn, render your custom properties redundant, and force you to clean up code for custom web parts.

Defining a custom field type

We'll need to define our custom field type within the interface of the project. In this example, we are creating a password field:

1. Start by opening the interface file within your `/src/webparts/{web-part-name}` folder. This is the `I{web-part-name}Props.ts` filename.

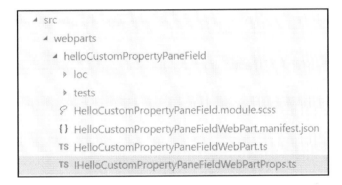

2. Within the file, modify the existing interface by adding your custom field type. In this example, we'll call it `password` and it will be a type of string:

```
export interface IHelloCustomPropertyPaneFieldWebPartProps {
  description: string;
  password: string;
}
```

3. Next, we'll need to import the custom field type to our `WebPart` class. The custom field type is now available as `PropertyPaneCustomField`, Visual Studio Code's fantastic Intellisense will help you right away:

```
2    import {
3      BaseClientSideWebPart,
4      IPropertyPaneConfiguration,
5      PropertyPaneTextField,
6      PropertyPaneCustomField
```
```
[⊘] PropertyPaneCustomField                    import PropertyPaneCustomField
[⊘] IPropertyPaneCustomFieldProps              sp-iouasii-suuset ,
```

4. Since SPFx has no knowledge of how our custom field type might work, or look visually, we need to provide code to actually render the element. We are going to create label element and input element of type `password`.

5. Since SPFx has no knowledge of how our custom field type might work, or look visually, we need to provide an internal element for rendering the field. This is achieved by adding the `innerHTML` element in the web part class as follows:

```
private _customPasswordFieldRender(
        elem: HTMLElement, context?: any): void {
    if (elem.childElementCount === 0) {
      let label: HTMLLabelElement =
          document.createElement("label");
      label.className = "ms-Label";
      label.innerText = "Password";
      elem.appendChild(label);
      let br: HTMLBRElement = document.createElement("br");
      elem.appendChild(br);
      let inputElement: HTMLInputElement =
          document.createElement("input");
      inputElement.type = "password";
      inputElement.name = context;
      this._customPasswordFieldChanged =
          this._customPasswordFieldChanged.bind(this);
      inputElement.addEventListener("keyup",
          this._customPasswordFieldChanged);
      inputElement.className = "ms-TextField-field";
      elem.appendChild(inputElement);
    }
}
```

6. Since our code needs to read the input value, we added an event listener to handle the keyup event. Here is the code for our event listener:

```
private _customPasswordFieldChanged(event: Event): void {
    let srcElement: HTMLInputElement =
        event.srcElement as HTMLInputElement;
    this.properties.password = srcElement.value;
}
```

7. Finally, within propertyPaneSettings, add your custom field type as you would add any field type and configure it accordingly:

```
PropertyPaneCustomField( {
  key: 'password',
  onRender: (domElement: HTMLElement, context?: any) => {
    this._customPasswordFieldRender(domElement, "password");
  }
})
```

8. This allows us to have a custom property field available within the property pane:

Summary

In this chapter, we took a detailed look at the Web Part property pane, which is also available in classic Web Parts within SharePoint. With SharePoint Frameworks' more modern capabilities the property pane is now much more useful, as it supports both reactive and non-reactive event handling. This provides a more fluid user experience as selections and changes within the property pane can be immediately reflected in the Web Part canvas for a user.

In addition to this chapter, we implementing multi-page property panes to better categorize a scenario where you might have multiple properties to fill out.

Finally, we implemented a custom property pane field that allows us to inject custom HTML within the property pane.

In the next chapter, you'll learn to use different JavaScript frameworks, including React and Angular, as part of our SharePoint Framework web parts.

9
Using React and Office UI Fabric React Components

In this chapter, we will cover how to use React and Office UI Fabric React frameworks within our code. React is an open source JavaScript library for building user interfaces. It is developed by engineers at Facebook and used in countless other services, including Instagram. Developers at Microsoft chose React for modern SharePoint development, but they carefully state that their choice shouldn't really limit your choices. You can use React as well, but you don't have to. After reading this chapter and doing the exercises, you will be equipped with the knowledge to make your own choice. With these two frameworks, we can create more consistent and modern applications with SharePoint Framework.

In this chapter, we'll cover the following topics:

- Understanding how React works and how it should be used
- Fabric React components and how to use them in your SharePoint Framework solutions
- Building a to-do list web part using both React and Office UI React

Overview

The fact that developers at Microsoft decided to use an open source JavaScript library to build their user interface, instead of creating their own, is very significant. If you are familiar with SharePoint 2013 search components, you learned how to use Display Templates. In essence, Display Templates is a relic from when Microsoft developers built solutions without third-party dependencies. Display Templates mix HTML and JavaScript and allow developers to customize the way search results look.

However, it is a SharePoint-only technology, which means that it is much more limited and not as well documented and supported than modern open source libraries. This decision was made for you, instead of you making your own decisions.

With Office UI Fabric, Microsoft offers an open source project for use. When using Office UI Fabric, you can stick with Fabric Core, which includes core elements, such as icons, colors, and the grid, or depending on your framework choice, you could utilize components from Fabric React, **Fabric JS** for JavaScript, or **ngFabric** for Angular. In addition, there is also Fabric iOS with native iOS styling and components written in Swift; however, in this chapter, we will focus on the Office UI Fabric React components.

Understanding React

So, as we discussed, React is a JavaScript library for building user interfaces in web and mobile applications that utilize JavaScript. Later on in this chapter, we will use React with TypeScript, instead of JavaScript, but for a short while, we will focus purely on React, and thus, deal with the only JavaScript. For a more in-depth documentation on React, refer to `https://facebook.github.io/react/`.

React is declarative

When we use React, we have an option to use JSX, which gives us a markup-style syntax, which is then compiled to procedural JavaScript code. JSX stands for Syntax Extensions for JavaScript. Consider the following statement:

```
const helloElement = <h3>Hello, {user.name}</h3>;
```

It is not pure JavaScript, nor is it pure HTML--it is something in between. It definitely mixes JavaScript and HTML in a very powerful and expressive way. In JSX, you wrap JavaScript inside the XML style markup using curly braces, and you can close your tag with `/>`, as follows:

```
const userPicture = <img src="{user.imageUrl}"/>;
```

A React element can have only one root element, but it can have nested elements. When you write JSX, there are some differences to it from HTML; for example, in the attribute names, you can't use attribute `class` (because it is a reserved name in ECMAScript 6), but, instead, you need to use `className`, and the attribute names are always written in camel case, `tagIndex` instead of `tagindex`:

```
const userCard = (
   <div className="userCard">
      <img src="{user.imageUrl}"/>
      <p>{user.name}</p>
   </div>);
```

React elements are not DOM elements, instead they are simple JavaScript objects, and React DOM takes care of updating the DOM to match React elements. This makes React very efficient. The JSX syntax may look strange to readers who have not seen it before. Remember that React is not a full framework; it is just a view engine.

React is component-based

In React, elements are building blocks of components. The simplest way to define a React component is to define a function:

```
function Greeter(props) {
   return <h3>Hello, {props.name}!</h3>;
}
```

However, you can also use ECMAScript 6 `class` to define a component:

```
class Greeter extends React.Component {
   render () {
      return <h3>Hello, {this.props.name}!</h3>;
   }
}
```

In React, React elements can represent DOM elements or React components:

```
const helloElement = <Greeter name="{user.name}"/>;
```

Also, real React apps are in fact composed of reusable components and elements, which are then rendered in a specific DOM element. This component model is very powerful and has some similarity to the notion of nested custom controls in ASP.NET, but is entirely implemented on the client side:

```
class Hello extends React.Component {
   render () {
```

```
      return <h3>Hello, {this.props.name}!</h3>;
    }
}

class HelloMakers() extends React.Component {
  render () {
    return (
      <div>
        <Hello name="Patrick"/>
        <Hello name="Vesa"/>
      </div>
    );
  }
}

ReactDOM.render(
  <HelloMakers />,
  document.getElementById('root')
);
```

As you saw in the previous examples, React components have properties called `props`. There is one very important rule in React when it comes to `props`, that is from the standpoint of the component, they are read-only. So, you can't modify `props` inside a component.

Components aren't static, however, since `state` allows React components to change their input over time without violating this rule. You don't have to use `state`--if you do, your React component is `stateful`, and if you don't, it is `stateless`:

```
class StatelessHello extends React.Component {  render () {
    return <h3>Hello, {this.props.name}!</h3>;
  }
}

class StatefulHello extends React.Component {
  constructor(props) {
    super(props);
    this.state = {
      fullName: props.firstName + " " props.lastName
    };
  }
  render () {
    return <h3>Hello, {this.state.fullName}!</h3>;
  }
}
```

If you are building stateful React components, you can only set the `state` directly in the `constructor`. After that, you will need to use the `setState` function, as follows:

```
// Wrong
this.state.fullName = "Mr " + this.state.fullName;
// Right
this.setState({
  fullName: "Mr " + this.state.fullName
});
```

From the component architecture point of view, a `state` is something that is internal to the component. Only the component knows whether it is stateful or stateless; a component can set the props for the child components but never the state. For the most part, this makes the solutions clear and easy to understand. However, there are situations where the state of a component needs to be available to other components--for example, if you are building a custom people picker and have a component that is holding the information about the selected user, you need to be able to communicate the information to other components. In React, this is called lifting the state up.

We lift the state by binding controls together with functions. Consider the following simple component with the `input` and `button` elements. When the value of `input` changes, the changed value is handled by the `handleChange` function, which in turn saves the new value in the component's `state`. When a button is clicked, the `saveClick` event occurs, and a function called `saveValue` is called, but that function is in the `props` of the component:

```
class SimpleComponent extends React.Component {
  constructor(props) {
    super(props);
    this.state = { value: ''};
    this.saveClick = this.saveClick.bind(this);
    this.handleChange = this.handleChange.bind(this);
  }
  handleChange(e) {
    this.setState({ value: e.target.value });
  }
  saveClick(e) {
    this.props.saveValue(this.state.value);
  }
  render() {
    return (
      <div>
        <input type="text"
          onChange={this.handleChange} />        <button type="button"
          onClick={this.saveClick}>Save</button>
      </div>
```

```
        );
    }
}
```

So, when we declare the component that is using this `SimpleComponent`, we are binding that component's function in the `props` of its child component so that property `saveValue` is, in fact, a function of the parent component, and the `state` value is communicated to the parent component:

```
class ParentComponent extends React.Component {
    constructor(props) {
        super(props);
        this.simpleComponentDone =
            this.simpleComponentDone.bind(this);
    }
    simpleComponentDone(valueFromSimpleComponent) {
        alert(valueFromSimpleComponent);
    }
    render() {
        return (
            <div>
                <SimpleComponent
                    saveValue={this.simpleComponentDone} />
            </div>
        );
    }
}
```

Introduction to Fabric React components

Office UI Fabric is the framework for building the Office and Office 365 user experience. This is a bit like Twitter Bootstrap, a framework primarily for CSS and UI. It was designed originally to help Office add-in developers get the look and feel of Microsoft Office applications. You don't have to use it, but if you want to build a consistent user experience for your web parts--something that fits right into the other components that are available in SharePoint sites--then Office UI Fabric is the way to go. Fabric Core includes the styles we have already used, and Fabric React includes a wide array of components that are built with React.

The idea here is not only to use the same design language and look and feel that Office 365 is using, but also to utilize reusable patterns.

Fabric React support

There are a few caveats you should be aware of when building SharePoint Framework solutions with Office UI Fabric. First, note that Fabric React doesn't support older IE versions, such as 9 and 10, so that is something you need to take into the consideration if you are running clients with an old browser base. The second caveat is a bit more complicated.

Microsoft is not done with Office UI Fabric and Fabric React, so styles and components will evolve. In practice, this means that in order to remain supported, you will need to ensure the following:

- SharePoint Framework web parts should have an explicit dependency to version 2.0 of Fabric React
- Fabric React components needs to be statically linked, which means that Fabric React components are bundled to your web part, and should the components change, it is not reflected in your web parts

The following are the differences between static and dynamic linking:

```
// static
import { Button } from 'office-ui-fabric-react/lib/Button';

// dynamic linking – usually works but not supported
import { Button } from '@microsoft/office-ui-fabric-react';
```

Since this is something that is likely to change in the future, you can double-check the current guidance at `https://dev.office.com/sharepoint/docs/spfx/web-parts/guidance/office-ui-fabric-integration`.

How to obtain Fabric React for your web part

The easiest way to start using Fabric React is to create a web part from the Yeoman template using React and then run the following command on Command Prompt while in the web part folder:

```
npm --save install office-ui-fabric-react
```

Next, in the file you will use a Fabric React component. Add the following import statement:

```
import { ColorPicker } from 'office-ui-fabric-react/lib/ColorPicker';
```

To add the Fabric React component inside your component, use the following pattern:

```
26    public render(): React.ReactElement<IHelloReactProps> {
27      return (
28        <div className={styles.helloReact}>
29          <ColorPicker color="gray" />
30        </div>
31      );
32    }
```

You should be able to see the Fabric React component in your web part. The component has all the Office UI Fabric styling applied automatically. You can take a look at the page source to see what was actually generated:

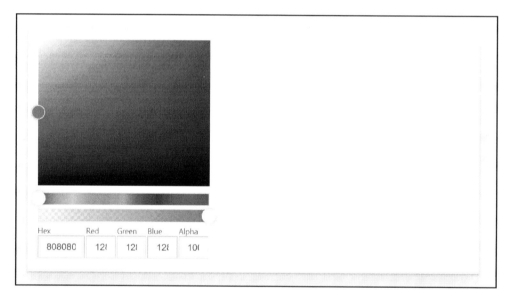

Using Fabric React components

To find out all Fabric React components that are currently available, as well as instructions, how to use them, navigate to `https://dev.office.com/fabric#/components`. Here, we will have a closer look at few of them.

Button

Fabric React's `Button` is a versatile component and can take many forms, which are called variants. In the earlier version of Fabric React, you could declare `Button` as `<Button />`, defining the desired `buttonType` to declare the variant that you want to use. But this has been deprecated and we recommend that you use a specific variant component, such as `<CommandButton/>`, in your definition. Using `Button` is a bit confusing because we already have an HTML button:

```
<!-- deprecated - don't use -->
 <Button iconProps={ { iconName: "addFriend"} }
buttonType={ButtonType.command}>Command</Button><!-- correct use of variant
button -->
 <CommandButton iconProps={ { iconName: "addFriend"}
}>Command</CommandButton>
```

Currently available button types are `CommandButton`, `CompoundButton`, `DefaultButton`, `IconButton`, and `PrimaryButton`. To use a specific style of button, import it at the start of the web part:

```
import { CommandButton, DefaultButton, IconButton } from 'office-ui-fabric-
react/lib/Button';
```

When the user clicks on the button, something needs to happen. This is done using `onClick` to bind the click event to the web part's function:

```
<IconButton iconProps={ { iconName: "mapDirections"} }
                   onClick={this._showMapDirections.bind(this)} />
```

You can enable or disable a button using the `disabled` property:

```
<DefaultButton disabled={this.props.defaultButtonDisabled}>
 Click me</DefaultButton>
```

Dialog

Dialogs are a powerful way to interact with the user when you want to show information or ask them to make a choice as part of the application flow. To do that, first, you import the types:

```
import { Dialog, DialogType, DialogFooter } from 'office-ui-fabric-
react/lib/Dialog';
```

Then, you can define a button that shows the dialog and the actual dialog:

```
<DefaultButton
  onClick={this._showDialog.bind(this)}>Show Dialog</DefaultButton>
<Dialog isOpen={this.state.showDialog}
  type={DialogType.normal}
  onDismiss={this._closeDialog.bind(this)}
  title="My Dialog Title"
  subText="Some more text here."
  isBlocking={false}
  containerClassName={styles.container}>
  <DialogFooter>
    <PrimaryButton onClick={ this._closeDialog.bind(this)
}>OK</PrimaryButton>
  </DialogFooter>
</Dialog>
```

We control the appearance of dialog through `this.state.showDialog` property. The buttons alter the component state, which is set as `false` in the constructor:

```
constructor(props: IHelloReactProps) {
  super(props);
  this.state = { showDialog: false };
}
private _showDialog(): void {
  this.setState({showDialog:true});
}
private _closeDialog(): void {
  this.setState({showDialog:false});
}
```

Here is what the dialog looks like in action:

TextField

The `TextFields` are simple but useful. Like other Fabric React components, `TextField` is very versatile. First, import the component in a normal fashion:

```
import { TextField } from 'office-ui-fabric-react/lib/TextField';
```

Then, you can define the actual component with `onChanged` binding to access the changed value:

```
<TextField label="Text field"
onChanged={this._textFieldChanged.bind(this)}/>
```

In the `_textFieldChanged` function, we set the state to reflect the changed text:

```
private _textFieldChanged(newValue: string): void {
  this.setState({textFieldValue: newValue});
}
```

We can control `disabled` and `required` properties of `TextField`:

```
<TextField disabled={this.state.textFieldDisabled} required={true}
label="Text field" onChanged={this._textFieldChanged.bind(this)}/>
```

We can also control other properties, such as `placeholder` and icon:

```
 <TextField placeholder="Enter date" iconClass="ms-Icon--Calendar ms-Icon"
label="Text field" onChanged={this._textFieldChanged.bind(this)}/>
```

This will be rendered as follows:

We can make `multiline` text input and control the number of rows:

```
<TextField placeholder="Type ingress text here" multiline rows={4}
label="Ingress text" onChanged={this._textFieldChanged.bind(this)}/>
```

Make the `TextField` control non-resizable or make the height automatically adjustable and control the maximum length of the input:

```
<TextField placeholder="Type ingress text here" multiline rows={4}
```

```
resizable={ false } label="Non-resizable text field" maxLength={255}/>

<TextField placeholder="Type ingress text here" autoAdjustHeight={true}
multiline label="Auto adjust height text field" maxLength={4096}/>
```

Both options work nicely depending on your user interface needs. You have the option to compose larger components out of these building blocks to allow component reuse:

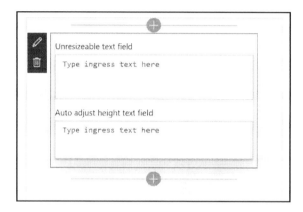

That was a quick overview of using Fabric React components. They are versatile and quite easy to use. When you have a few hours to spare, go through all of them at `https://dev. office.com/fabric#/components` so that when you need a UI control, you will have knowledge of the options.

Now, it is time to create a web part and learn more about how to work with React and Office UI Fabric React components in SharePoint Framework.

Using React and Office UI Fabric React components in SharePoint Framework web parts

When you are using React and Fabric React, it is practical to create your web parts using the Yeoman template with React and use npm to install `office-ui-fabric-react` components.

Creating the SharePoint Framework React To-do web part

We will now build a React web part to implement a mockup to-do list--like a poor man's planner in Office 365. It will not save the to-do list, but if you want, you can implement that using the CRUD list item operations we went through in `Chapter 7`, *Working with SharePoint Content*.

The following screenshot shows the actual web part user interface we are building:

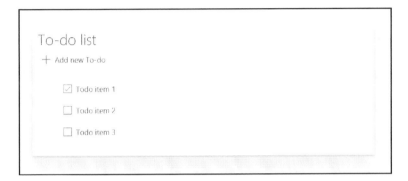

Web part has a title, command button, and list of to-do items. The icon in the to-do item shows whether it has been done or not. When the user clicks on the **Add new To-do** button, we will show a panel with a user interface to fill in the **To-do item** information:

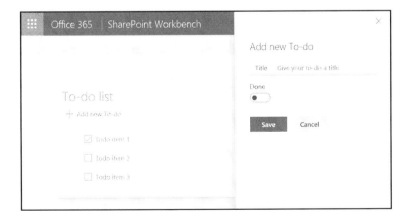

When the user clicks on an existing **To-do item**, we will see an edit panel, with a button to **Delete this item**:

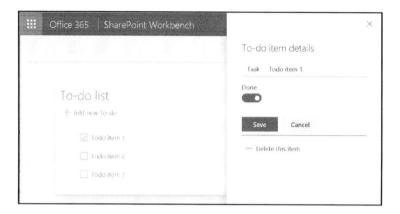

Step 1 - Creating a React web part project

First, we will create a folder for the web part, for example, `react-todo-webpart` and start the Yeoman generator to create the SharePoint Framework web part. React is selected for the framework:

```
C:\Users\olli>md react-todo-webpart

C:\Users\olli>cd react-todo-webpart

C:\Users\olli\react-todo-webpart>yo @microsoft/sharepoint


                      |  Welcome to the       |
                      |  SharePoint Client-side |
                      |  Solution Generator    |



Let's create a new SharePoint solution.
? What is your solution name? react-todo-webpart
? Which type of client-side component to create? WebPart
? What is your WebPart name? ReactTodo
? What is your WebPart description? ReactTodo description
? Which framework would you like to use?
  No JavaScript framework
> React
  Knockout
```

We then wait until the generator finishes.

Step 2 - Adding Office UI Fabric React to the project

While we are still at Command Prompt, type in the following command to add Fabric React to the project:

```
npm --save install office-ui-fabric-react
```

The `--save` parameter means that the package will appear in the project's dependencies.

Step 3 - Examining the React project structure

Then, start Visual Studio Code, or open a new window if you already have it opened, and open your project's folder. You can, of course, use another editor if you prefer.

Let's examine the project structure:

The web part file and the folder structure is similar but not the same as in the no-framework project. The main difference is that there is a `components` folder under the `src\webparts\reactTodo` web part folder. We can see that, in the `ReactTodoWebPart.ts` file, there is an `import` statement, which imports the `ReactTodo` class from `components/ReactTodo`. Also, if we examine the `ReactTodoWebPart` class, we can see that in the `render` function, instead of creating the HTML directly, we are actually creating a React element using the class definition of `ReactTodo` and then calling `ReactDom` to render it to the web part's `domElement`:

```
18    public render(): void {
19      const element: React.ReactElement<IHelloReactProps> = React.createElement(
20        HelloReact,
21        {
22          description: this.properties.description
23        }
24      );
25
26      ReactDom.render(element, this.domElement);
27    }
```

Next, we open `ReactTodo.tsx` from the `components` subfolder and examine that file:

```
6    export default class HelloReact extends React.Component<IHelloReactProps, void> {
7      public render(): React.ReactElement<IHelloReactProps> {
8        return (
9          <div className={styles.helloReact}>
10           <div className={styles.container}>
11             <div className={`ms-Grid-row ms-bgColor-themeDark ms-fontColor-white ${styles.row}`}>
12               <div className="ms-Grid-col ms-u-lg10 ms-u-xl8 ms-u-xlPush2 ms-u-lgPush1">
13                 <span className="ms-font-xl ms-fontColor-white">Welcome to SharePoint!</span>
14                 <p className="ms-font-l ms-fontColor-white">Customize SharePoint experiences using Web Parts.</p>
15                 <p className="ms-font-l ms-fontColor-white">{escape(this.props.description)}</p>
16                 <a href="https://aka.ms/spfx" className={styles.button}>
17                   <span className={styles.label}>Learn more</span>
18                 </a>
19               </div>
20             </div>
21           </div>
22         </div>
23       );
24     }
25   }
```

We can see that the web part does exactly the same action as a web part that is not using a JavaScript framework, but this time it does it in a React fashion. Note that in line 15, the `escape` function is used to make sure that the evil user is not trying to inject JavaScript or HTML into the page as is the case with no-framework web part projects. However, this time, it isn't actually necessary because React will do it automatically for us.

Start the project at a local workbench with `gulp serve`, and you will see how double escaping works:

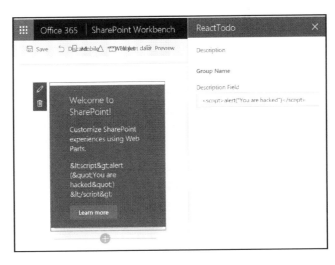

Then, remove the `escape` function call by replacing line 15 with the following code:

```
<p className="ms-font-l ms-fontColor-white">{this.props.description}</p>
```

You will see that it works more like expected without the use of the `escape` function, and we are still protected from the evil user input. Script tags are escaped so that the script will not run:

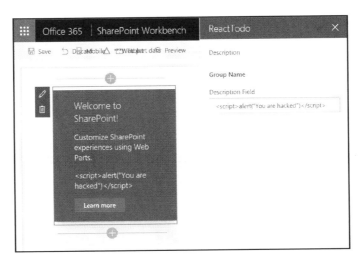

Enough examining is done at this point; let's start to create our data model.

Step 4 - Creating the ITodoItem interface and mockup data

Create a new file called `ITodoItem.ts` in the web part's `src\webparts\reactTodo` folder, and insert the following code and save the file:

```
export interface ITodoItem {
    Id: number;
    Title: string;
    Done: boolean;
}
```

As you can see, we kept the data model very simple. It will be a **POJO (Plain old JS object**--wait, that's Java, oh well!)--this would be the model if we were doing a more conventional MVC pattern. It has only three properties that can easily be implemented in the SharePoint list as well.

Next, create a new file called `TodoClient.ts` in the web part's `src\webparts\reactTodo` folder, and insert the following code and save the file:

```
import { ITodoItem } from "./ITodoItem";

export default class TodoClient {
private _todoItems: ITodoItem[] = [
    { Id: 1, Title: "Todo item 1", Done: true },
    { Id: 2, Title: "Todo item 2", Done: false },
    { Id: 3, Title: "Todo item 3", Done: false },
];

private _lastItemId: number = 3;
public getItems(): Promise<ITodoItem[]> {
        return new Promise<ITodoItem[]>((resolve) => {
        resolve(this._todoItems);
    });
}

public add(NewItemTitle: string, NewItemDone: boolean): Promise<number> {
    this._lastItemId += 1;
    this._todoItems.push({
        Id: this._lastItemId,
        Title: NewItemTitle,
        Done: NewItemDone
    });
    return new Promise<number>((resolve) => { resolve(this._lastItemId);
});
}
```

```
public edit(TodoItem: ITodoItem): Promise<boolean> {
    this._todoItems.forEach((existingItem: ITodoItem) => {
        if (existingItem.Id === TodoItem.Id) {
            existingItem.Title = TodoItem.Title;
            existingItem.Done = TodoItem.Done;
            return new Promise<boolean>((resolve) => { resolve(true); });
        }
    });
    return new Promise<boolean>((resolve) => { resolve(false); });
}

public get(ItemId: number): Promise<ITodoItem> {
    this._todoItems.forEach((existingItem: ITodoItem) => {
        if (existingItem.Id === ItemId) {
            return new Promise<ITodoItem>((resolve) => {
                resolve(existingItem);
            });
        }
    });
    return new Promise<ITodoItem>((resolve) => { resolve(null); });
}

public delete(ItemId: number): Promise<boolean> {
    this._todoItems.forEach((existingItem: ITodoItem) => {
        if (existingItem.Id === ItemId) {
            const ind: number = this._todoItems.indexOf(existingItem);
            this._todoItems.splice(ind, 1);
            return new Promise<boolean>((resolve) => { resolve(true); });
        }
    });
    return new Promise<boolean>((resolve) => { resolve(false); });
}
}
```

We have declared all the basic operations as well as mockup data. With `getItems`, we can list all items--`add` creates a new item working with the item ID in a similar fashion as the SharePoint list does, `edit` modifies an existing item, `get` returns an item by `Id`, and `delete` removes item by `Id`. We will use `Promise`, which makes things a bit more complex with the need of `then` when we call the functions, but it is also more realistic as actual data operations will be asynchronous and require the same pattern.

Step 5 - Implementing a to-do list in React and Fabric React components

Now that we have the data model and client class capable of connecting to data, we will add these to the web part. There are quite a few things to do, but we will start with a few simple modifications to the web part file.

Modifying the web part file

Open `ReactTodoWebPart.ts` and add the following code at the end of import statements, before the class definition begins:

```
import TodoClient from "./TodoClient";
```

Next, replace the existing `render` function with the following code:

```
public render(): void {
    const element: React.ReactElement<IReactTodoProps> =
React.createElement(
        ReactTodo,
        {
          description: this.properties.description,
          todoClient: new TodoClient()
        }
    );
    ReactDom.render(element, this.domElement);
}
```

As you can see, as part of `IReactTodoProps`, we are passing a new `TodoClient` object. At this point, Visual Studio Code will note that `IReactTodoProps` doesn't include `TodoClient`, so we open `IReactTodoProps.ts` under the `components` folder to fix it. Replace the contents with the following code:

```
import TodoClient from '../TodoClient';
export interface IReactTodoProps {
  description: string;
  todoClient: TodoClient;
}
```

We won't use `description` in this web part, but we leave it there in case you want to modify the web part later to use web part properties and use it as an example. React components use props and states, as described earlier in this chapter. When we are using TypeScript with React, it is good practice to declare the properties as strongly typed objects, and this is what the `IReactTodoProps` interface is for.

Modifying the ReactTodo component

Next, create a new file in the `components` folder, name it `IReactTodoState.ts`, and copy the following code to the file and save it:

```
import {ITodoItem} from "../ITodoItem";
export interface IReactTodoState {
    todoItems?: ITodoItem[];
    showNewTodoPanel?: boolean;
    newItemTitle?: string;
    newItemDone?: boolean;
}
```

Here, we declare all objects and variables that we are using to describe the state of our `ReactTodo` component. Note that all of them are marked as optional with a question mark. When we change the state of our component with the `this.setState` function, we don't always want to change all of the values, and by making them optional, TypeScript allows us to change just one or a few of them.

In the interface that is used to describe the state of `ReactTodo` component, the most important property is `todoItems`, into which we will save the array of to-do items. Then, we have three properties to handle a new to-do item, as you will soon see.

Now, it is time to open `ReactTodo.tsx`. This file will define our main React component, which is loaded in the web part file. First, add the following `import` statements, and as you can see, there are quite many of them:

```
import { ITodoItem } from '../ITodoItem';
import { IReactTodoState } from './IReactTodoState';
import TodoItemComponent from './TodoItemComponent';
import { CommandButton, PrimaryButton, DefaultButton } from 'office-ui-
fabric-react/lib/Button';
import { Panel, PanelType } from 'office-ui-fabric-react/lib/Panel';
import { Toggle } from 'office-ui-fabric-react/lib/Toggle';
import { TextField } from 'office-ui-fabric-react/lib/TextField';
```

We first import `ITodoItem`, which is our data model, and `IReactTodoState`, which we just declared, to be able to save the state of our component. Then, we import another component called `TodoItemComponent`, which represents a single to-do item. The rest of the imports are Office UI Fabric components.

Handling state is an essential part of building React solutions. For the ReactTodo component, we start by adding a constructor for the class. Add the following code inside the class definition:

```
constructor(props: IReactTodoProps) {
  super(props);
  this.state = {
    todoItems: [],
    showNewTodoPanel: false
  };
  this.props.todoClient.getItems()
  .then((resolvedTodoItems) => {
    this.setState({
      todoItems: resolvedTodoItems
    });
  });
}
```

Whenever you are doing React component constructors, first call super(props). Then, set the state's initial values. At the time of an object instantiation, todoItems will be an empty array and showNewTodoPanel, the boolean variable controlling the visibility of the panel with a UI to add a new item, is false. The only place in a React component where you can, and should, set the state directly is the constructor function.

It might seem odd, but just after we set the state directly, we will set the value of this.state.todoItems asynchronously. We do this to make sure that we have an empty array of items when the render function is called initially by React. When then happens, we will use the setState function to change the value of todoItems. When the state changes, React will call the render function again automatically.

Next, replace the existing render function with the following code:

```
public render(): React.ReactElement<IReactTodoProps> {
  const items: any[] = [];
  this.state.todoItems.forEach((todoItem: ITodoItem) => {
    items.push(
      <li>
        <TodoItemComponent
          itemId={todoItem.Id}
          itemTitle={todoItem.Title}
          itemDone={todoItem.Done}
          edit={this.edit.bind(this)}
          delete={this.delete.bind(this)}>
        </TodoItemComponent>
      </li>
    );
```

```
    });
    return (
      <div className={styles.reactTodo}>
          <div className={styles.container}>
            <div className="ms-font-xxl">To-do list</div>
            <CommandButton
              iconProps={{iconName:"Add"}}
              onClick={this.addItem.bind(this)}>
              Add new To-do
            </CommandButton>
            <Panel
                isOpen={this.state.showNewTodoPanel}
                type={PanelType.smallFixedFar}
                onDismiss={this.closeNewTodoPanel.bind(this)}
                headerText="Add new To-do"
                onRenderFooterContent={ () => {
                return (
                  <div>
                    <PrimaryButton
                      onClick={this.saveNewTodo.bind(this)}
                      style={ { 'marginRight': '8px' } } >
                      Save
                    </PrimaryButton>
                    <DefaultButton
                      onClick={this.closeNewTodoPanel.bind(this)}>
                      Cancel
                    </DefaultButton>
                  </div>
                );
              } }>
              <TextField
                label="Title"
                underlined
                placeholder="Give your to-do a title"
                value={this.state.newItemTitle}
                onChanged={this.newItemTitleChange.bind(this)}  />
              <Toggle
                label="Done"
                checked={this.state.newItemDone}
onChanged={this.toggleNewItemDone.bind(this)} />
            </Panel>
            <ul className={styles.todoList}>
              {items}
            </ul>
          </div>
      </div>
    );
  }
```

The `render` function starts by building an array of to-do items, as follows:

```
67   const items: any[] = [];
68   this.state.todoItems.forEach((todoItem: ITodoItem) => {
69     items.push(
70       <li>
71         <TodoItemComponent
72           itemId={todoItem.Id}
73           itemTitle={todoItem.Title}
74           itemDone={todoItem.Done}
75           edit={this.edit.bind(this)}
76           delete={this.delete.bind(this)}>
77         </TodoItemComponent>
78       </li>
79     );
80   });
```

Each item is enclosed in an HTML `<li></li>`, and inside them is `TodoItemComponent`, which we will be building later on. We will pass props for each to-do item component and bind two props to `ReactTodo` component's functions to lift the state from the child component to parent.

Let's study the `return` statement of the `render` function in the following statement:

```
81   return (
82     <div className={styles.reactTodo}>
83       <div className={styles.container}>
84         <div className="ms-font-xxl">To-do list</div>
85         <CommandButton
86           iconProps={{iconName:"Add"}}
87           onClick={this.addItem.bind(this)}>
88           Add new To-do
89         </CommandButton>
90       <Panel ···
120      </Panel>
121      <ul className={styles.todoList}>
122        {items}
123      </ul>
124      </div>
125    </div>
126  );
```

In our `return` statement, we have a title element in line 85 and `Add new To-do` command button in lines 86-90. By clicking on a button a function is called, and it will change the state so that the add new to-do panel in lines 91-120 will be visible. Lastly, in lines 121-123, we render the list of to-do `items` to the user.

The add new to-do panel is a bit longer, but not too complicated. We declared some properties such as the header text and footer content with two buttons. The important part is to understand how we bind the functions of this component to the child component's props. When a user interacts with the Fabric React component, our function will handle the situation. Consider the following code snippet:

```
90    <Panel
91        isOpen={this.state.showNewTodoPanel}
92        type={PanelType.smallFixedFar}
93        onDismiss={this.closeNewTodoPanel.bind(this)}
94        headerText="Add new To-do"
95        onRenderFooterContent={ () => {
96        return (
97          <div>
98            <PrimaryButton
99              onClick={this.saveNewTodo.bind(this)}
100             style={ { 'marginRight': '8px' } } >
101             Save
102           </PrimaryButton>
103           <DefaultButton
104             onClick={this.closeNewTodoPanel.bind(this)}>
105             Cancel
106           </DefaultButton>
107         </div>
108       );
109     } }>
```

The actual contents of the panel are declared inside the `<Panel>` element:

```
110   <TextField
111       label="Title"
112       underlined
113       placeholder="Give your to-do a title"
114       value={this.state.newItemTitle}
115       onChanged={this.newItemTitleChange.bind(this)}  />
116   <Toggle
117       label="Done"
118       checked={this.state.newItemDone}
119       onChanged={this.toggleNewItemDone.bind(this)} />
```

`TextField` is used to get a user input for the title of the to-do item, and `Toggle` is used to ask the user whether the to-do item has been done already.

Finally, add the following code that includes the bind functions:

```
private addItem(): void {
  this.setState({showNewTodoPanel: true});
}
private closeNewTodoPanel(): void {
  this.setState({
```

```
      showNewTodoPanel: false,
      newItemDone: false,
      newItemTitle: ""
    });
  }
  private saveNewTodo(): void {
    this.props.todoClient
      .add(this.state.newItemTitle, this.state.newItemDone).then(() => {
        this.setState({newItemDone: false, newItemTitle: "",
showNewTodoPanel: false});
        this.refreshTodoItems();
      });
  }
  private newItemTitleChange(value: string): void {
    this.setState({newItemTitle: value});
  }
  private toggleNewItemDone(e: any): void {
    this.setState((prevState, props) => ({
      newItemDone: !prevState.newItemDone
    }));
  }
  private delete(Id: number): void {
    this.props.todoClient.delete(Id);
    this.refreshTodoItems();
  }
  private edit(TodoItem: ITodoItem): void {
    this.props.todoClient.edit(TodoItem);
    this.refreshTodoItems();
  }
  public refreshTodoItems(): void {
    this.props.todoClient.getItems().then((resolvedTodoItems: ITodoItem[]) =>
{
      this.setState({
        todoItems: resolvedTodoItems
      });
    });
  }
```

The addItem function changes the component state by setting the value of this.state.
showNewTodoPanel to true, which means that the add new to-do item panel will be
rendered visible. The closeNewTodoPanel function will do the opposite--it will hide the
panel, but it will also clear the values for newItemTitle and newItemDone so that closing
the panel will also clear the user input.

The saveNewTodo function, which is called when the **Save** button of the new to-do item
panel is called, uses the TodoClient object that is in props of this class to call the add
function of the client and save data to the to-do list.

This is lifting the state in React. After that, we clear the state related to the new to-do item and call our helper function `refreshTodoItems` to retrieve a current array of `todoItems` and set it to the `state`.

The `newItemTitleChange` and `toggleNewItemDone` functions are bound to `TextField` and `Toggle` components in the new to-do item panel. They will take the user input and set `state` to match it.

Then, we will declare `delete` and `edit` functions that we passed as props for `TodoItemComponent`. That component will use these functions to lift the state to its parent, the `ReactTodo` component.

Open `ReactTodoModule.scss` and add the following CSS fragment after `.container` element; the SCSS file extension stands for Sassy CSS, which allows us to write smart syntax close to CSS to avoid the usual complexity that comes with larger CSS files:

```scss
.todoList {
  list-style-type: none;
}
```

Our to-do items are rendered as an HTML list, and this will remove the bullet point from the start of each list item.

Creating TodoItemComponent

Finally, we will create `TodoItemComponent`. It is responsible for rendering a to-do item and has a UI for the edit panel and the delete button.

We will create three files in the `components` folder. First, create a file named `ITodoItemProps.ts` and insert the following code; the parent component will communicate to-do item details as well as the bound functions to `edit` and `delete` the to-do item:

```ts
export interface ITodoItemProps {
  itemId: number;
  itemTitle: string;
  itemDone: boolean;
  edit: any;
  delete: any;
}
```

Next, create `ITodoItemState.ts` and insert the following code:

```
export interface ITodoItemState {
  itemId?: number;
  itemTitle?: string;
  itemDone?: boolean;
  showPanel?: boolean;
}
```

Again, all the properties in state interface are optional. For each to-to item, we are interested in its data. In addition, we use `this.state.showPanel` to control the visibility of the edit to-do item panel.

Create the final file, `TodoItemComponent.ts`, in the same `components` folder and copy the following code to the file:

```
import * as React from 'react';
import {ITodoItemProps} from "./ITodoItemProps";
import {ITodoItemState} from "./ITodoItemState";
import { CommandButton, PrimaryButton, DefaultButton } from 'office-ui-
fabric-react/lib/Button';
import { Panel, PanelType } from 'office-ui-fabric-react/lib/Panel';
import { Toggle } from 'office-ui-fabric-react/lib/Toggle';
import { TextField } from 'office-ui-fabric-react/lib/TextField';
import { ITodoItem } from "../ITodoItem";

export default class TodoItemComponent extends
  React.Component<ITodoItemProps,ITodoItemState> {
constructor (props: ITodoItemProps) {
  super(props);
  this.state = {
      itemDone: this.props.itemDone,
      itemTitle: this.props.itemTitle,
      itemId: this.props.itemId,
      showPanel: false
  };
}
public closePanel(): void {
  this.setState({
      itemTitle: this.props.itemTitle,
      itemDone: this.props.itemDone,
      showPanel: false
  });
}
public showPanel(): void {
  this.setState({
      showPanel: true
  });
```

```
  }
  private itemClicked(e: any, Id: number): void {
      this.setState({showPanel: true});
  }
  private titleChange(value: string): void {
      this.setState({ itemTitle: value});
  }
  private toggleDone(e: any): void {
    this.setState((prevState, props) => ({
      itemDone: !prevState.itemDone
    }));
  }
  private saveClick(): void {
      const changedItem: ITodoItem = {
          Id: this.state.itemId,
          Title: this.state.itemTitle,
          Done: this.state.itemDone
        };
      this.props.edit(changedItem);
      this.setState({showPanel: false});
  }
  private deleteClick(): void {
    this.props.delete(this.state.itemId);
    this.setState({showPanel: false});
  }
  public render(): React.ReactElement<ITodoItemProps> {
    const resolvedIconName: string =
      (this.props.itemDone) ? "CheckboxComposite" : "Checkbox";
    return (
        <div>
      <CommandButton
        iconProps={{iconName: resolvedIconName}}
        onClick={(e) => this.itemClicked(e,this.props.itemId)}>
        {this.props.itemTitle}</CommandButton>
      <Panel
        isOpen={this.state.showPanel}
        type={PanelType.smallFixedFar}
        onDismiss={this.closePanel.bind(this)}
        headerText="To-do item details"
        onRenderFooterContent={ () => {
        return (
          <div>
            <PrimaryButton
              onClick={this.saveClick.bind(this)}
              style={ { 'marginRight': '8px' } } >
              Save
            </PrimaryButton>
            <DefaultButton
```

```
              onClick={this.closePanel.bind(this)}>
              Cancel
            </DefaultButton>
            <hr/>
            <CommandButton
              iconProps={{iconName:"Remove"}}
              onClick={this.deleteClick.bind(this)}>
              Delete this item
            </CommandButton>
          </div>
        );}}>
          <TextField
            label="Task" underlined
            value={this.state.itemTitle}
            onChanged={this.titleChange.bind(this)}  />
          <Toggle
            label="Done"
            checked={this.state.itemDone}
            onChanged={this.toggleDone.bind(this)} />
        </Panel>
      </div>
    );
  }
}
```

This component follows the same principles as the ReactTodo component does. With React, it is all about getting props from the parent component, handling the state inside the component to respond to the user input, and finally lifting the state with functions that are bound to props when the user does something that needs to be handled outside the component.

The following are some key points to highlight and summarize:

1. Set the initial value of state in a constructor, often reading the initial values from this.props:

```
12    constructor (props: ITodoItemProps) {
13      super(props);
14      this.state = {
15          itemDone: this.props.itemDone,
16          itemTitle: this.props.itemTitle,
17          itemId: this.props.itemId,
18          showPanel: false
19      };
20    }
```

2. Our user input should be tied to a `state` property. When the `state` changes, React will call the `render` function to change the user interface accordingly:

```
36    private titleChange(value: string): void {
37        this.setState({ itemTitle: value});
```

3. When *lifting the state*, call the parent components function via `this.props`. This child component is only responsible for a single item--it doesn't worry about the whole list:

```
79        <DefaultButton
80          onClick={this.closePanel.bind(this)}>
81          Cancel
82        </DefaultButton>
```

4. When rendering React components, use `props` to bind `this` of the event handling functions into this instance of the component:

```
84        <CommandButton
85          iconProps={{iconName:"Remove"}}
86          onClick={this.deleteClick.bind(this)}>
87          Delete this item
88        </CommandButton>
```

5. In case, you need to communicate information to the bound function, that is not in the `state` but is available in the `render` function, you can do it by following the pattern shown in line 64. We are using an arrow function, but adding another parameter to it. In this case, it doesn't make real sense, as `itemId` is already known from a `state` property, but be aware of this possibility in case you run into a situation where you need it:

```
62    <CommandButton
63      iconProps={{iconName: resolvedIconName}}
64      onClick={(e) => this.itemClicked(e,this.props.itemId)}>
65      {this.props.itemTitle}</CommandButton>
```

Summary

This chapter gave us a deep dive into React and Office UI Fabric React. We went through all the key building blocks of React and tried to understand how it works through declarative UI, reusable components, and props and state of each component. We also discussed how to communicate information back to parent components. All this information was showcased in the to-do list web part.

In the next chapter, we'll work with other JavaScript frameworks that you might already be using, but this time with SharePoint Framework.

10
Working with Other JavaScript Frameworks

In this chapter, you will learn about working with other JavaScript frameworks in addition to React and Office React components. We'll discuss at a general level what we need to take into account when using different JavaScript frameworks and libraries.

One of the main changes in SharePoint Framework, compared to the model of software distribution Microsoft has given to SharePoint developers, is embracing the open source and giving the developer liberty to choose whatever framework or library he or she wants to use. One of the problems with previous SharePoint development approaches is that we have felt isolated from the broader development community, particularly in the world of web development. The SharePoint Framework is flexible enough to allow a developer in the future to be able to use new JavaScript tools and frameworks that don't yet exist.

In this chapter, you'll do the following:

- Learn how to use jQuery inside SharePoint Framework
- Take a deep dive inside the Knockout web part in order to understand how this library works with SharePoint Framework web parts
- Discuss AngularJS and Angular and what you need to take into consideration if you want to use these web app frameworks in your projects
- Learn a great deal about SharePoint PnP JavaScript Core Library and how to use it from SharePoint Framework solutions
- Learn how to use JavaScript libraries without existing type definitions

Overview

There are a few important considerations you face when you start using third-party frameworks and libraries in your SharePoint Framework web parts. First, you must take TypeScript type definitions, which will allow you to use tools like Intellisense, into account and then you need to decide whether you want to load the external dependencies from CDN or you want to bundle them to your web part.

One of the strengths of TypeScript is type definitions, and when you include third-party libraries and frameworks to your project, it is best to go with the libraries that have type definitions available. With the constantly evolving world of modern web development, this will likely give you a headache at some point. There are versions of libraries and libraries with mismatching type definition versions. Also, the version of TypeScript can come into play because SharePoint Framework is using one version of TypeScript and type definitions available to third-party frameworks or libraries can be compiled with the newer version of TypeScript. In this case, you need to do some troubleshooting and specify the versions you want to use as type definitions as well as which library or framework version you are using.

Loading something from CDN instead of bundling it to your web part is almost always a better choice, but it will add a dependency to the CDN service in question. The CDN service needs to be trustworthy and reliable. A good CDN service is faster than SharePoint Online when the client is downloading the library, and using CDN services, in general, will make your compiled web part JavaScript file a lot lighter and faster to load for the user.

Using jQuery in SharePoint framework web parts

For some developers, jQuery is an integral part of JavaScript development. From a broader perspective, jQuery is just a DOM manipulation library, but the popularity of the library is unquestionable. With only a few lines of code, jQuery allows developers to handle DOM manipulation, event handling, and Ajax calls in a very simplified manner. Using jQuery helps developers write browser independent code, although this is not a significant advantage in SharePoint Framework development since TypeScript already does that.

The obvious downside is that by loading external frameworks, such as jQuery, you're effectively adding to the overall page payload, which in turn might not be helpful in the long run if you only use jQuery for a simple feature.

Loading jQuery from CDN

First, we install typings for jQuery with the following command on the project's root folder:

```
npm install --save @types/jquery@2.0.48
```

Next, open the `config.json` and add the following external dependency:

```
"jquery": "https://code.jquery.com/jquery-2.2.4.min.js"
```

The hard part with jQuery is matching the jQuery version to the typings version close enough not to give you an additional headache. At the time of writing this book, you can't really use the latest 3.x versions of the typings because they are compiled with a newer version of TypeScript than what SharePoint Framework is using.

When you want to use jQuery in a TypeScript file, add the following `import` statement:

```
import * as $ from "jquery";
```

At this point, we are able to actually write jQuery statements on our web parts. The following example will first render standard `HelloWorld` web part contents and then, when the document is fully loaded, we use the jQuery selector to find `div` with a `class` defined in `styles.helloFrameworks` and replace the contents of the elements with hello world text:

```
17    public render(): void {
18      this.domElement.innerHTML = `
19        <div class="${styles.helloFrameworks}">
20          <div class="${styles.container}">
21            <div class="ms-Grid-row ms-bgColor-themeDark ms-fontColor-white ${styles.row}">
22              <div class="ms-Grid-col ms-u-lg10 ms-u-xl8 ms-u-xlPush2 ms-u-lgPush1">...
29              </div>
30            </div>
31          </div>
32        </div>`;
33      $(document).ready(() => {
34        $("."+styles.helloFrameworks).html("Hello World from jQuery!");
35      });
36    }
```

Bundling jQuery to the web part package

If you want to bundle jQuery to your web part package, use npm to save it as part of the package. If you choose to load jQuery from a CDN, you might accidentally use the wrong version.

```
npm install jquery@2.2.4 --save
npm install @types/jquery@2.0.48 --save
```

Again, pay attention to the versions you are using. If you try to load the latest version, everything may seem to be working just fine:

```
C:\Users\olli\hello-frameworks2>npm install jquery --save
hello-frameworks-2@0.0.1 C:\Users\olli\hello-frameworks2
`-- jquery@3.2.1

npm WARN optional SKIPPING OPTIONAL DEPENDENCY: fsevents@^1.0.0 (node_modules\chokidar\node_modules\fsevents):
npm WARN notsup SKIPPING OPTIONAL DEPENDENCY: Unsupported platform for fsevents@1.1.2: wanted {"os":"darwin","arch":"any
"} (current: {"os":"win32","arch":"x64"})

C:\Users\olli\hello-frameworks2>npm install @types/jquery --save
hello-frameworks-2@0.0.1 C:\Users\olli\hello-frameworks2
`-- @types/jquery@3.2.9

npm WARN optional SKIPPING OPTIONAL DEPENDENCY: fsevents@^1.0.0 (node_modules\chokidar\node_modules\fsevents):
npm WARN notsup SKIPPING OPTIONAL DEPENDENCY: Unsupported platform for fsevents@1.1.2: wanted {"os":"darwin","arch":"any
"} (current: {"os":"win32","arch":"x64"})
```

But when you actually `import` the type definition file in your web part file and then start the project with `gulp serve`, you could get about a thousand errors:

```
[10:10:52] Starting subtask 'typescript'...
[10:10:52] [typescript] TypeScript version: 2.2.2
[10:10:54] Error - typescript - node_modules\@types\jQuery\index.d.ts(40,46): error TS1005: ',' expected.
[10:10:54] Error - typescript - node_modules\@types\jQuery\index.d.ts(130,27): error TS1005: ',' expected.
[10:10:54] Error - typescript - node_modules\@types\jQuery\index.d.ts(2896,12): error TS1005: ',' expected.
[10:10:54] Error - typescript - node_modules\@types\jQuery\index.d.ts(2896,23): error TS1005: ',' expected.
[10:10:54] Error - typescript - node_modules\@types\jQuery\index.d.ts(2896,34): error TS1005: ',' expected.
[10:10:54] Error - typescript - node_modules\@types\jQuery\index.d.ts(2910,12): error TS1005: ',' expected.
[10:10:54] Error - typescript - node_modules\@types\jQuery\index.d.ts(2910,23): error TS1005: ',' expected.
[10:10:54] Error - typescript - node_modules\@types\jQuery\index.d.ts(2923,12): error TS1005: ',' expected.
[10:10:54] Error - typescript - node_modules\@types\jQuery\index.d.ts(2923,25): error TS1005: ',' expected.
[10:10:54] Error - typescript - node_modules\@types\jQuery\index.d.ts(2933,18): error TS1005: ',' expected.
[10:10:54] Error - typescript - node_modules\@types\jQuery\index.d.ts(2942,13): error TS1005: ',' expected.
[10:10:54] Error - typescript - node_modules\@types\jQuery\index.d.ts(2942,26): error TS1005: ',' expected.
[10:10:54] Error - typescript - node_modules\@types\jQuery\index.d.ts(2954,39): error TS1005: ',' expected.
```

To clear out the errors, uninstall jQuery and the type definitions and try again with different versions:

```
npm uninstall @types/jquery --save
npm uninstall jquery --save
gulp clean
```

Knockout

Knockout (`http://knockoutjs.com`) is a good option if you want to use a **Model-View-ViewModel** (**MVVM**) approach to building your web parts. The fundamental difference between MVVM and other MVx patterns is that View and ViewModel are linked by data-binding. Following the MVVM pattern, Knockout separates the development of a UI in the form of an HTML template from the business logic (the data model). In practice, this means that there is a model (HTML template), view (TypeScript class), and binder (Knockout internal code) that work together to achieve a UI reflecting the changes in the data. Knockout is really just a data-binding library rather than a full framework in its own right.

Microsoft's SharePoint Yeoman template includes the possibility to build a `HelloWorld` web part using Knockout and it is the best place for us to start. Create the web part as any web part, but this time select `Knockout` as a framework:

Let's examine how Knockout works in SharePoint Framework. First, open `HelloKnockoutWebPart.ts` and compare the differences to the regular no-framework version of the file. In line 1, the `knockout` library is imported as `ko` and in 10, `HelloKnockoutViewModel` is imported. Also, note that this web part keeps account of the `_instance` number in line 13:

```
1    import * as ko from 'knockout';
2    import { Version } from '@microsoft/sp-core-library';
3  ⊟ import {
4       BaseClientSideWebPart,
5       IPropertyPaneConfiguration,
6       PropertyPaneTextField
7    } from '@microsoft/sp-webpart-base';
8
9    import * as strings from 'helloKnockoutStrings';
10   import HelloKnockoutViewModel, { IHelloKnockoutBindingContext } from './HelloKnockoutViewModel';
11   import { IHelloKnockoutWebPartProps } from './IHelloKnockoutWebPartProps';
12
13   let _instance: number = 0;
```

The actual web part class has a few differences as well. Properties `_id`, `_componentElement`, and `_koDescription` are defined in lines 16 to 18, and a `_shouter` object is created at line 23:

```
15   export default class HelloKnockoutWebPart extends BaseClientSideWebPart<IHelloKnockoutWebPartProps> {
16      private _id: number;
17      private _componentElement: HTMLElement;
18      private _koDescription: KnockoutObservable<string> = ko.observable('');
19
20      /**
21       * Shouter is used to communicate between web part and view model.
22       */
23      private _shouter: KnockoutSubscribable<{}> = new ko.subscribable();
```

The `onInit` function is taking care of housekeeping, tracking the web part instance number, creating `this._componentElement`, and saving the web part's property `description` value to `this._koDescription` property, as well as taking care of the all required Knockout subscriptions and bindings:

```
28    protected onInit(): Promise<void> {
29      this._id = _instance++;
30
31      const tagName: string = `ComponentElement-${this._id}`;
32      this._componentElement = this._createComponentElement(tagName);
33      this._registerComponent(tagName);
34
35      // When web part description is changed, notify view model to update.
36      this._koDescription.subscribe((newValue: string) => {
37        this._shouter.notifySubscribers(newValue, 'description');
38      });
39
40      const bindings: IHelloKnockoutBindingContext = {
41        description: this.properties.description,
42        shouter: this._shouter
43      };
44
45      ko.applyBindings(bindings, this._componentElement);
46
47      return super.onInit();
48    }
```

Our `render` function will create the component element if needed and take care that any changes to web part's description property are reflected in `this._koDescription`:

```
50    public render(): void {
51      if (!this.renderedOnce) {
52        this.domElement.appendChild(this._componentElement);
53      }
54
55      this._koDescription(this.properties.description);
56    }
```

Finally, examine the `_registerComponent` function. In essence, it will combine the view model and HTML template file together:

```
64    private _registerComponent(tagName: string): void {
65      ko.components.register(
66        tagName,
67        {
68          viewModel: HelloKnockoutViewModel,
69          template: require('./HelloKnockout.template.html'),
70          synchronous: false
71        }
72      );
73    }
```

Now, open `HelloKnockoutViewModel.ts` and examine the class definition. The `description` property is defined as `ko.observable` but the other properties are basically constants but available in the HTML template file:

```
9   export default class HelloKnockoutViewModel {
10    public description: KnockoutObservable<string> = ko.observable('');
11
12    public labelClass: string = styles.label;
13    public helloKnockoutClass: string = styles.helloKnockout;
14    public containerClass: string = styles.container;
15    public rowClass: string = `ms-Grid-row ms-bgColor-themeDark ms-fontColor-white ${styles.row}`;
16    public buttonClass: string = `ms-Button ${styles.button}`;
17
18    constructor(bindings: IHelloKnockoutBindingContext) {
19      this.description(bindings.description);
20
21      // When web part description is updated, change this view model's description.
22      bindings.shouter.subscribe((value: string) => {
23        this.description(value);
24      }, this, 'description');
25    }
26  }
```

Finally, open the `HelloKnockout.template.html` file and examine its contents. As you can see, this file is rather a standard HTML markup. The only notable difference is the `data-bind` attributes which include references to data values following the notation used by Knockout:

```
1   <div data-bind="attr: {class:helloKnockoutClass}">
2     <div data-bind="attr: {class:containerClass}">
3       <div data-bind="attr: {class:rowClass}">
4         <div class="ms-Grid-col ms-u-lg10 ms-u-xl8 ms-u-xlPush2 ms-u-lgPush1">
5           <span class="ms-font-xl ms-fontColor-white">Welcome to SharePoint!</span>
6           <p class="ms-font-l ms-fontColor-white">Customize SharePoint experiences using Web Parts.</p>
7           <p class="ms-font-l ms-fontColor-white" data-bind="text:description"></p>
8           <a href="https://aka.ms/spfx" data-bind="attr: {class:buttonClass}">
9             <span data-bind="attr: {class:labelClass}">Learn more</span>
10          </a>
11        </div>
12      </div>
13    </div>
14  </div>
```

As we can see, using Knockout requires a few special tweaks compared to aq no-framework approach or the way React is used with SharePoint Framework. If you are new to Knockout, these may seem complex, but as you work your way through building more complex web parts, you will learn that this is just the way you control how Knockout takes care of the view model and how it is presented in the UI. Further reading for Knockout is available at `http://learn.knockoutjs.com/`.

AngularJS and Angular

AngularJS (also known as angular.js or angular.js 1.X) is a full SPA (Single Page Application) framework and popular open-source JavaScript web application framework mainly maintained by Google. It broadly follows the **Model-View-Controller** (**MVC**) pattern to separate presentation, data, and logic components. It uses scoping, bootstrapping and two-way data binding. The latest version of AngularJS at the time of the writing is 1.6.4.

In 2014, the Angular team decided to embark on a rewrite, and originally called it Angular 2. Now, Angular 4 is often referred to as just *Angular*. Angular is not backward compatible with Angular1/AngularJS and is fundamentally different in design. Angular (also known as Angular 2 or Angular 2+) is a complete rewrite from the same team that wrote AngularJS. It doesn't use scoping but hierarchical components, has simpler expression syntax, is more modular and aimed to serve modern browsers, and actually recommends the use of Microsoft's TypeScript. Angular is also written using TypeScript. The latest version of Angular at the time of the writing is 4.2.4.

If you are new to AngularJS and/or Angular, you must understand that these two share the name but are different frameworks, and they are both alive and evolving. When reading information about one, it only applies to that given framework and the topic could be completely different in the other.

If you take a look at the SharePoint Framework web part samples available at `https://github.com/SharePoint/sp-dev-fx-webparts/tree/master/samples`, you will find a number of AngularJS web parts but, at the time of writing, only one Angular web part. Microsoft has chosen React to build OOB web parts and modern pages because they had to focus on one approach for consistency in their internal development. Inevitably this has meant that there are more samples for React than Angular in the Microsoft documentation. This does not mean that AngularJS is a bad choice or is not supported. This doesn't make things easy for Angular developers and it just highlights the fact that in this case you just can't rely on the latest version of a framework. Much of the existing work is done with AngularJS, and it will be used in the future as well.

Use the following commands if you want to include AngularJS in your project as bundled content. Note that we need to refer to AngularJS as `angular`:

```
npm install angular --save
npm install @types/angular --save
```

AngularJS applications are made of controllers and data services. Controllers control how the application behaves and data services control the access to the data, for example, to SharePoint list. AngularJS applications always include the scope on which they are run. Different web parts on the same page have the same application but work in a different scope.

In-depth coverage of AngularJS and Angular is out of the scope of this book. We recommend that you familiarize yourself with the sample web parts at GitHub and, for example, blog posts by *Waldek Mastykarz*:

- `https://github.com/SharePoint/sp-dev-fx-webparts/tree/master/samples`
  `https://blog.mastykarz.nl/building-sharepoint-framework-client-side-web-parts-angular/`

Using SharePoint patterns and practices JavaScript Core Library

One of the most useful libraries for SharePoint Framework developers is SharePoint PnP JavaScript Core Library. This library was created to help SharePoint developers work with SharePoint content, simplifying the common operations with a REST wrapper required in most SharePoint applications. It has a simple and powerful API, which uses SharePoint REST API under the hood, but makes operations very easy and as straightforward as possible. It also includes a number of utility and helper functions. The library is currently in version 2.0.

To install SharePoint PnP JavaScript Core Library to your SharePoint Framework project, we use the following command in the project's root folder:

```
npm install sp-pnp-js --save
```

In the TypeScript file, we want to use the library. We insert the following import statement:

```
import pnp from "sp-pnp-js";
```

Now, we are able to utilize the library in a rather straightforward, promise-based pattern:

```
public render(): void {
  this.domElement.innerHTML = `<p>Loading...</p>`;
    pnp.sp.web.get().then((web: any) => {
      const webTitle: string = web.Title;
      const webUrl: string = web.Url;
      const webTemplate: string = web.WebTemplate;
      this.domElement.innerHTML =
        `<p>webTitle: ${webTitle}</p>
          <p>webUrl: ${webUrl}</p>
          <p>webTemplate: ${webTemplate}</p>`;
    });
}
```

As you can see, we are accessing the current web and reading some its properties to be able to show them inside the web part:

You can also use TypeScript types defined in our code. It starts by referencing what you need in the `import` statement:

```
import { Web } from "sp-pnp-js";
```

Then, you can use the actual typed objects in your code and gain Intellisense support. In addition to just querying of the data, you can also do `update` statements:

```
const web: Web = new Web("https://opax.sharepoint.com/pnp");
web.update({Title: "PnP JS Core Library Rules!"}).then(() => {
  console.log("Site title updated.");
});
```

Next, we are going to go through some of the basic operations when working with SharePoint PnP JavaScript Core Library.

Accessing user profiles

We can access the user profile of the current user through `pnp.sp.profiles.myProperties`:

```
public render(): void {
  this.domElement.innerHTML = `<p>Loading...</p>`;
  pnp.sp.profiles.myProperties.get().then((userProfile: any) => {
    const userCard: string =
      `<div>
        <a href="${userProfile.PersonalUrl}">
```

```
            ${userProfile.DisplayName}
        </a>
      </div>`;
    this.domElement.innerHTML = userCard;
  });
}
```

Sending email

It is possible and easy to send email using SharePoint PnP JavaScript Core Library. You can do it by defining an object based on the `EmailProperties` interface, and send it using the `utility.sendEmail` function:

```
const emailProperties: EmailProperties = {
    To: ["olli@opax.onmicrosoft.com"],
    CC: [],
    Subject: "Testing PnP JavaScript send email functionality",
    Body: "This email has been sent using JavaScript",
};
pnp.sp.utility.sendEmail(emailProperties).then(() => {
    this.domElement.innerHTML = `<p>Email has been sent.</p>`;
});
```

This function doesn't send the email as the user in whose context we are working but as SharePoint Online system. You don't have to be tenant admin to send this email:

Testing PnP JavaScript send email functionality

OI Onsight Intranet <no-reply@sharepointonline.com>
    Today, 10:33 AM
    Olli Jääskeläinen ⌄

    This email has been sent using JavaScript

A word of caution here: based on our testing, this functionality currently only works on classic SharePoint sites but not in modern Team Sites. It is also highly likely that the email will not appear in the focused email box but can end up in clutter or even spam folders. Also, while we could send an email from one tenant to another, sending outside Office 365 doesn't seem to work. Under the hood, SharePoint PnP JavaScript Core Library is using REST endpoint `/_api/sp.utilities.utility.sendemail`, which you can also use without the library.

Working with lists and list items

There are multiple ways to access lists and they all start from the `Web` object. You can access a list if you know the list's web relative URL address, title, or ID:

```
// get list by web relative url
pnp.sp.web.getList("/Shared Documents").get().then((list: List) => {
  console.log(list);
});

// get list by title
pnp.sp.web.lists.getByTitle("Documents").get().then((list: List) => {
  console.log(list);
});

// get list by id
pnp.sp.web.lists.getById("267acf5a-151b-4dbf-
b65b-545ed382a425").get().then((list: List) => {
  console.log(list);
});
```

In the previous example, we are using the `console.log` object, which is an excellent way to examine the returned object. You can easily find out all of the properties of the object via your browser's developer tools **Console** window:

In some cases, we need to change the type of the returned object to `any`, in order to actually access all properties. For example, `list.AllowContentTypes` is not visible if you are using the object as List. This is because not all properties are defined in the type definition used by this library:

```
pnp.sp.web.lists.getById("267acf5a-151b-4dbf-
b65b-545ed382a425").get().then((list: any) => {
    console.log(list.AllowContentTypes);
});
```

We can easily create new lists and modify their settings or the settings of the existing lists. In the next example, we will create a new custom list and then modify it to allow content types:

```
pnp.sp.web.lists.add("Custom List 1").then((value: ListAddResult) => {
    value.list.update({"AllowContentTypes": true, "ContentTypesEnabled":
true}).then(() => {
        console.log("List created and then modified to allow the use of content
types.");
    });
});
```

Naturally, we can also delete lists:

```
pnp.sp.web.lists.getByTitle("Custom 1").delete().then(() => {
  console.log("List deleted.");
});
```

There are multiple ways to access list items. The most straightforward are using the `items` property of the `list` object. It is reasonable as long as there are only a few list items in the list. If your list has hundreds of list items, this is not a viable pattern for accessing them:

```
pnp.sp.web.lists.getByTitle("Custom 1").items.get().then((items: any[]) =>
{
  items.forEach(element => {
    console.log(element.Title);
  });
});
```

The best method for accessing items depends on the item count (accessible via `List.ItemCount`) and the use of metadata fields. In cases where you really need to iterate through items, and there hundreds of items to go through, you can use the `getPaged` function of the list's items property to access the items in workable batches. The paged item collection has two properties, `results` containing the list items of the current page and `hasNext` indicating whether there are more results available. In that case, you can go retrieve them using the `getNext` function. Even in this case, you should only call `getNext` when the user needs the next items, for example, when she or he clicks the next page icon, to keep the network load minimum and user experience as smooth as possible:

```
109   pnp.sp.web.lists.getByTitle("Custom 1").items.getPaged().then((pagedItems: PagedItemCollection<any>) =>
110     pagedItems.
111   });        🔾 getNext              (method) PagedItemCollection<any>.getN  ×
112              🔾 hasNext              ext(): Promise<PagedItemCollection<any
113   }          🔾 results              >>
114   protected get dataVersion(): Version {
115     return Version.parse('1.0');    Gets the next set of results, or resolves to null if no
116   }                                  results are available
```

Using metadata queries is the usual way to limit the retrieved list items to only those we are really interested in. SharePoint PnP JavaScript Core Library offers two different alternatives to achieve this.

The first way is to utilize OData filters. In the following example, we are adding first OData parameter `top`, using it as a function to state that we are interested only in one item, and then setting a `filter` that the `title` field value must equal the string we are providing. This will still result in an array, although there will only be one item in the array. Sometimes, our queries will result in multiple items and we might need to go through them page by page as in the previous example:

```
pnp.sp.web.lists.getByTitle("Custom 1").items.top(1).filter("Title eq
'First item'").get().then((items: any[]) => {
  items.forEach(item => {
    console.log("item.Title = " + item.Title);
  });
});
```

The other way to query list items is CAML query. This is an old way of retrieving SharePoint list items. For the most part, CAML queries are helpful for backward compatibility, using SharePoint specific XML schema to build queries for list items. However, it is possible that some very specific queries can only be achieved via CAML, and thus we need to know that we have the option. To do a CAML query, first create an object with the `ViewXml` property and then pass it as an argument to the `list.getItemsByCAMLQuery` function:

```
const camlQuery: CamlQuery = {
  ViewXml: "<View><Query><Where><Eq><FieldRef Name='Title' /><Value
Type='Text'>Second item</Value></Eq></Where></Query></View>"
};
pnp.sp.web.lists.getByTitle("Custom
1").getItemsByCAMLQuery(camlQuery).then((items: any[]) => {
  items.forEach(item => {
    console.log("item.Title = " + item.Title);
  });
});
```

To add a new list item, we use the same pattern that we did when we were creating a new list to the web's collection of lists. We call the `add` function and provide list item metadata as the property object collection in the arguments:

```
pnp.sp.web.lists
  .getByTitle("Custom 1").items
  .add({ Title: "New item added via code."})
  .then((value: ItemAddResult) => {
    console.log(value);
  });
```

You can also add a batch of list items with a single REST query when we need to improve performance. Batching actually works in many situations when you are working with SharePoint data and using SharePoint PnP JavaScript Core Library. It allows us to execute changes in a single query, making our code very effective. First, we create a batch object, and then we use a special `inBatch(batch)` function to add multiple items without actually executing the query. Finally, we execute the query using the `batch.execute` function:

```
let batch: any = pnp.sp.web.createBatch();
const list: any = pnp.sp.web.lists.getByTitle("Custom 1");
let i: number;
for (i = 1; i <= 10; i++) {
  list.items.inBatch(batch)
  .add({ Title: "New item "+i+" added via code."})
  .then(() => {
    console.log(i);
  });
}
batch.execute().then(()=> {
  console.log("Added 10 items as single batch.");
});
```

Updating list items work in a similar fashion. We first get the specific item we want to update and then call the `update` function supplying the changes as an argument:

```
pnp.sp.web.lists.getByTitle("Custom 1").items
  .getById(1)
  .update({Title: "Updated list item title"})
  .then(() => {
    console.log("List item updated.");
  });
}
```

Deleting list items, again, follows the same pattern as when we were working with lists. First, we get the specific item we want to delete and then we call the `delete` function:

```
pnp.sp.web.lists.getByTitle("Custom 1").items
  .getById(2)
  .delete().then(() => {
    console.log("List item deleted.");
  });
}
```

You can see that working with list items using SharePoint PnP JavaScript Core Library is rather straightforward. The code we write is quite short. Using asynchronous REST calls using the `then` function makes the code more readable and easier to understand. There is a lot of nesting sometimes we do operation after operation, which all might be asynchronous, and this only works in the simple execution flow of the code. Try to make your code simple by avoiding too complex loops with multiple asynchronous calls.

Working with JavaScript libraries

As an example, how we make a third-party JavaScript library work with SharePoint Framework and TypeScript, we use a simple but useful library called `Markup.js` by Adman Mark. This is a simple templating library which converts JavaScript objects into HTML. You can find the library on GitHub: `https://github.com/adammark/Markup.js/`. This library does not come with typing but we can create our own.

We can use npm to install the package as part of our web parts. Type the following command to Command Prompt when you are in the root folder of the project:

```
npm install markup-js --save
```

We need to add a type definition file to make Intellisense and type-checking work in our web part project. Luckily, this is very simple because `Markup.js` only has one function. Add a new file called `markup-js.d.ts` in the `typings` folder of the web part project with the following contents:

```
declare module "Mark" {
  function up(context: any, template: string): string
}
```

We are declaring module `Mark` with a single function called `up`. This function has two parameters: `context`, of the type `any`, because it can be really just about anything, and `template`, which is a `string`. The function returns a `string` variable. If you are using a more complex JavaScript library, you need to do a lot more work with the type definition file. If the library in question is something you work for yourself, you might want to transform it to TypeScript instead, but now we are simply using this nice JavaScript library which needs minimal type definition.

For example, the context could be a collection of list items, and the template defines that those list items are shown in an HTML list:

```
public render(): void {
  let context: any = {
    list: {
      Title: "Sample list",
      ItemCount: 3
    },
    listItems: [
      { ID: 1, Title: "First item"},
      { ID: 2, Title: "Second item"},
      { ID: 3, Title: "Third item"},
    ]
  };
  let template: string = "<h3>{{list.Title}}
({{list.ItemCount}})</h3><ul>{{listItems}}<li>{{Title}}</li>{{/listItems}}<
/ul>";
  let result:string = Mark.up(template, context);
  this.domElement.innerHTML = result;
}
```

Which will render nicely with this small library? Context can include multiple different objects which are referenced in the template. You can use repeating elements like list items and render them as you want. This is just a very quick demonstration how `Markup.js` works:

Please note that we are using Markup.js as an example and not saying that you should use it rather than other options we have presented to create HTML markup. We are simply using this library as an example of how to work with third-party JavaScript libraries.

Additional considerations

In order to fulfill business requirements with limited resources, we are often in situations where using third-party libraries and frameworks makes a lot of sense. Depending on the experience of the developers and the expectations of the customer, we will end up choosing a specific framework or set of libraries. Some of them are very easy to incorporate to SharePoint Framework, like React and Fabric React as well as AngularJS or Angular 1+. Others might work just as well, but the lack of guidance and examples might steer us away from them. Experience in both using the specific frameworks or libraries and SharePoint Framework will guide us through, and you will learn by doing and resolving issues when needed.

Among the first questions we face is whether to bundle your project or not. If the source files are very small, it is probably easiest and most convenient to bundle the libraries or frameworks as part of our web part projects. But for bigger libraries or libraries that are used by a variety of solutions, it is much more convenient to load them from CDN services.

The next question is how to deal with TypeScript type definitions of third-party libraries. Luckily, they are available for the most popular libraries and the problem is solved easily. For some other libraries, we might end up doing some work to get the type definitions working.

In SharePoint Framework, one of the greatest changes from the previous SharePoint development models is the embrace towards open-source development. For example, Microsoft is using React, a library built originally for Facebook and Instagram, to build SharePoint web parts. But they are not saying everybody should use React. We can use any library we want. That is a major change, and the greatest benefit is that the development tomorrow is not tied to the technology of today.

Summary

This chapter gave us an overview of how to use different JavaScript libraries and frameworks in SharePoint Framework solutions. Utilizing existing libraries and frameworks requires a lot of planning.

In this chapter, you learned how to use jQuery in SharePoint Framework solutions. We can now load the jQuery from CDN or bundle it as part of our web part project. The benefit of using jQuery is that it will save a lot of time for the developer and it is also likely that by saving that time by not writing custom code, the developer will make fewer bugs as well. This, of course, is true of using libraries generally, not just jQuery.

Then, we took a dive into the Knockout HelloWorld web part and examined what it is made of and how data-binding works in the context of SharePoint Framework. Knockout is a nice lightweight library using the MVVM pattern.

We also talked briefly about the basics of AngularJS (Angular 1+) and Angular (Angular 2+). These are two different frameworks, originally made by the same team at Google. Both of them can be made to work with SharePoint Framework, but the guidance to do so with Angular 2+ is currently still lacking. Unfortunately, it is also out of the scope of this book.

Then, we spent some time learning to use SharePoint Patterns and Practices JavaScript Core Library. It is a great open-source library, which allows us to access SharePoint content in our web parts with a minimal amount of code. We can read and update SharePoint web properties, work with the user profiles, send email, and fulfill a lot of other requirements using SharePoint PnP JavaScript Core Library. You learned how to operate with SharePoint lists as well as list items.

Finally, we went through an example of how to incorporate a JavaScript library with no TypeScript type definitions to our SharePoint Framework web part. We used `Markup.js` as an example because it only has one module and one function in that module that needs type definitions to make it work with the TypeScript we use in SharePoint Framework.

In the next chapter, we'll learn some important ways to perform debugging and troubleshooting for your SharePoint Framework code.

11
Troubleshooting and Debugging SharePoint Framework Solutions

In this chapter, we'll first go through the typical troubleshooting tips developers can use to fix certain errors when developing solutions with the SharePoint Framework. As the development model consists of numerous different tools and platforms, including Webpack, Node.js, npm, Yeoman, and Gulp, different issues might arise when you least expect them. Not all possible scenarios are clear enough for debugging, but often times, it is found to be useful to run through the typical troubleshooting approaches if you run into problems.

In addition, we'll show how you can configure the Google Chrome browser and Visual Studio Code for debugging and troubleshooting.

This chapter will teach you to do the following things:

- Performing troubleshooting for the core tools you use with the SharePoint Framework
- Optimizing your code and load libraries externally from CDN
- Using debugging features in VS Code and Chrome

Troubleshooting

Troubleshooting your code, especially when working with SharePoint, is often time-consuming and generally quite complex. You have to factor in the inner workings of SharePoint, possibly Office 365 also, and your code and deployment approach. The following guidance will walk you through the necessary tasks that are especially helpful when working with the toolchain that the SharePoint Framework requires. Occasionally, even if everything seems to be in order, it helps to fix your development environment if you walk through these simple steps.

Ensuring an up-to-date npm

Sometimes, you'll run into unforeseen issues while developing for the SharePoint Framework. These issues might include different errors during your development cycle, such as when you generate a new project with Yeoman.

One of the basic things to do is to update npm, the **Node Package Manager**, that you installed in Chapter 3, *Getting Started with the SharePoint Framework*.

In order to force an update on npm, use npm and run the following command:

```
npm install -g npm
```

This is a simple process, and after it completes, you can verify your npm version with the following command:

```
npm -v
```

At the time of writing this book, the latest stable version of npm was *5.4.2:*

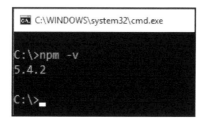

Updating the Yeoman template version

Yeoman generator, which you installed after Node.js and npm, tends to get frequent updates from Microsoft. When developing for SharePoint Online using the SharePoint Framework, you should always choose the latest stable Yeoman templates by running the following command:

```
npm install -g @microsoft/generator-sharepoint
```

This pulls in the latest version from `https://www.npmjs.com/package/@microsoft/generator-sharepoint` and installs the necessary templates.

To verify the current version of Yeoman templates, use the following command:

```
npm list -g | find "sharepoint"
```

This should print out the version number. At the time of writing this book, the latest version was 1.2.0:

If, however, you are aiming to create the SharePoint Framework solutions for SharePoint 2016 that together with SharePoint Feature Pack 2 (FP2) provides limited support for SPFx, you may need to switch to a different version corresponding to the version of the Yeoman templates.

First, you'll need to verify which version of Yeoman templates is supported at the time of installation. This might very well be the latest version, thus, no action is needed. It might also be a different version from SharePoint Online's required version, which presumably is the latest stable version.

Before switching to the Yeoman template version, you will need to uninstall the currently installed version with the following command:

```
npm uninstall  -g @microsoft/generator-sharepoint
```

Next, you can install a specific version of Yeoman template by specifying the exact version with the following syntax:

```
npm install -g @microsoft/generator-sharepoint@1.0.2
```

The `1.02` stands for version, and at the time of writing, this is the version that is supported with **SharePoint 2016 Feature Pack 2**. For SharePoint Online, you should always go with the latest version--at the time of writing, this was *1.2.0*.

After installing an older version, you can once again verify your currently installed version with the following command:

```
npm list -g | find "sharepoint"
```

This should print out the specific version, such as `@microsoft/generator-sharepoint@1.0.2`.

Troubleshooting the npm cache

Sometimes, you run into weird-looking errors with npm or while serving your solutions with Gulp. Since version 5, npm cache has had a self-healing mechanism that guarantees data to be valid.

If you need to verify that the npm cache is intact, run the following command:

```
npm cache verify
```

This prints out the verification statistics:

```
C:\>npm cache verify
Cache verified and compressed (~\AppData\Roaming\npm-cache\_cacache):
Content verified: 2010 (51567153 bytes)
Index entries: 3125
Finished in 6.945s
```

You should never need to clean the npm cache, other than to free up more disk space. You can force the cache to empty its contents with the following command:

```
npm cache clean --force
```

Run `verify` once again to verify that the cache was cleaned:

```
C:\>npm cache verify
Cache verified and compressed (~\AppData\Roaming\npm-cache\_cacache):
Content verified: 0 (0 bytes)
Index entries: 0
Finished in 0.017s
```

Optimization

Ever since developers moved to more managed development languages, such as C# and .NET in general, the need for optimization has become less important. This is not to say that optimizing your code is not important--on the contrary, it still is, and it is important to understand as a SharePoint developer that items you implement and package to your solutions will affect the overall page payload for your users. As a developer, this might not seem such a big problem, but considering the fact that your page might get hundreds or thousands of active users, the lack of optimization soon starts to take its toll.

Optimizing the SharePoint Framework packages

When you start building solutions with SPFx, there's a nice way to view what kind of packages you are producing. As part of the toolchain, Microsoft has included Webpack Visualizer, which produces a nice overview of your overall bundle. This overview is accessible under /temp/stats, in a .html file:

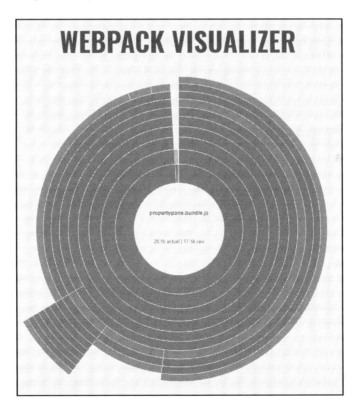

This sample SPFx web part project is about 20 KB without any optimizations.

To deploy code in production, as discussed in Chapter 6, *Packaging and Deploying Solutions*, use the ship parameter with gulp bundle to minify the dependent packages:

```
C:\dropbox\SP\SPFX\propertypane-webpart\temp\stats>gulp bundle --ship
[09:49:40] Working directory changed to C:\dropbox\SP\SPFX\propertypane-webpart

Build target: SHIP
[09:49:42] Using gulpfile C:\dropbox\SP\SPFX\propertypane-webpart\gulpfile.js
[09:49:42] Starting gulp
[09:49:42] Starting 'bundle'...
```

We can see from the preceding output that instead of a DEBUG build, this will be a SHIP build. The **WEBPACK VISUALIZER** now shows an, even more, slimmed-down release:

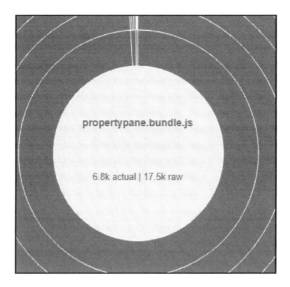

From roughly 20 KB down to 6.8 KB, this is about 65 % smaller with just one command. This is even more evident in larger projects.

Loading external packages

If your project requires external libraries, such as jQuery or similar, commonly used libraries, you might consider loading these from CDN. You can always bundle them within your project, but this means that your packages that are deployed will grow in size. Also, maintaining or updating these external libraries quickly becomes time-consuming, as you need to manually track what version of each library is being loaded on a page.

A solution for this is to load these external libraries from a CDN. The process is quite straightforward:

1. First, install the npm package for your library. In our example, this would be jQuery:

   ```
   npm install jquery --save
   ```

2. Next, run the npm install to ensure that all packages are updated:

   ```
   npm i
   ```

3. Then, open the `config/config.json` file within your project and look up the `externals` portion of the file. Update this to reflect that you'll load jQuery from a CDN, with a `globalName` of `jQuery`. Your external configuration in the file should look like this:

   ```
   "externals": {
   "jquery": {
   "path": "https://code.jquery.com/jquery-2.1.1.min.js",
   "globalName": "jQuery"
   }
   }
   ```

4. Now, open your web part project file and import the following library:

   ```
   import * as $ from 'jquery';
   ```

5. Finally, use jQuery within your code. A simple test would be an alert in your `render()` method:

   ```
   public render(): void {
   $(function(){
   alert('hi');
   });
   ```

6. Run `gulp serve` to verify that your code compiles and loads up in SharePoint Workbench. You should see an alert when the web part is added on the page:

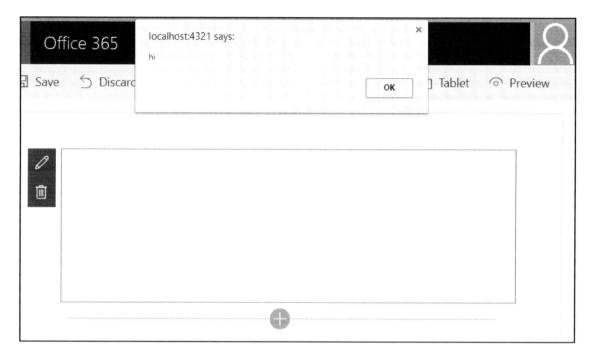

When you now run `gulp bundle -ship`, you can verify that jQuery is not packaged as part of your web part--it is referenced externally.

Debugging solutions

As a developer, you'll often need to debug your code, either while writing it or during deployment. Sometimes, debugging happens at a later stage when your code is already deployed to production and unforeseen issues are found.

With the SharePoint Framework, debugging primarily happens within your browser's developer tools.

Debugger statements using browser developer tools

Debugger statements are an ingenious way to add simple breakpoint-style elements to your code that can be tripped with developer tools in your browser.

1. To start with the debugger statements, add the `debugger;` statement anywhere within your TypeScript code, for example, as soon as you enter the `render()` function:

```
public render(): void {
debugger;
$(function(){
alert('hi');
});
```

2. Run `gulp serve` to bundle the solution and wait for SharePoint Workbench to load.

3. Add the web part on the canvas like you normally would.

4. Press *Ctrl + Shift + I* in Chrome to run Developer Tools.

5. Reload the page to trip over the `debugger;` statement in your code.

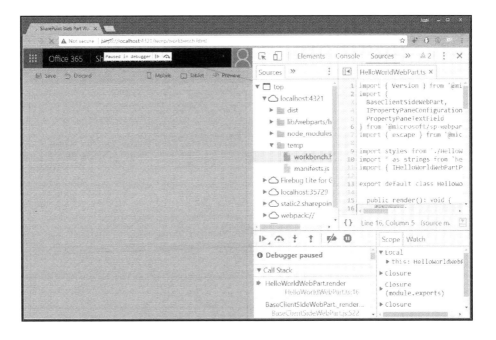

Debugging with source maps

Source maps are a great feature that aid in debugging, especially when your source files might be minified and bundled. You can force the building of a source map for all of your client-side scripts and files, and then navigate the generated map during debugging. They also allow you to enable breakpoints on any file part of your solution without the need to go to Visual Studio Code to try and find out which file and which line you need.

The SharePoint Framework automatically generates source maps, and they are also enabled when you debug code through Visual Studio Code through a separate configuration setting.

When you're running Developer Tools in Chrome, press *F1* to verify that you have JavaScript source maps enabled, as follows:

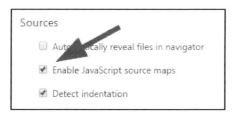

While debugging in Chrome, you can now travel through the sources. This also includes `webpack://` in the source tree that provides you with a fantastic way to reveal what is loaded and where:

You can now travel through all the assets that your web part has loaded. For individual files, you can add breakpoints by double-clicking on a line:

Refreshing the SharePoint Workbench page now captures the breakpoints you've set through source maps:

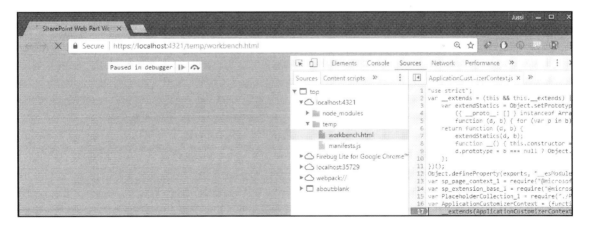

Debugging in Visual Studio Code

There's an extension available for Google Chrome for Visual Studio Code that greatly helps when debugging SPFx projects. To start using the extension, first install it in VS Code:

1. Click on the **EXTENSIONS** pane in VS Code (or press *Ctrl + Shift + X*):

2. Search for **Debugger for Chrome** and click on **Install**. Remember to reload VS Code window by clicking on the reload button to load this new extension.
3. Now, we will need to introduce Chrome debugging for VS Code. Start by clicking on the debug icon on the left (or *Ctrl + Shift + D*):

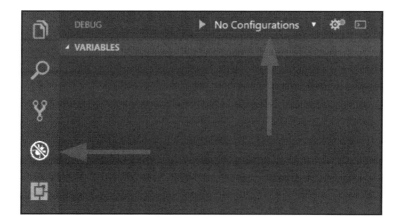

4. Then, click on **No Configurations** and on **Add configuration**:

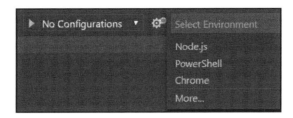

5. Select **Chrome** from the drop-down list.
6. This creates a new `launch.json` configuration file to parametrize the configuration for debugging with Chrome. Remove all contents in the file and replace it with following:

```
{
    "version": "0.2.0",
    "configurations": [
        {
            "name": "Local workbench",
            "type": "chrome",
            "request": "launch",
            "url":
"https://localhost:4321/temp/workbench.html",
            "webRoot": "${workspaceRoot}",
            "sourceMaps": true,
            "sourceMapPathOverrides": {
                "webpack:///../../../src/*":
"${webRoot}/src/*",
                "webpack:///../../../../src/*":
"${webRoot}/src/*",
                "webpack:///../../../../../src/*":
"${webRoot}/src/*"
            },
            "runtimeArgs": [
                "--remote-debugging-port=9222"
            ]
        }
    ]
}
```

7. The configuration adds a new parameter for Chrome, `--remote-debugging-port`, which in turn enables remote debugging in Chrome. With this configuration, we can run Chrome's own remote debugger in one instance and our code in another instance and see the debugging details within the remote debugger.

Once the configuration is done, you can try debugging your code using the following steps:

1. First, configure a new breakpoint in your code. You can choose any line of code for the breakpoint, such as something in the `render()` method of your web part. Press *F9* to insert a breakpoint or click on the left side of the line number:

2. We'll now need to run the project within a local SharePoint Workbench but without a browser instance. When we start debugging, we will have a browser window, thus, the one that `gulp serve` normally executes is not needed. Run the following command:

```
gulp serve --nobrowser
```

3. Start debugging by pressing *F5* in Visual Studio Code. This will now open a Chrome instance with remote debugger enabled and show the **DEBUG** window within VS Code.

4. Switch to the new browser window, and add the web part to the canvas.

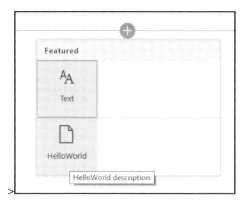

5. Note how the breakpoint lights up in red now when the web part is added to the canvas.

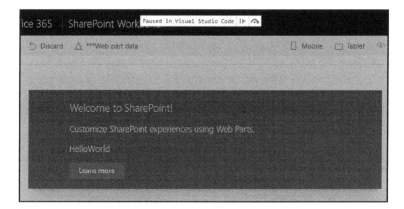

6. Reload SharePoint Workbench by pressing *Ctrl + R* in your browser. The breakpoint is now caught, and VS Code allows you to perform traditional debugging against your code. The code execution within the browser is paused:

Properties of your code are now available for inspection in VS Code:

Call Stack is also visible to aid in debugging:

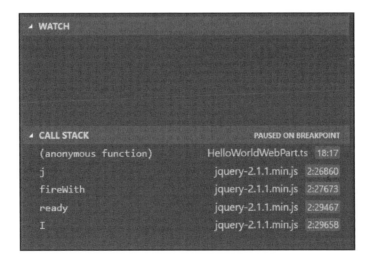

7. When you click on **VARIABLES | Local | this: #document**, you can immediately see a lot of interesting data about your running code:

Debugging with Chrome remote debugging in a locally hosted SharePoint Workbench is a good way to perform the majority of your troubleshooting and code debugging. It is, however, a good practice to also run your code against the hosted SharePoint Workbench in SharePoint Online. You can use the exact same approach, but you'll need to change the `url` property in the `launch.json` to point to `https://{tenant}.sharepoint.com/_layouts/workbench.aspx`.

As you'll typically need both, the `Local workbench` and `Hosted workbench`, for debugging, it's a good idea to add another configuration:

1. Open `launch.json` that you created earlier.
2. Add another configuration under the `configurations` node and name it `Hosted workbench`. Copy the configuration from the `Local workbench` configuration, but change the `url` to reflect SharePoint Online. Your configuration should now look like this:

```
{
  "version": "0.2.0",
  "configurations": [
  {
    "name": "Local workbench",
    "type": "chrome",
    "request": "launch",
    "url": "https://localhost:4321/temp/workbench.html",
    "webRoot": "${workspaceRoot}",
    "sourceMaps": true,
    "sourceMapPathOverrides": {
      "webpack:///../../../src/*": "${webRoot}/src/*",
      "webpack:///../../../../src/*": "${webRoot}/src/*",
      "webpack:///../../../../../src/*": "${webRoot}/src/*"
    },
    "runtimeArgs": [
      "--remote-debugging-port=9222"
    ]
  },
  {
    "name": "Hosted workbench",
    "type": "chrome",
    "request": "launch",
    "url":
"https://{tenant}.sharepoint.com/_layouts/workbench.aspx",
    "webRoot": "${workspaceRoot}",
    "sourceMaps": true,
    "sourceMapPathOverrides": {
      "webpack:///../../../src/*": "${webRoot}/src/*",
      "webpack:///../../../../src/*": "${webRoot}/src/*",
      "webpack:///../../../../../src/*": "${webRoot}/src/*"
    },
    "runtimeArgs": [
      "--remote-debugging-port=9222"
    ]
  }
  ]
```

```
}
```

3. Verify that you now have two debug configurations, **Local workbench** and **Hosted workbench**, in the top drop-down list under VS Code **DEBUG**:

4. If you select **Hosted workbench** and initiate debugging by pressing *F5* in VS Code, a new browser session opens and navigates you directly to SharePoint Online's **Hosted workbench**.

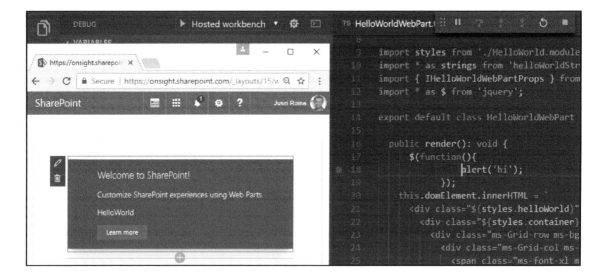

Summary

In this chapter, we took a look at troubleshooting common toolchain issues with the SharePoint Framework. As the framework, along with its hooks into open source tools and platforms continues to evolve rapidly, it is not too uncommon to run into new issues and errors in your projects. The approaches we showed aim to quickly help you isolate the issues and better help you understand why your code does not deploy or compile as expected.

Then, we covered analyzing and optimizing your code primarily through the use of not bundling larger libraries in your deployable package. You can reference these common libraries as external libraries with the use of CDNs.

In addition, we also configured Visual Studio Code to support debugging through Google Chrome with the use of Chrome's remote debugging capabilities. This approach also works for the hosted version of SharePoint Workbench in SharePoint Online.

In the next chapter, we will take a look at security and APIs in SharePoint.

12
SharePoint APIs and Microsoft Graph

In this chapter, we will take a deeper look into SharePoint's APIs, especially the REST APIs. As part of development work, your solutions often need a way to connect with SharePoint directly or get data from other APIs to use within your solutions. It is not often easy to differentiate between the numerous interfaces SharePoint provides, as some still have a strong historical value while others are more recent but might not be as well documented yet. One goal of this chapter is to provide a clear understanding of the different approaches to help you choose when to use which API or approach when integrating your solutions and data with SharePoint.

In this chapter, you'll learn the following topics:

- How and where SharePoint APIs reside
- How to access SharePoint through REST APIs directly and use the SharePoint **Client-Side Object Model (CSOM)** SDK
- What Microsoft Graph is
- How to access Microsoft Graph from SharePoint Framework

SharePoint APIs

SharePoint has, for the better part of its history, been very supportive of customization and providing access through the use of APIs. This, in turn, has resulted in numerous ways that help developers to read, write, and modify data stored within SharePoint, regardless of whether this is SharePoint Online or an on-premises SharePoint server.

Before SharePoint Online was available, the APIs within SharePoint were where mostly older SOAP-based web services reside under the `/_vti_bin/` virtual directories in SharePoint. One such older web service is `listdata.svc`, which is located under `/_vti_bin/listdata.svc`. Although some of these are still available even with SharePoint 2016, one should not rely on them, as they are mostly provided for backward compatibility and either deprecated or a newer (and typically better) interface is available.

SharePoint REST APIs

For SharePoint Online, API support is a bit of a mess. On one hand, developers can directly access most REST-based APIs from `https://{tenant}.sharepoint.com/_api/`, and when they develop solutions, this is often a valid way of directly communicating with SharePoint.

All APIs available through REST are documented at `https://dev.office.com`, and a more comprehensive walk-through of constructing the API addresses is found at `https://dev.office.com/sharepoint/docs/sp-add-ins/get-to-know-the-sharepoint-rest-service`.

Figuring out the API locations is quite easy, as they all follow the same patterns. The base address (`https://{tenant}.sharepoint.com`) is always the same. By adding `/_api/`, we can then choose what scope of data we will need to access. The available scopes are the **site** for a site collection and the **web** for a single SharePoint site. They map directly to the server-side object model naming conventions, where `SPSite` is the site collection and `SPWeb` is a single site.

The way to access these APIs is to use plain old HTTP operations toward APIs under these two scopes. The APIs currently supported are listed at `https://msdn.microsoft.com/en-us/library/office/jj860569.aspx#Reference`, and as you can see from the list, all major operations in SharePoint are supported and accessible.

An example API location would be `https://{tenant}.sharepoint.com/_api/web/webs`, which lists all subsites in a given SharePoint Online site collection. You can call this URL directly in your browser if you first access your SharePoint Online site at `https://{tenant}.sharepoint.com` to get a valid authentication token.

You can call the APIs with your preferred approach. Typically, a good practice is to employ SharePoint Online Client Components SDK, which is frequently updated and published as a NuGet package. This, however, calls against the SOAP-based web services through CSOM and acts as a wrapper to hide the complexity of the SharePoint API's. You can obtain its latest package from `https://www.nuget.org/packages/Microsoft.SharePointOnline.CSOM/`.

Accessing SharePoint Online with CSOM using a console app

Before we construct our calls directly to the REST APIs SharePoint exposes, let's do a quick exercise using the traditional CSOM approach. This is part of the SDK, and depending on your usage, it will access SharePoint through the SOAP-based Web Services, such as `sites.asmx` that resides in `/_vti_bin/sites.asmx`.

Let's try creating a simple console application first to see how things were working until now:

1. Open Visual Studio 2015/2017 and create a new project from **File** | **New** | **Project...**:

2. Select a **Console App** from the list of available templates, as follows:

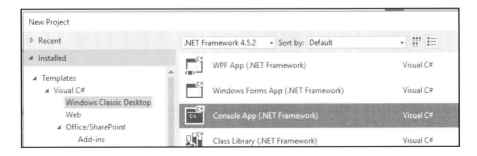

3. Name the app as you like, and click **OK**.

4. If you choose C# as the programming language, a `Program.cs` open with a skeleton class. You'll need to get the SharePoint Online Client Components SDK first; to do it, click on **Tools** |**NuGet Package Manager** | **Package Manager Console**:

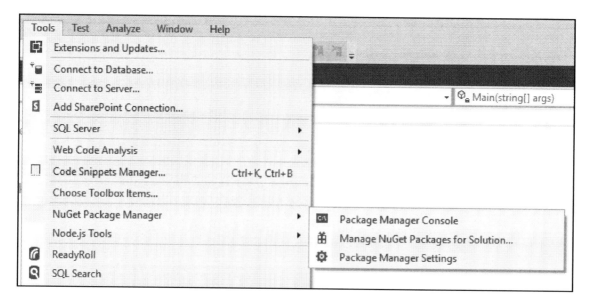

5. The **Package Manager Console** opens in a separate window; by default, it opens in the bottom area of Visual Studio. Type the following command to initiate the installation of the Client Components SDK for your project:

```
Install-Package Microsoft.SharePointOnline.CSOM
```

6. If you're not sure what the NuGet package name is, you can always search for the correct package within the Package Manager Console with the following command:

```
Find-Package keyword
```

To find all packages that are intended for SharePoint development, use `Find-Package sharepoint`:

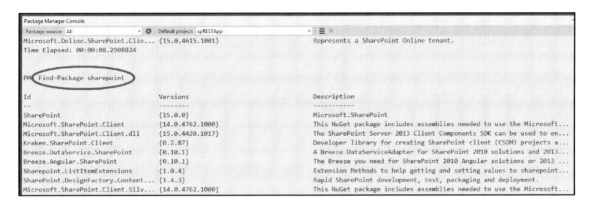

7. Its installation takes a moment and confirms that packages are now added to your project:

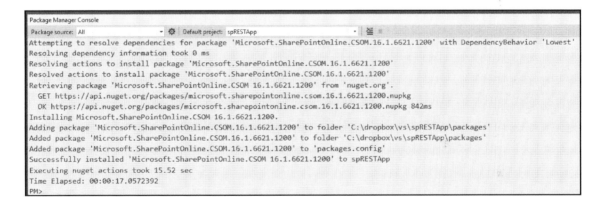

8. Verify within **Solution Explorer** that your project now has references to additional libraries:

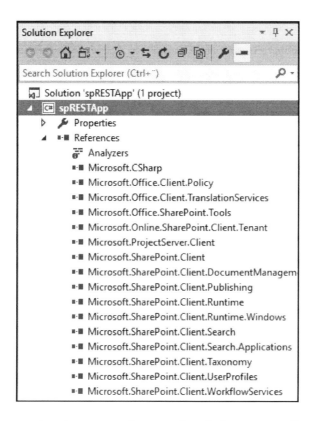

We are now ready to start implementing the actual code for our small console app; to do that, follow these steps:

1. Add a `using` statement for `Microsoft.SharePoint.Client` at the beginning of `Program.cs`:

   ```
   using Microsoft.SharePoint.Client;
   ```

2. Next, to keep our sample code clean and simple, let's introduce a few variables in the `Main()` method of our program to hold the credential information:

   ```
   var username = "user@domain.onmicrosoft.com";
   var password = "password123";
   var tenanthost = "domain";
   ```

3. Replace the credential information with proper values for your own tenant. You'll also need to convert the password to a `SecureString`, so let's add that directly underneath:

```
var securePassword = new SecureString();
foreach (var c in password)
{
securePassword.AppendChar(c);
}
```

4. Then, you'll just need to put these two together with a `SharePointOnlineCredentials()` method, which is part of the `Microsoft.SharePoint.Client` namespace:

```
var credentials = new SharePointOnlineCredentials(username,
securePassword);
var tenant = "https://" + tenanthost + ".sharepoint.com";
```

5. Now that we have your credentials, in order to authenticate with our SharePoint Online tenant, the only thing needed is a `ClientContext`, which helps us to retrieve the data we need. In the following bit of code, we will use the `ClientContext` to query for the `Title` property of the root website of our tenant:

```
using (var cc = new ClientContext(tenant))
{
cc.Credentials = credentials;
    cc.Load(cc.Web, w => w.Title);
    cc.ExecuteQuery();

    Console.WriteLine(cc.Web.Title);
}
```

When we run this, the output is a simple printout of our SharePoint site's title, as follows:

Looking at this through Fiddler, a tool that allows us to inspect the traffic we're generating, we will note that the call goes directly to

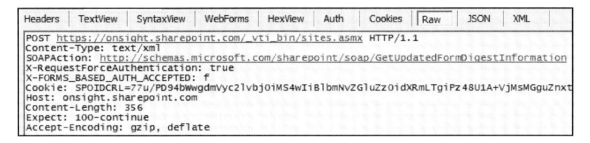

The following is the request we will get:

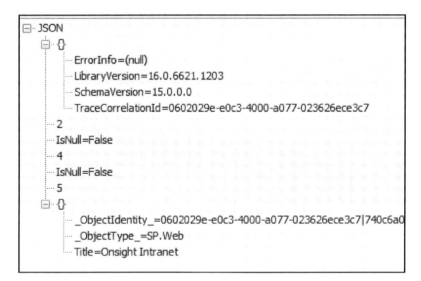

The preceding screenshot shows us that we only retrieve the `Title` property of the `SP.Web-object`.

So, with this simple exercise, we've started calling SharePoint Online directly with the classic SOAP-based Web Services. Let's next move on to REST-based APIs that are a bit more modern.

Accessing SharePoint Online with REST using a console app

You can continue working on the same console app project in Visual Studio you started previously. Simply add a new class file and mark that as the startup method in your app:

1. Right-click on your project in **Solution Explorer** and click on **Add | New Item...**:

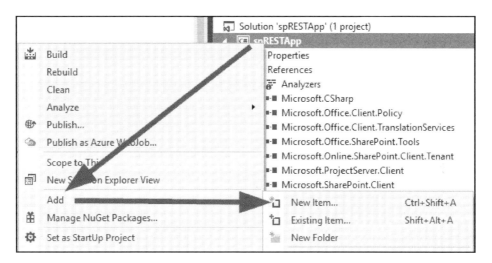

2. The class is selected by default, so enter a name, such as spREST.cs and click on **Add** to add a new class file in the project.

3. Next, right-click again on your project in **Solution Explorer** and select **Properties**:

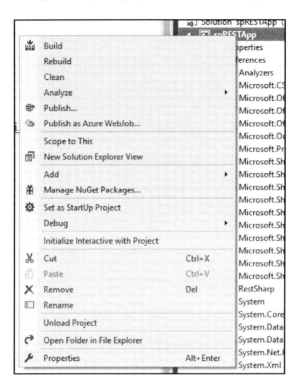

4. In the **Properties** window, click on the **Startup object** to reveal a drop-down menu, and then select the new class you added as the startup object:

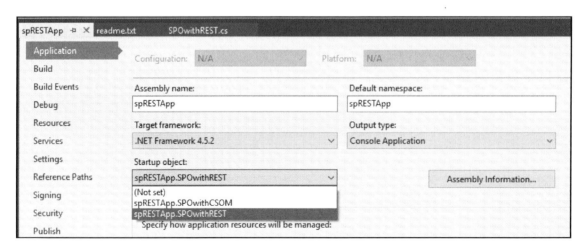

5. You can now run your code in the new app without having to remove the SOAP-based app from the same project.

To start building your new console app that uses REST APIs to access SharePoint Online, perform the following:

1. First, as we need to access REST APIs, it's beneficial to use a helper tool to perform the REST calls. For this, we suggest using `RestSharp`, which is a well-known and widely used package. We can install `RestSharp` with the Package Manager Console. Simply run the following command in the console:

```
Install-Package RestSharp
```

2. This adds a `RestSharp` library in our references.

3. Next, add a using-statement for `Deserializers` of `RestSharp`, as we will deserialize the content SharePoint Online sends as a response:

```
using RestSharp.Deserializers;
```

4. The start of the code in `Main()` is identical to the preceding sample, so add the following:

```
var username = "user@domain.onmicrosoft.com";
var password = "Password123";
var tenanthost = "domain";

var securePassword = new SecureString();
foreach (var c in password)
{
securePassword.AppendChar(c);
}
var credentials = new SharePointOnlineCredentials(username,
securePassword);
var tenant = "https://" + tenanthost + ".sharepoint.com";
```

5. From here, we'll need to instantiate a new `RestClient` (via RestSharp) to perform our API calls. With `RestSharp`, things get much easier, as we do not have to worry about the underlying HTTP calls. In the following bit of code, we'll indicate that the call will go to `/_api/web`, and we're accepting JSON back. Finally, we will set the authentication token by retrieving the cookie from our `SharePointOnlineCredentials`:

```
var client = new RestClient(tenant + "/_api/");
var getWebTitleRequest = new RestRequest("web", Method.GET);
getWebTitleRequest.AddHeader("Accept", "application/json");
//authentication cookie
client.CookieContainer = new CookieContainer();
client.CookieContainer.SetCookies(new Uri(tenant),
credentials.GetAuthenticationCookie(new Uri(tenant)));
```

6. The only thing left now is a client-side call to the API, where we also choose the property or data that we want to retrieve. As we're getting the whole result back, it's easier to deserialize the call and simply pick the value we need. In this case, that will be the `Title` result of the `SP.Web-object`.

```
JsonDeserializer deserial = new JsonDeserializer();
var result = deserial.Deserialize<Dictionary<string,
string>>(client.Execute(getWebTitleRequest));
Console.WriteLine(result["Title"]);
```

When we execute the preceding code, we will note that the HTTP GET is going toward `/_api/`:

```
Headers | TextView | SyntaxView | WebForms | HexView | Auth
GET https://onsight.sharepoint.com/_api/web HTTP/1.1
Accept: application/json
User-Agent: RestSharp/105.2.3.0
Host: onsight.sharepoint.com
Cookie: SPOIDCRL=77u/PD94bWwgdmVyc2lvbjOiMS4wIiBlbmNvZ
Accept-Encoding: gzip, deflate
```

Also, the HTTP response with the full body is returned:

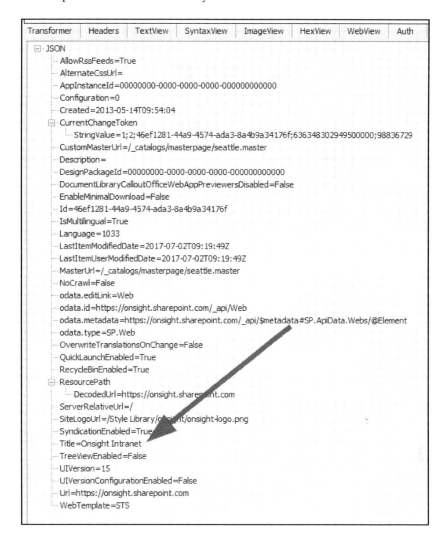

As you can see, calling REST APIs directly from SharePoint Online is more or less as simple as calling any regular REST API, with the slight addition of providing `SharePointOnlineCredentials` with the call.

Accessing REST APIs with SharePoint Framework

By now, you might be wondering how things change when we switch our underlying platform from a console app that runs on the server or workstation side to SharePoint Framework that always runs on the client side in a browser. As it turns out, it's not much different as you can still access the same REST APIs through SharePoint Framework. The main difference between our next example and the two previous examples is that everything runs within the constraints of SharePoint Framework, thus, development is done with TypeScript and through REST, not CSOM or JSOM (the JavaScript version of CSOM).

Let's create our new project first:

1. Create a new folder in the desired location, and run the following command in a Command Prompt:

   ```
   yo @microsoft/sharepoint
   ```

If it's been a while since you last ran Yeoman template generator, you might receive a notification that Yeoman can be updated:

2. Simply cancel the current process (*Ctrl* + *C*) and run the following command:

   ```
   npm install -g yo
   ```

3. In the generator, select the usual (default) settings, and choose a **No JavaScript framework** for the framework selection:

```
Welcome to the
SharePoint Client-side
Solution Generator

Let's create a new SharePoint solution.
? What is your solution name? spfxrest-sample
? Which type of client-side component to create? WebPart
? What is your WebPart name? HelloWorld
? What is your WebPart description? HelloWorld description
? Which framework would you like to use? (Use arrow keys)
> No JavaScript framework
  React
  Knockout
```

4. Start VS Code after scaffolding is complete, and open up the main code file for your web part.

5. Since we plan on communicating through REST, we will need the `SPHttpClient` and its counterpart `SPHttpClientResponse` in our project. Add the following after the existing import statements:

```
import { SPHttpClient, SPHttpClientResponse } from
'@microsoft/sp-http';
```

6. `SPHttpClient` is used to perform REST calls against SharePoint, and it takes care of adding the default headers and managing the digest if you write values back. If you need to call a REST API that is not SharePoint-hosted, you should use `HttpClient`.

7. Next, let's add a new private method that performs the actual call to SharePoint. To keep things simple, we're not too worried about error handling, and we assume that our calls will be against SharePoint Online in the hosted SharePoint Workbench, not the local SharePoint Workbench:

```
private _getWebTitle(): Promise<{Title: string}> {
  return
this.context.spHttpClient.get(this.context.pageContext.web.abso
luteUrl + `/_api/web?$select=Title`,
```

```
    SPHttpClient.configurations.v1)
        .then((response: SPHttpClientResponse) => {
          return response.json();
        })
    }
```

8. So, there's quite a bit of logic happening here. Let's do a quick dissection of this method.

First, we use a promise to get an interface, since our call will be asynchronous. This way, we can ensure that our code is completed when we actually need to retrieve the values. We expect to get a string named `Title`.

Next, we get the context object from SharePoint and use `spHttpClient` to call `/_api/web`. We could make a native JavaScript call with `XMLHttpRequest` but it is much more convenient to use `spHttpClient` JavaScript API that comes with SPFx. In order to be more efficient, we will get the `Title` property through the use of an `odata` query operator.

We will then get the response in JSON and return that through the promise using the following steps:

1. Now, let's move to the `render()` method of our web part and add the following right after the method starts:

```
    let webtitle: string = "";

        this._getWebTitle()
        .then((web: {Title: string}): void => {
          webtitle = web.Title;
          document.getElementById('webtitle').innerHTML = webtitle;
```

2. We will use a local variable named `webtitle` to store the property value from the REST call. In order to get it populated, we will call our `_getWebTitle` private method. As the call is still asynchronous and we'd like to see the result, we could use a simple `console.log()` approach to print it out for browser developer tools console. However, to make this cleaner, we will manipulate the DOM and find an element to print out the value.

3. Thus, we will need to add the element; so to finalize the code, modify any of the existing HTML elements to include a `<div>` element named `webtitle`:

```
    <span class="ms-font-xl ms-fontColor-white"><div
    id="webtitle"></div></span>
```

4. You can now run `gulp serve` and open the hosted SharePoint Workbench from SharePoint Online. The address for this is `https://{tenant}.sharepoint.com/_layouts/workbench.aspx`.

5. Add your web part on the page, and it should print out the `Title` property of your SharePoint Online root site:

6. To verify we're actually calling the correct APIs, we can once again employ Fiddler to track the calls from the client (our browser) to the server (SharePoint Online).

7. The initial page load for `/workbench.aspx` is first:

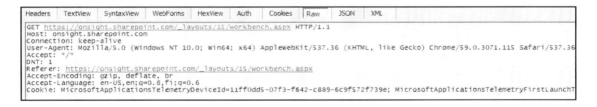

8. Right after this, we should have another call to `/_api/web`:

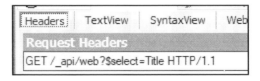

9. We will get the following result:

So, by now, we've completed three different approaches to access data on SharePoint Online.

Microsoft Graph

Now that you are able to call SharePoint directly through SharePoint Framework, you might be wondering if this is all there is to know about APIs and SharePoint. Sadly or happily, depending on your point of view, there is more!

We will next spend a little bit of time to walk through Microsoft Graph, which, without a doubt, is one of the largest and most ambitious services Office 365 currently supports and uses.

What is Microsoft Graph?

While the topic of Microsoft Graph is very interesting, it's also fairly large, and this book wouldn't be able to accommodate everything there is to know about this service.

In simple terms, Microsoft Graph is a unified platform that offers a single endpoint for accessing Office 365 and certain Microsoft Azure services including **Microsoft Azure Active Directory** (**Azure AD**). This removes the need for developers to learn multiple different APIs, where typically each API acts a little bit differently from each other, depending on the service they communicate with.

The benefit of using Microsoft Graph is evident; by authenticating with Microsoft Graph, a developer can create code that can easily access most major Office 365 services, including SharePoint Online, OneDrive for Business, Exchange Online, and Office 365 Groups. In addition, Microsoft Graph also provides visibility to Azure Active Directory-stored entities, such as users and groups, individual files (Excel, OneNote), and numerous other services.

Microsoft has been actively expanding the reach of Microsoft Graph, as it's a central service that Office 365 also uses internally for provisioning services and communicating between different services. This is especially obvious for a service, such as Microsoft Teams, which actively works within, and with an Office 365 Group, as well as Skype for Business.

Accessing Microsoft Graph with Graph Explorer

To access Microsoft Graph, Microsoft provides Graph Explorer. It's a free and open source tool that allows developers a nice way to query the Graph APIs. You can download the code from `https://developer.microsoft.com/en-us/graph/graph-explorer` if you want to see how it works but there's no need for that because you can just use the tool at `https://graph.microsoft.io`.

You can use the tool with sample data, or you can log in with your Microsoft or Organizational account to get full benefits. This way, you can query against live data. Just be careful as the data is yours and you could accidentally modify or delete critical items.

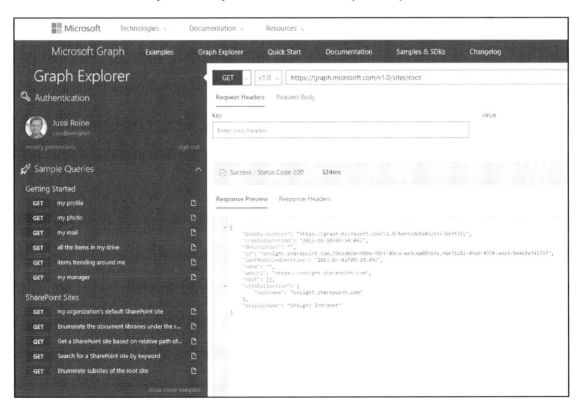

Queries against Graph API can be entered in the query bar, in the form of `https://graph.microsoft.com/{version}/{target}`. The version at the time of writing this book is either 1.0 (for stable endpoints) or beta (for upcoming features). Typically, you would call Graph APIs through `https://graph.microsoft.com/v1.0/{target}`. SharePoint is accessible as a separate target called **sites**, and since Graph Explorer has IntelliSense support, you can easily start finding your way around the APIs.

When you click on **More samples** on the left-hand navigation, you can enable sample queries for SharePoint sites:

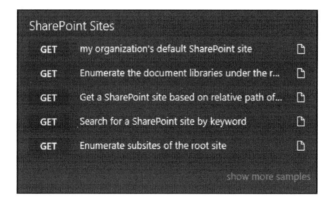

As an example, a query to search all available sites with a keyword would look like follows:

```
https://graph.microsoft.com/v1.0/sites?search=jussi
```

Results are listed in JSON by default:

```json
{
    "@odata.context": "https://graph.microsoft.com/v1.0/$metadata#sites",
    "value": [
        {
            "createdDateTime": "2013-09-13T12:05:54Z",
            "id": "onsight.sharepoint.com,59215d25-958d-44fa-b0ec-a7cb0475c0e5,3f
            "lastModifiedDateTime": "2016-05-10T06:15:31Z",
            "name": "Jussi",
            "webUrl": "https://onsight.sharepoint.com/sites/Jussi",
            "displayName": "jussi"
        },
```

Microsoft Graph evolves rapidly, and you can always view the up-to-date syntax at `https:/` `/developer.microsoft.com/en-us/graph/docs/api-reference/v1.0/resources/users`.

Accessing Microsoft Graph with SharePoint Framework

Now that we are more familiar with Microsoft Graph, it's time to start using it by initiating calls directly to the Graph API from SharePoint Framework. We could build our own HTTP requests for Microsoft Graph, but we also have to get an access token and add to the authorization header, unlike for SharePoint REST API (against which we are already authenticated). But fortunately, the SPFx comes with a built-in `GraphHttpClient` which is similar to `spHttpClient` and makes our job a lot easier.

In the simplest scenario, we'll simply call the Graph API to retrieve the `Title` property of the root SharePoint site at `https://{tenant}.sharepoint.com`.

1. Once again, initiate the scaffolding of a new SharePoint Framework web part project with the following command:

   ```
   yo @microsoft/sharepoint
   ```

2. Choose the defaults, and ensure that you select **No JavaScript framework** for the framework, as this keeps things a bit simpler for us.

3. Open the project folder in VS Code, and navigate to the main web part source file.

4. We'll first need to import the client for MS Graph, the `GraphHttpClient`. As it's similar to `spHttpClient`, we'll also need the `HttpClientResponse`:

   ```
   import { GraphHttpClient, HttpClientResponse } from
   '@microsoft/sp-http';
   ```

5. Next, let's follow the pattern we set earlier and create a private method called `_graphCall` to initiate the call to Microsoft Graph:

   ```
   private _graphCall(): Promise<{displayName: string}> {
       return this.context.graphHttpClient.get(`v1.0/sites/root`,
   GraphHttpClient.configurations.v1)
         .then((response: HttpClientResponse) => {
           console.log(response.status);
           return response.json();
         })
   }
   ```

6. The method is almost identical to the approach we used when accessing REST APIs from SPFx, but since the endpoint exposes a slightly different set of properties, we are not expecting a property named `Title`, but a property named `displayName`. The call via `graphHttpClient` is aimed at `v1.0/sites/root`, as the `graphHttpClient` already knows the base address for Microsoft Graph-- `https://graph.microsoft.com`.

Through this call, we will get the response as JSON. We've added a `console.log` just to make sure that the call is actually getting through and resulting in an HTTP's 200 OK response.

7. Next, in `render()`, we'll add a call to our private method. It's identical to the one we created in the preceding example, only the method name is different:

```
let webtitle: string = "";

this._graphCall()
.then((web: {displayName: string}): void => {
  webtitle = web.displayName;
  document.getElementById('webtitle').innerHTML = webtitle;
});
```

8. Finally, in our HTML, we will need to add a `<div>` somewhere to print out the values:

```
<p class="ms-font-l ms-fontColor-white"><div
id="webtitle"/></p>
```

9. When you run this with `gulp serve`, the web part should successfully show the root site's `Title` property:

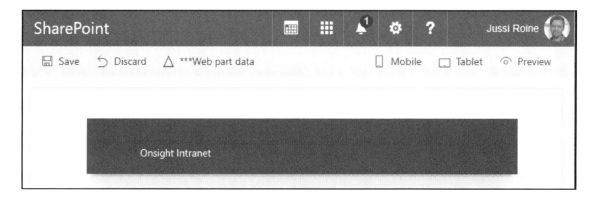

10. To verify that our call is truly going through as intended, we can check the actual calls via Fiddler. The HTTP GET looks like the following:

11. The call seems to go correctly to `https://graph.microsoft.com`, thus; we can see that the response is also available on Fiddler:

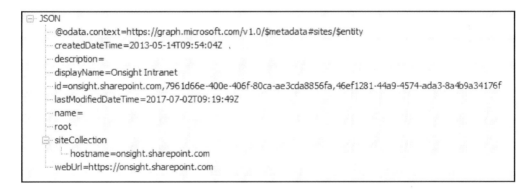

In this example, we saw how easy it is to call Microsoft Graph directly with `graphHttpClient`, without the need to craft the `REST-calls` manually.

Summary

In this chapter, we discussed how to access SharePoint-hosted APIs, such as the `/_api/web` endpoint via REST and console applications. In addition, we accessed Microsoft Graph, which provides us with a centralized collection of APIs that in turn allow us to access SharePoint Online in a unified way.

In the next chapter, we will wrap up the topic on SharePoint Framework and take a look at the near future and how things will move forward.

13
The Future of SharePoint Customizations

Throughout this book, we've looked at the SharePoint Framework--how it enables developers to create powerful SharePoint customizations with modern tools and a lightweight approach.

Before the SharePoint Framework was made available, we had numerous models, patterns, and best practices for bending and customizing many aspects of SharePoint, both in Office 365 and SharePoint on-premises. We took a look at the history of SharePoint customizations in `Chapter 1`, *Introducing SharePoint Online for Developers*. In this chapter, let's take a look at the following topics:

- The possible future of SharePoint customizations
- SharePoint 2016's support for the SharePoint Framework
- The future and relevance of the SharePoint Framework for developers

The future of SharePoint developers

As SharePoint as a platform has been available since the early 2000s, there have been many ways for developers to work with it. As the SharePoint Framework's general availability and a more stable release were announced in early 2017, it is still very early for this development approach.

Currently, developers still heavily use the full-trust code, as this is probably what most developers are comfortable with if they've been working with SharePoint for years. Also, Microsoft has stated that the FTC approach is not being phased out and is still fully supported in SharePoint 2016. It might be safe to assume that certain elements of the FTC functionality will also be present in a possible future version of SharePoint on-premises builds. As such, we will see a long but narrow road for FTC developers, as most new and interesting capabilities will be announced as part of the SharePoint Framework. Developers working with older versions of SharePoint (but not SharePoint Online) will probably stick with FTC, and to a certain degree, app model-based customizations, as these versions will not support the SharePoint Framework.

In a way, this reminds us of the approach we saw with Microsoft Azure and its Classic (ASM) versus Resource Manager (ARM). As you may note, Azure was initially made available with the Classic model that was a monolithic approach to Azure's services and capabilities. When the more modern Resource Manager approach was made available, new services were generally being made available only on the ARM side, while the older ASM portion of Azure was still healthy, but shrinking. As such, developers working with older deployments of services in Azure tend to work more focused with ASM, such as Cloud Services, unless they're being forced to migrate to ARM by Microsoft.

Such drastic pushes from Microsoft for developers to be forced to migrate to the SharePoint Framework is not something we're envisioning, as FTC-based and other legacy code cannot simply be ported to SPFx-style customizations. The thinking is different, development languages are different (typically C# versus JavaScript), and typically the platform is different (on-premises versus online).

Some developers will have a more challenging task, as they might need to keep existing code bases in working order with on-premises services and start creating new customizations for SharePoint Online and/or SharePoint 2016. The challenge of ramping up with the SharePoint Framework is notable but something that all SharePoint developers need to do at some point if they wish to continue working with newer SharePoint versions.

During customization projects, there are always requirements and requests for features that might not be possible or reasonable to do with the SharePoint Framework. In FTC, developers often found a workaround, as they had unrestricted access to the platform. With the SharePoint Framework, this tends to result in non-optimal JavaScript or Frankenstein-style deployments where certain bits are being offloaded to another platform in hopes of circumventing limitations that the developers feel should not be there.

A real-world example is what we witnessed with a customer who had migrated to SharePoint Online several years ago: A customer needed to have a list of available site collections as a kind of landing page, where each site collection would be shown as a link. Instead of using the SharePoint Framework, or an add-in to find a solution for this request, the developer opted to use server-side .NET-based code, that is, FTC.

The result was a large .NET project with several custom DLLs, a complex configuration file, and an executable that needed to be run once per day manually on a workstation. Inherently, this isn't necessarily a bad approach, but there would have been so many ways to create an efficient solution for this. It is also clear that most developers familiar with .NET and maybe SharePoint tend to find a solution with the tools they already know.

Our recommendations for developers

We hope that with this book we've been open and clear about what SharePoint developers need to learn and understand about the SharePoint Framework. For now, SPFx is by no means a perfect framework, but it's rapidly becoming one.

With FTC, the App Model, custom JavaScript's inject on pages, and other older approaches, we tended to have a monolithic and slow-moving framework that did not update frequently enough.

With SPFx, we note a combination of community work, agile development models, and lightweight tooling that quickly create customizations for SharePoint.

As such, our recommendation for developers is to keep using the SharePoint Framework, as it evolves based on customer needs, requests, and feedback. If you're fully rooted in FTC code, do not worry, as FTC has been around for a long time. However, ensure that you put some time aside to start using SPFx as best as possible.

Ensure that you start using Visual Studio Code, even if you're mostly working within Visual Studio these days. It's a fine tool and allows for rapid development, and as such will benefit from rapid releases and new features faster than Visual Studio.

It might very well be that in coming years, Microsoft, once again, chooses an alternative path for SharePoint customizations and SPFx will be left on the sidelines. However, based on current experiences, it seems that SPFx is very much here to stay and will evolve over time.

The SharePoint Framework support in SharePoint 2016

In September 2017, Microsoft announced the availability of Feature Pack 2 for SharePoint Server 2016. This update includes initial support for the SharePoint Framework-based customizations in locally hosted SharePoint 2016 farms.

The update is available through the September 2017 Public Update, and the bits can be downloaded for your SharePoint 2016 farm from `https://technet.microsoft.com/en-us/library/mt715807%28v=office.16%29.aspx`.

As the support does not--at least in the initial release--have parity with all the SharePoint Framework functionalities Microsoft supports with SharePoint Online, it is more limited but still very usable. Now, developers can target their code for on-premises and cloud-based deployments, with minimal, if any, changes to their code. In time, Microsoft will provide further updates to SharePoint 2016, which makes using SPFx a logical choice as a development approach.

Customers who are still running older versions of SharePoint, such as 2013 or 2010, do not get support for the SharePoint Framework. This might require too much work for Microsoft to make it a viable approach, and most customers are typically either planning to migrate to SharePoint Online or upgrade to a newer SharePoint version in the future. As discussed in the earlier chapters of this book, customizations created with models other than SPFx are not automatically migrated as part of a version change and will require additional work or even rewrite. In these cases, developers should switch to the SharePoint Framework, as it is the current model that evolves and provides support for both cloud and on-premises platforms.

Is SharePoint Framework the final framework for SharePoint developers?

We've had this question posed to us over the years multiple times. Just replace the SharePoint Framework with any of the previous development models, and you'll see this question is something that is impossible to answer with certainty. For now and for the past few years since Microsoft announced SPFx to be a first-class development framework for SharePoint, the answer has been a solid yes. We're seeing SPFx pick up a lot faster than previous models, and the support that both Microsoft and the community are providing has been excellent so far.

A major influence on the adoption of SPFx has been through the Office Developer Patterns and Practices, which is a highly active program to educate and evangelize the SharePoint Framework, among other things.

While we're seeing enthusiastic reception for SPFx, we're also seeing developers who are still not yet ready or willing to move to this new development model. They might have seen too many development models for SharePoint in the past 15+ years and may simply not yet be convinced of the investment of time and resources to learn it. This is perfectly fine, and the previous development models are still very much alive and supported. It's still important to note that all future investments from Microsoft for SharePoint development models are aimed at the SharePoint Framework. As such, customers will eventually request features that make more sense to implement with the SharePoint Framework rather than in some other way. These requests will force developers to migrate over to SPFx, often in a hurry, to implement customer solutions in a supported and reasonable way.

We would encourage developers to follow up on SPFx releases and news, and if they do not want to fully move over to this model, at least keep track of the possibilities and limitations. This way, when the time comes, you are more than ready to use SPFx while also continuing with other development approaches you might still need or want to use.

Summary

We hope you've enjoyed reading and learning about the SharePoint Framework with this book. For us, learning about the SharePoint Framework, recalling details about past development models, and seeing how Microsoft actively expands the reach of these new development models to SharePoint 2016 and beyond has been exciting. Throughout the months leading up to this chapter, we've written, tested, deployed, redeployed, and configured SharePoint Online and SharePoint 2016. We're certain that the SharePoint Framework is here to stay, but at the same time, it will evolve rapidly in the coming months and years. For now, it seems that this model is the one that has stuck, and yet another development model is not around the corner. Developers are free to pick whichever features they seem comfortable with and choose not to use other aspects of SPFx; that is the beauty of this more open and more rapidly evolving model, a model that SharePoint has not seen before.

Thank you for reading this book, and all the best in your future SharePoint development adventures!

Index

mockup data
  creating 278
Model-View-Controller (MVC) 301
Model-View-ViewModel (MVVM) 297

N

ngFabric 262
Node Package Manager 316
Node.js
  installation link 80
non-reactive mode 255
npm
  about 56
  reference 56

O

OAuth 130
OData 130
Office 365 license
  about 19
  B (Business) license 20
  E (Enterprise) license 20
  reference 20
  selecting 20
Office 365
  reference 21, 221
  used, for business process 135
Office Dev PnP repository
  reference 70
Office Dev PnP
  contributing 71
  reference 71
Office Developer Patterns and Practices
  about 67
  references 69
  subcategories 69
  using 68
Office UI Fabric 262
Office UI Fabric React components
  using, in SharePoint Framework web parts 272
Office UI Fabric React
  adding, to project 275
optimization 319

P

packaging
  overview 167
Platform as a Service (PaaS) 41, 52
POJO (Plain old JS object) 278
Project Online 27
property field events
  handling 254
property pane
  custom properties, implementing 256
  fields 245
  fields, implementing 246
  groups, implementing 246
  headers, implementing 246
  implementing 244
  multiple pages, implementing 251

R

React web part project
  creating 274
React
  about 262
  as component-based 263
  as declarative 262
  project structure, examining 275
  reference 262
  to-do list, implementing 280
  using, in SharePoint Framework web parts 272
reactive mode 255
ReactTodo component
  TodoItemComponent, creating 287
REST APIs
  about 31
  reference 33

S

sandbox solutions 39
Script Editor Web Part (SEWP) 42
server-side object model (SSOM) 130
SharePoint 2001-2003 37
SharePoint 2007 38
SharePoint 2010 39
SharePoint 2013 41
SharePoint 2016 Feature Pack 2 318

Printed in Great Britain
by Amazon